QUALITY IMPROVEMENT

*Teamwork Solutions from the UK
and North America*

EDITORS:

LESLEY MUNRO-FAURE
RICHARD TEARE
EBERHARD E. SCHEUING

CASSELL

Cassell
Wellington House
125 Strand, London WC2R 0BB

PO Box 605
Herndon, VA 20172

First published 1998

British Library Cataloguing-in-Publication Data
A catalogue record for this book is available from the British Library.

ISBN 0-304-70311-7 (paperback)

Typeset by Kenneth Burnley in Irby, Wirral, Cheshire.
Printed and bound in Great Britain by Redwood Books, Trowbridge, Wilts.

CONTENTS

CONTENTS

EDITORS AND CONTRIBUTORS

EDITORS

Lesley Munro-Faure is a graduate engineer with many years' experience of implementing performance improvement and organizational change programmes within leading international businesses. Lesley is the Executive Director of the National Society for Quality Through Teamwork and she is the co-author of two leading *Financial Times* books: *Implementing Total Quality Management* and *The Success Culture,* together with a practical handbook on ISO9000 for The Institute of Management.

Richard Teare PhD, DLitt is Granada Professor and Director, University for Industry, Oxford Brookes University, and Revans' Professor and Academic Chair, International Management Centres. Richard is a Non-Executive Director and current Chairman of the NSQT, Editor of the *International Journal of Contemporary Hospitality Management* and a Consulting Editor for Cassell. He is a Fellow of the Hotel and Catering International Management Association (HCIMA) and directs the HCIMA's Worldwide Hospitality and Tourism Trends project. He has co-written and edited eighteen books and 80 articles and book chapters on aspects of service industry management.

Eberhard E. Scheuing PhD is Professor of Marketing, Director of the Business Research Institute and Director of Executive Education at St. John's University, New York, USA. As Founder and President of the International Service Quality Association (ISQA), Eb co-chairs the prestigious series of international conferences on Quality in Services (QUIS) and is co-editor of *The Service Quality Handbook.* He has published more than 500 articles and 25 books on aspects of purchasing management, customer service, new product management and strategic partnering.

CONTRIBUTORS

Beth Aarons is Group Training Manager at The Savoy Group plc where she is responsible for the training and development of some 2,000 employees in six units. Beth studied psychology at university and began her career with Travellers Fare. In 1991, Beth joined Manpower plc as a training executive where she was instrumental in setting up an induction programme now used in Manpower branches throughout the UK. Beth is a qualified trainer with the Hospitality Training Foundation, a member of the HCIMA, and an NVQ Assessor for Customer Service.

Roger Armstrong MPhil, MA, DMS, Cert.Ed is Senior Lecturer in Management Development and Programme Director of the MBA at Lancashire Business School, University of Central Lancashire. He is a recent Chairman of SAGSET, an international Society of Interactive Learning and is a member of the *Yearbook* Editorial Board. He is the co-author of many management development and training manuals on aspects of personal and professional development, managerial effectiveness, problem-solving and decision-making, quality and customer service.

David Atkinson is a Senior Engineer with the Total Industrial Engineering Group, Denso Manufacturing UK Limited.

Gerald Barlow MSc, MBA is Senior Lecturer in Operations Management at UCE Business School. His main areas of research centre around the service industries, especially the use of techniques developed within manufacturing industries and adopted for use in the service sectors. Over the past four years, he has published over twenty articles and conference papers in these areas together with chapters in three operations management and quality books.

Colin Benefer is the head of UK Human Resources for Kennametal Hertel Ltd. His research interests are based around employee development issues within manufacturing industries.

John Bicheno is Reader in Operations Management at the University of Buckingham and author of four books, including the best-selling texts *The Quality 50* and *Cause and Effect JIT* in the area of Just-in-Time Manufacturing and Total Quality, both fields with strong links to teamworking. Prior to his current post he was a practitioner in the field of operations management and he has also held the post of Associate Professor of Industrial Engineering at the University of the Witwatersrand, South Africa.

Jackie Brander Brown is a Senior Lecturer and Research Co-ordinator, Department of Accounting and Finance, Manchester Metropolitan University; she has also taught at Cornell University, USA. Jackie is an associate member of the Institute of Chartered Accountants and a Fellow of the British Association of Hotel Accountants. Her research interests include the relationship between organizational culture, management control systems and organizational effectiveness, and she is currently completing a PhD degree, on a part-time basis, at Oxford Brookes University.

Roger J. Callan PhD is Principal Lecturer in the Department of Hotel, Catering and Tourism, Manchester Metropolitan University. He is currently Vice President of EuroCHRIE (the European chapter of the association of international hospitality educators) and will be President in 1998–99. After a career in hotel management, he opened a country guest house with his wife, which they operated for eighteen years. He is a member of the review panels of three international journals and has authored more than thirty articles and conference papers in the fields of service quality and hotel grading.

Janet Coburn began her career with Glaxo Wellcome twenty-six years ago at the Barnard Castle site in Co. Durham. She started as a process operator in the packaging department and progressed to Senior Supervisor in both packaging and printing departments. Janet is currently the Continuous Improvement Co-ordinator, Tropicals Department where she acts as mentor and facilitator to numerous self-directed continuous improvement teams who are seeking to improve departmental performance and promote the Glaxo Wellcome goal to be 'the supplier of choice'.

David Davies DPhil is Deputy Principal, Westhill College of Higher Education in Birmingham. He has considerable experience in developing and managing large-scale programmes of continuing education for universities and colleges. David's experiences at the Open University and the University of Cambridge helped to shape his belief in developing learning which is available to all those who need it in the world of work, continuing and professional development. He has published in these areas and more widely in the fields of work-based learning and credit accumulation and transfer.

Margaret Erstad is a Training Adviser to Forte Hotels and a Researcher with the School of Hotel and Restaurant Management at Oxford Brookes University. She recently completed her MSc Degree at the University of Nevada, Las Vegas in Hotel Administration. Margaret is also a Research Manager (Europe) for the HCIMA's Worldwide Hospitality and Tourism Trends project.

Linda Fleming has worked in the NHS since the 1970s in a variety of administrative and managerial posts in the Glasgow area. She has been working in her present post as Director of Contracts within Yorkhill NHS Trust since 1994. Her work involves the co-ordination of the Trust's business planning strategy, negotiating with Health Care Commissioners to secure the Trust's income and providing a strategic overview to the Trust Board of child and maternal health care. She is an ex-officio member of the Trust Board.

Nick Hadley BSc joined what is now the Rover Organization in 1977. A graduate of the University of Bristol, Nick began working in the Personnel function and since then has held a range of positions in learning and development and employee relations. He is currently the Communication and Involvement Manager at Land Rover Vehicles where he participates in business strategy deployment among other activities. Nick also lectures on internal communication and employee motivation at the University of Birmingham's School of Continuing Studies.

Richard Hale is a partner in the international consultancy The Asset Partnership and author of several books on the subject of personal and organizational change, including *The Power of Personal Influence* (McGraw-Hill, 1995) and *Towards the Virtual Organization* (McGraw-Hill, 1997). His initial corporate experience was with the GEC Marconi Group and BSkyB. He has contributed to the competency movement in the UK and consulted with organizations such as Coca Cola, Nestlé, Motorola, Esselte and Blackwell's in the area of organizational change and team development.

Nigel Hemmington PhD is Reader and Director of Research and Consultancy in the School of Hotel and Restaurant Management at Oxford Brookes University. He is also President of the HCIMA, the professional body for the international hospitality industry. A graduate of the University of Surrey, his main interests are in the areas of consumer behaviour, relationship marketing, customer satisfaction and professional development. He has worked in both the hotel and foodservice industries and has extensive experience of consultancy in the hospitality industry.

Anthony Ingold PhD is Reader and Director of Research at Birmingham College of Food. Tony trained as a medical biologist, specialized in microbial ecology and later diversified as he became interested in the application of research methodology to a variety of problems. Tony has worked with Land Rover before and has co-authored work relating to their CQI programme. His publications include a recent co-authored book on yield management systems.

Hadyn Ingram graduated from Middlesex University and worked as a manager in luxury hotels in London and Yorkshire before taking on the running of a busy pub in the suburbs of London. He received his MSc from Oxford Brookes University in 1993 and spent four years as a Senior Lecturer at Bournemouth University. He now owns a sixteen-bedroom hotel in Salisbury and teaches at the University of Surrey. He was awarded a DPhil by International Management Centres in 1997, and his publications and research centre around teamwork and performance in the hospitality industry.

Nick Johns PhD is Senior Research Consultant and Reader, The Research Centre, City College Norwich, a Regional College of Anglia Polytechnic University, where his writing and research focus on quality and productivity in service operations. Nick has written extensively in the field and he is an Associate Editor of the *International Journal of Contemporary Hospitality Management.* His most recent book addresses the application of research methods in service industry management.

Matt Johnson is a Quality Development Consultant in Legal & General's Sales & Marketing Division, Kingswood, Surrey. He joined the company in 1990, working in a variety of customer-facing roles before moving to the Quality Team. His quality role involves managing projects across the Legal & General Group, coaching managers in implementing quality initiatives and analysing and driving changes identified by group-wide staff feedback.

Alison King is the Training and Development Manager in the Human Resources Department at Case United Kingdom Ltd. She is a graduate member of the Institute of Personnel and Development.

Conrad Lashley is Head of the Centre for Hospitality Management, Nottingham Business School, Nottingham Trent University. Conrad has researched and published extensively on employee empowerment and the management of employees in the service sector. He has particular interest in the contribution of employees to service quality enhancement. He holds a BA in Social Science, an MA in Industrial Relations and he is a Fellow of the Royal Society for Arts.

Edward Matier is the Vice President and General Merchandise Manager for Sears Canada's Footwear, Children's Men's and Cosmetics divisions. He is responsible for over $1 billion ($Cnd) in retail and catalogue sales annually. A twenty-six-year retail industry veteran, Ed was chosen as Business Manager of the Year in 1995 after the successful rollout of the Merchandise Procurement Re-engineering Project.

EDITORS AND CONTRIBUTORS

Malcolm Munro-Faure is a Chartered Accountant who specializes in working with management teams to improve the performance of multinational businesses. He has been actively involved in developing a practical approach to the continuous improvement of quality, and is particularly interested in the application of Total Quality Management to non-manufacturing businesses. He is the co-author of two leading *Financial Times* books: *Implementing Total Quality Management* and *The Success Culture,* together with a practical handbook on ISO9000 for The Institute of Management.

Paul Newton is a full-time instructor/assessor at RHP Bearings. Paul was the project team leader and the author of the 'Mission Impossible' team log book. This was Paul's first project involving teamwork and he is now promoting the further use of teams to solve work-related problems and to contribute to the success of the business.

David Omholt is a Manager in Andersen Consulting's Chicago office and has wide experience of business process design and operational excellence, and improvement projects in retail and consumer products companies. David also serves as a trainer in Andersen Consulting's Business Integration/Value group using the Andersen Consulting Economic (ACE) and Business Case Economic Impact (BCEI) models which aim to assist clients to improve shareholder wealth. David served on the Andersen Consulting/Sears Canada project for two years.

John Sparrow PhD is Professor and Director of Research at UCE Business School. As a chartered psychologist he has conducted a wide range of research into human behaviour and associated management/policy issues for government, industrial federations and companies. He acts as a consultant in task, job and work analysis and has published over fifty applied research papers.

Sue Temperton joined Legal & General in 1988 at the height of the housing boom. She managed several administrative departments before moving into a process re-engineering/crisis management role in 1995. A spell in public relations as spokeswoman on Legal & General's electronic commerce initiatives followed and she was recently appointed Services Development Manager, responsible for ensuring that the customer's transition from the sales experience to after-sales service is smooth and seamless.

Don Watt works in the human resource department at RHP Precision Bearings. He has particular interest in total quality management and employee training and development. Don has developed the training and assessment systems which have enabled the company to become an approved centre for Manufacturing NVQs. He has recently completed an NVQ Level 4 in learning development and is an associate member of the Institute of Personnel and Development. Don was the team facilitator for 'Mission Impossible'.

Nigel Williams is one of a team of Continuous Quality Improvement Advisers at Britannia Airways, Luton Airport. He joined Britannia in September 1991 and is currently part of the team responsible for the design and implementation of the Continuous Improvement Programme throughout the company. This involves the design and delivery of training courses and supporting continuous improvement teams at all levels. Prior to joining Britannia Airways, Nigel served as an Airframe Technician with the Royal Air Force.

THE COMPANIES

Andersen Consulting is a leading global management and technology consulting firm whose mission is to help its clients change to be more successful. The firm works with over 5,000 client organizations from a wide range of industries to align their people, processes and technology with their strategy to achieve best business performance. *Consultants News,* the leading authority in the consulting industry, ranked Andersen Consulting as No. 1 in its annual survey of the largest management consulting firms. Andersen's organization has approximately 49,000 people with offices in forty-seven countries and is growing at an average annual rate of approximately 20 per cent.

Britannia Airways Limited is the world's largest charter airline and Britain's second largest airline, carrying over eight million people from seventeen airports to more than 100 destinations worldwide. Founded in 1962, Britannia became part of the Thomson Corporation in 1965. The company has a reputation for innovation – it was the first airline to offer its holiday passengers hot meals, it was the first European operator of the Boeing 737-200, it was the first UK holiday airline to offer passengers free inflight entertainment and it pioneered charter flights from the UK to Australia.

Case United Kingdom Limited, based in Doncaster, is part of the Case Corporation, a multinational marketing organization which has been producing a comprehensive range of agricultural equipment and construction machinery for the past 150 years. The Case plant at Doncaster operates with a workforce of 1,200 people, who assemble more than 12,000 tractors every year – of which 85 per cent are destined for export. These tractors are widely considered to be among the most technically advanced in the world – as are the manufacturing facilities at Doncaster, which now comprise the Corporation's European Centre for Excellence for Tractor Assembly.

Denso Manufacturing UK Limited is a joint venture company established by Denso of Japan and Magneti-Marelli of Italy. The company was established in August, 1990 and occupies a 53-acre site (factory is 54,700 square metres) in

Telford, Shropshire. There were almost 900 employees on site by mid-1997. Principal products are climate control units and heat exchangers for the automotive industry.

Glaxo Wellcome has six manufacturing plants in the UK, employing some 7,500 people. The 63-acre Barnard Castle site is a major manufacturing centre where 'active' ingredients are converted into a wide range of medicines. Products include ampoules, syringes, vials, inhaled liquids, ointments and creams. These forms of medicines are used to treat a variety of conditions including hay fever, ulcers, migraine, nausea, eczema and asthma. More than 80 per cent of the factory's output is exported to over 100 countries.

Kennametal Hertel Limited is a division of Kennametal Inc. (USA) with European headquarters in Germany. During the fiscal year for 1996 the Kennametal group had world sales in excess of $1 billion, and is pursuing an aggressive sales growth programme aimed at doubling this figure by the year 2000. The UK operations are based at Kingswinford in the West Midlands and a Scottish Office in East Kilbride. The main activities in the UK involve design and manufacture of cutting tools, tool holders and tooling systems for the global metalworking industry.

Land Rover Vehicles is a business unit within Rover Group plc, a wholly-owned subsidiary of BMW since 1994. There are over 7,000 people employed at Land Rover Vehicles' Solihull Manufacturing site, where 130,000 four-wheel-drive vehicles are made each year. Production volume and sales records have been broken in each of the last three years and the Solihull site has seen massive capital investment and recruitment over these years of rapid business expansion. Seventy per cent of the world-famous products (Range Rover, Discovery, Defender and Freelander) are exported, and the business is one of the largest earners of export revenues in the UK.

Legal & General is a household name in the financial services industry, with its well-recognized umbrella logo and more than 160 years of experience in meeting the demands of its customers. Today 2.5 million people rely on the assurance society for insurance, pensions, mortgages and investments. Legal & General Group plc reached the finals of the VarityPerkins European Quality Awards with two separate entries: the Customer Service division at Hove, East Sussex, which has 1,014 staff, responds to queries from life assurance and pensions customers on their policies; the Sales & Marketing division at Kingswood, Surrey, with 1,751 staff, is responsible for the development, marketing and selling of financial products through various distribution channels in the UK.

Magnox Electric plc is based at Berkeley in Gloucestershire and owns nine Magnox stations, six of which are still operating and three in the process of being decommissioned. The company also owns one hydroelectric station at Maentwrog in Wales. The VarityPerkins submission relates to Dungeness 'A' power station, which was commissioned in 1966 in the heyday of Magnox nuclear technology. In 1997, the station employed just under 10 per cent of the total workforce of Magnox Electric.

NSK Bearings, Europe was established in the UK in 1975 to supply Europe with 'popular' metric sizes of single row, deep groove, ball bearings. NSK was the first Japanese-owned company to have a manufacturing plant in the North East of England (Peterlee, Co. Durham). From the initial five sizes of ball bearings, the company now produces a range of forty-seven sizes, of which there are many variants. NSK is headquartered in Tokyo and is a truly global organization with manufacturing plants and sales offices throughout the world.

RHP Precision Bearings is a specialist division of NSK-RHP Bearings, one of the world's largest bearings manufacturers. NSK, of Japan, acquired the company in 1990 and operates manufacturing sites across Europe. The markets served are very broad based and include automotive, aerospace, machine tool and general industrial with customers including Ford, Rover, Rolls Royce, Pratt & Whitney, British Aerospace and Bearing Services Ltd.

The Savoy Group plc manages four luxury hotels in London and one hotel in the Cotswolds. In addition to hotels, the Group's business portfolio consists of traditional restaurants and the Savoy Theatre. At present, the Group employs approximately 2,000 people. In 1995, Ramon Pajares became the Group's Managing Director and brought with him plans to revitalize the company which had seen its products and services become tired with time. A strategic plan known as The Savoy 2000 was devised that required heavy investment in the Group's products and human capital. The results for 1997 indicate very strong growth and evidence of the success of The Savoy 2000 strategy.

Sears Canada is Canada's largest single retailer of general merchandize, with department and speciality stores as well as catalogue-selling units located across Canada. The company emphasizes quality and service in appealing to a broad cross-section of Canadian consumers. Sears' vision is to be Canada's most successful retailer by providing its customers with total shopping satisfaction. It associates with opportunities for career advancement and personal growth and its shareholders with superior returns on their investment. The organization has experienced an average annual sales growth rate of more than 15 per cent.

Yorkhill NHS Trust is one of Scotland's principal centres of Maternal and Child Health. It comprises Scotland's largest children's hospital, one of the area's foremost maternity hospitals, several community services and houses seven academic departments of the University of Glasgow. Yorkhill cares for more than 25,000 in-patients, 26,000 new out-patients and around 9,000 day-patients each year. In addition, in excess of 33,000 children attend the Accident & Emergency department and the Queen Mother's Hospital accommodates the birth of around 3,600 babies every year. Uniting this multidisciplinary body of skills, expertise and resources is the common cause of caring for the health of mothers and children in the area.

THE NATIONAL SOCIETY FOR QUALITY THROUGH TEAMWORK

TEAMWORK DRIVES PERFORMANCE IMPROVEMENT

Business leaders identify two critical factors which drive success in world class organizations:

- constantly improving performance by becoming better, faster, cheaper and more effective; and
- involving 100 per cent of the minds and passion of all their people in identifying problems and resolving them.

Every organization has to deliver more for less. The challenge is to develop the structure, culture and leadership style which encourages individuals to get involved, and use the power of teamwork to deliver real performance improvements.

The NSQT was founded in 1982 to support organizations which want to improve performance and increase competitiveness by getting their people involved.

CONTINUOUS IMPROVEMENT

World class companies seek to improve performance in every area of their work:

- understanding customer requirements and improving performance to meet customer needs more effectively;
- understanding processes – cutting out waste and inefficiency – working better, cheaper and faster;
- improving communications between departments – breaking down internal barriers;
- getting employees involved – improving performance and working in teams to improve morale and support the development of individuals.

IMPROVING QUALITY THROUGH TEAMWORK

The benefits to organizations of involving their people in improving performance are significant – but it requires real commitment on the part of the organization, its managers and all employees to be successful. Managers must encourage open discussion about means to improve performance, the identification of problems and the implementation of solutions to them. They must create a framework which helps people to work together to identify means to improve performance and resolve problems, and secure commitment and support from every level in the organization.

The senior management team are responsible for defining the framework for the continuous improvement process. They must create and maintain a culture in which managers:

- recognize the importance of involving their people in teams to tackle problems and improve the performance of processes for which they are responsible;
- create an environment which helps employees to feel committed to the organization – and supported by the management team – if they want their people to put in the effort required to improve things.

Managers must also support their teams by working together to improve the performance of processes which involve more than one function.

EMPLOYEE INVOLVEMENT – THE STRENGTH OF TEAMWORK

Performance improvement can only be achieved by improving the processes within an organization. Processes are designed and operated by people so the only way to improve performance is through people.

Effective continuous improvement therefore depends on the ability of managers to ensure that everyone becomes actively involved in improving performance, working effectively in teams to analyze processes, investigate problems and implement solutions. Successful performance improvement depends on the effective operation of two principal types of team, described in Figure 1:

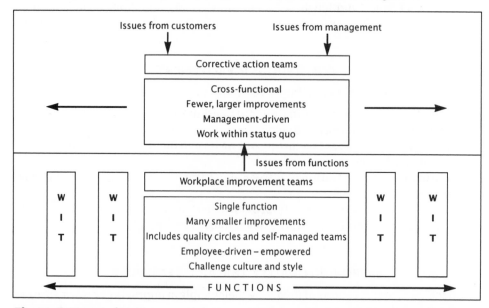

Figure 1: Types of team

CORRECTIVE ACTION TEAMS

Corrective Action Teams are set up to improve the operation of specific processes, or to analyse and solve particular problems which affect more than one function.

Managers select the appropriate team leader who is usually responsible for choosing individual team members. On completion of the project, the Corrective Action Team is disbanded. New teams are selected to work on new projects – allowing the appropriate mix of individuals to be pulled together for each circumstance.

Corrective Action Teams are generally easy to establish and maintain because they do not challenge the basic way the organization is managed. They are management-led and can lead to employee participation but not true employee involvement.

WORKPLACE IMPROVEMENT TEAMS

Workplace Improvement Teams involve people from the same work area, or those who work on the same process. Often with a voluntary membership, these teams select the work-related problems which they intend to address, and then meet regularly to analyse and resolve them. Workplace Improvement Teams are important because they drive improvements in individual functions or in the performance of individual processes. They can also provide the foundation for changing the culture of the organization – providing a basis for involving everyone in the continuous improvement of performance.

As these teams grow in competence and confidence, organizations typically find that they become able to take on more responsibility and get increasingly involved in making day-to-day decisions. If managers are prepared to delegate the necessary authority, these Workplace Improvement Teams can grow in stature until they take full responsibility for complete work areas, and may eventually evolve into self-managed teams.

However, some organizations find that these teams present too much of a challenge for their existing management-driven structure. They challenge the culture of the organization by involving employees in decision-making and changing the way the organization is managed. But they can enable organizations to realize significant benefits by releasing the full potential of all their employees – enabling them to apply their skills and experience in the efficient running of operations with which they are intimately familiar.

Successful continuous improvement programmes need to embrace both types of team:

- *Workplace Improvement Teams* to bring about many smaller improvements involving everyone, delegating decision-making and changing the culture of the organization.
- *Corrective Action Teams* to resolve the bigger issues which are outside the remit of Workplace Improvement Teams but which prevent them and the organization working effectively.

The organizations featured in this book provide leading-edge examples of the successful operation of both these types of team. They represent different types of organization and have adopted different solutions to improve performance but they all have one key feature in common; they have a deep-rooted conviction in the need to constantly improve their performance through believing in and involving their people.

Lesley Munro-Faure
Executive Director, NSQT

THE NATIONAL SOCIETY FOR QUALITY THROUGH TEAMWORK

Launched in 1982 by twenty founder companies, the National Society for Quality through Teamwork is a registered charity whose purpose is to promote the Achievement of Quality through the involvement of all employees. With more than 400 member organizations today, the Society is the UK's leading authority on employee involvement and participation. Utilizing the experience of our experts and the skills of our members, our aim is to encourage UK organizations to improve their ability to compete in today's marketplace.

Joining the NSQT enables members to benefit from the following services:

- Rapid and easy access to some of the UK's leading quality and teamwork experts.
- Free access to the programme of regional meetings where you can hear how different organizations have tackled specific problems, network with other members, learn new ideas, benchmark performance.
- Priority access, including a substantial discount, to the NSQT Annual Teamwork Conference, the largest teamwork event in Europe. This is an excellent opportunity to experience the benefits of the latest tools and techniques.
- A regular newsletter to keep you up-to-date with developments.
- Discounts on books, videos and training material produced by major publishers.
- The opportunity to achieve recognition for your organization and the work of individual teams by entering for one of our prestigious awards.

For further details on the NSQT please contact Judy Wilson on:

Phone	44 (0) 1722 326667
Fax	44 (0) 1722 410983
E-mail	nsqt@dial.pipex.com.

THE NSQT'S QUALITY AND TEAMWORK AWARDS

The NSQT is delighted to work with a number of leading organizations to promote and recognize the importance of using teamwork to achieve performance improvement, through the sponsorship of three major awards:

THE MICHELIN EXCELLENCE AWARD FOR IMPROVEMENT TEAMS

The Michelin Excellence Award is acknowledged as the UK's leading award which recognizes the contribution made by teams to the improvement of performance in businesses throughout the UK. The award is open to any type of improvement team, and from any type of organization or business.

Teams can be entered in either of the following award categories:

- *Single problem/management promoted teams.* These teams are formed to tackle an identified problem or improve the operation of a specific process.
- *Continuous improvement/self-directed teams.* These teams select their own problems and remedies, and membership is usually voluntary.

The judges are looking for teams which demonstrate success achieved by the involvement of all team members, a clear sense of direction, careful analysis of the problem, clear communication with colleagues and an effective programme to guide the implementation and monitoring of improvement actions.

The Michelin teamwork programme has evolved over the past fifteen years and has included within its past achievements being winners of the VarityPerkins Award. Their programme has been based on maximizing people involvement and ownership. Many forms of teamwork are used and they are one of the UK leaders in developing self-managing teams. Market share growth to become the world's number one tyre manufacturer indicates the extent of their success.

THE VARITYPERKINS EUROPEAN QUALITY AWARD

The VarityPerkins European Quality Award has been internationally acknowledged since 1988 as the leading award for achievements in Quality Improvement. The success of past winners – such as Philips, Texas Instruments, Michelin, Land Rover and Glaxo Wellcome – is testimony to the prestige of the award.

THE NSQT'S QUALITY AND TEAMWORK AWARDS

The judges are looking for companies which deliver continuous improvements in performance through the total involvement of their staff, and the excellence of their teamwork. The aim has been to find organizations which can demonstrate successful change throughout the company and not simply the achievement of a defined standard. Companies which have recently started to adopt a Total Quality Programme based on people involvement and teamwork are just as likely to become finalists as those which are several years into a programme.

The VarityPerkins total quality programme includes several hundred teams which are actively engaged in performance improvement throughout the Group. Their approach to performance improvement, bringing together process owners to focus on processes and crossing functional boundaries, is fundamentally changing the way the organization works and driving their continued success.

THE WEDGWOOD NHS TEAM OF THE YEAR AWARD

The Wedgwood-sponsored NHS Team of the Year Award, now in its sixth year, has achieved significant national status. The purpose of the award is to recognize excellence in teams and to encourage the development of teamworking throughout the NHS as a means to promote continuous improvement.

As sponsors of the NHS Team of the Year Award, Wedgwood has successfully operated a Continuous Improvement Programme for the last eighteen years. The company first went in this direction in 1980 to improve communications and drive forward improvement programmes across the six group factories. To date, Wedgwood has over 200 teams operating within the group and these include Quality Circles, Action Improvement Teams and Total Productive Maintenance Teams. The Board of Directors at Wedgwood has pledged its ongoing support for the Continuous Improvement Programme. The success of teamwork and the advantages created have led to a renewed vigour in the push for total quality.

Teamwork is the driving force for performance improvement and change, and is recognized as an essential element in the continued success of Michelin Tyres, Josiah Wedgwood & Sons and VarityPerkins.

FOREWORD

THE JOURNEY OF A THOUSAND MILES BEGINS WITH ITS FIRST STEP

Whenever we consider something new and challenging it is comforting to understand how others have responded and what they have achieved. This book provides just that opportunity to understand the ways in which others have applied the methods of continuous improvement to enhance their competitive advantage through the utilization of the skills and knowledge of all the workforce.

This book also provides a unique opportunity to celebrate the successes which have been achieved: not a very British trait, but one which is fundamental to the philosophy of total quality. So, whether you are considering embarking on this journey, or you are well down the road, I commend these case studies to you.

I want to take this opportunity to express again my belief, built up over the past fifteen years, that quality improvement through people involvement remains the fundamental way forward. I have been privileged in my role as President of the NSQT to witness how harnessing the skills and knowledge of all employees has helped companies to meet the ever-changing requirements of their customers in an increasingly competitive marketplace. This process has gained momentum over the years and many organizations have come to understand and benefit from devolving responsibility, thereby gaining not only the support but, more importantly, the active involvement of all their employees.

As someone who cut his teeth in the 1970s' environment of confrontation, I have no doubts that the total quality way is a much better way of doing business for everyone. Within my own company, Blue Circle Industries, we are experiencing the benefits which are derived from the growth of mutual trust and respect, and from creating an environment in which employees have experienced growth in self-confidence and pride in meeting customer requirements and being actively involved in the success of the organization.

Improvement through Involvement embraces all the fundamentals of best practice and I wish you every success on your journey.

Peter Mutter
President, NSQT, and Personnel Director, Blue Circle Industries plc

PREFACE

Throughout the UK and in most parts of the world the importance of continuous improvement in the drive for continued success is well recognized. It is also widely acknowledged that competitive advantage can be achieved most effectively by utilizing the knowledge and experience of all employees. It is clear from the entries for the Michelin, Wedgwood and VarityPerkins Awards that diversity in teamwork is wide and that its application throughout UK business is growing at an ever-increasing rate.

This book aims to provide case examples of teamworking, quality improvement and innovation drawn from fourteen British and North American organizations. It seeks to provide a practical guide for practitioners and a versatile resource for teaching and learning by providing illustrations, ideas for class discussion and for case study work. The material is grounded in the experiences of the participants so as to provide an accessible style and a realistic view of the issues involved in planning, implementing and evaluating a quality improvement strategy. Specifically, the case illustrations examine how quality improvement impacts on the organization as a whole and/or team performance. The thirteen UK organizations featured here were national finalists in the NSQT's 1997 Quality and Teamwork Awards.

The **Michelin Excellence Awards** are given each year to up to three teams who have demonstrated excellence in the way they have identified a problem, solved it and then implemented an effective solution. Accordingly, the six chapters in Part 1 concentrate on 'the project and the result' so as to bring out the most interesting aspects of the project work undertaken in two categories:

1. Single problem/management-promoted team projects.
2. Continuous improvements made by self-directed teams.

1. Single problem/management-promoted team projects are:
- The Double Sided Designers (NSK Bearings Europe Ltd, Peterlee, Co. Durham). This engineering/manufacturing process group was given the task of reducing soft ring manufacturing costs on one particular bearing size in order to make

their plant more cost-effective. By drawing upon each team member's own field of expertise they were able to re-think the production process, thereby enabling them to achieve the given objectives.

- *Mission Impossible Team* (RHP Precision Bearings, Newark). This manufacturing-based team tackled a rework problem which was limiting daily factory output. The team identified several possible causes, of which the main ones were people-related and therefore potentially very sensitive. This chapter describes how the team worked together to solve the problem and how this has minimized rework, reduced manufacturing costs beyond all initial expectations and increased individual motivation.

- *Project 60* (Denso Manufacturing UK Ltd, Telford). The Project 60 team was set up to reduce the evaporator scrap from 170 per day to a maximum of 60 per day. The evaporator process is very sensitive with a large number of variables. The cross-departmental team performed many investigations and implemented many countermeasures to understand, improve and standardize the process. Over eighteen months the scrap has been successfully reduced to less than 60 per day and is now heading towards 40 per day.

- *Value Added Team* (Kennametal Hertel UK, Kingswinford, West Midlands). This cross-functional team worked on reducing the number of customer complaints that resulted in the issue of a credit note. The team targeted problems arising from pricing and procedural errors. Investigations showed that incorrect discounts and accepting orders with incorrect prices contributed to the problem. By updating customer records held on computer and improving procedures the team successfully reduced the credit notes and eliminated discount errors.

2. Continuous improvements made by self-directed teams are:

- *The Streamline Team* (Glaxo Wellcome Operations, Barnard Castle, Co. Durham). The challenge facing this self-directed work team was how to reduce the team sizes in the department. Their answer was simple – releasing staff from existing lines; they used multiple activity charts to share tasks, trained everyone, wrote procedures and sold the idea. They saved £117,000 per year in the first instance and the savings have since increased.

- *The Wombats* (Britannia Airways Ltd, Luton). The 'Wombats' represent Britannia Airways and work in the avionic workshop. Their initial data-gathering proved that Britannia's main aircraft batteries were making too many workshop visits. The team set out to improve the utilization of the batteries and the chapter explains how they successfully completed the project.

- *'No Sweat Again'* (NSK Bearings Europe Ltd, Peterlee, Co. Durham). This group, who work in the soft machining process, took up the challenge of reducing the amount of dropped bearing races from within the tooling zone of their multi-spindle automatic lathes and thereby increasing material utilization. By calling on their process skills and experience as small-group activity members, they were able to exceed the targets they had set themselves.

- *The Pioneers* (Denso Manufacturing UK Ltd, Telford). The Pioneers investigated problems involved in the manufacture of car air conditioning systems. Using PDCA and the tools of QC, they investigated, analysed and successfully counter-measured a major quality problem for their line.

PREFACE

The **VarityPerkins European Quality Award** is presented to the organization which best demonstrates its continuing commitment to a programme of total involvement, with quality and employee activities as key elements. VarityPerkins criteria include: the quality journey; the deployment of quality improvement throughout the organization; quality education and training; the systems of measurement applied; achievements as recorded by the measurement system; management commitment and the recognition process; future continuous improvement plans. The featured organizations are:

- *Case United Kingdom Limited* (Doncaster). Case Corporation is a multi-national marketing organization producing, for the past 150 years, a full line of agricultural and construction equipment. Following a worldwide restructuring programme and an £8 million investment, the Doncaster tractor assembly plan is now the 'European Centre of Excellence' for assembly operations.
- *The Savoy Group plc* manages some of the world's most luxurious hotels and restaurants. Employing some 2,000 staff the Group believes that an hotel must be a haven with its own personality, traditions and history, identifying completely with its surroundings. To meet guest expectations in a luxury hotel environment, employees must work together to demonstrate flair, virtuosity and professionalism at all levels and in attending to the smallest details. The Group prides itself in its commitment to excellence in style and service.
- *Legal & General,* Customer Services, Hove. Legal & General is one of the UK's largest financial services companies with more than 160 years of experience and some 2.5 million current customers. The customer service division at Hove is the centre which responds to any queries which their life assurance and pensions customers have about their policies. Together with its salesforce, they are committed to delivering a consistently high quality of service to all their customers.
- *Legal & General,* Sales & Marketing, Kingswood. Legal & General's Sales & Marketing Division specializes in the provision of life, pensions, savings and protection policies throughout the UK. The Division operates a multi-distribution approach and Legal & General is the leading company still to do so.
- *Magnox Electric plc,* Dungeness 'A' Power Station, Romney Marsh. Dungeness 'A' is one of six operating nuclear power stations of Magnox design, owned and run by Magnox Electric plc. Commissioned in 1966, the station is located on the south-east coast of Kent and is one of the largest industrial employers in the area.
- *Land Rover Vehicles* is a business unit within Rover Group and more than 12,000 people are employed at the Solihull site which produces the Defender, Range Rover and Discovery vehicles among others. The manufacturing site at Solihull has received significant investment in recent years as production and sales volumes increased. The site now has some of the most modern manufacturing facilities in the UK.

PREFACE

The **Wedgwood NHS Team of the Year Award** seeks to recognize excellence in teams and to encourage the development of teamworking throughout the NHS as a means to promote continuous improvement. The winner in 1997 was Yorkhill NHS Trust:

- *What's up Doc? – the Bugs Bunny Project* (Yorkhill NHS Trust). Pulling together a multi-disciplinary group, this team undertook a project to re-design their health services around customer needs by developing a plan to deal with the annual winter influx of children suffering from respiratory illnesses. The case study shows how the multi-disciplinary team, working to achieve a clear and meaningful patient-centred goal set about exploring the problem and implementing real organizational change.

One of the goals of the **Achieving Quality Performance** series, and this its third volume, is to learn from leading-edge work in North American organizations. The Sears Canada and Andersen Consulting strategic partnering approach to value creation provides an outstanding example of how teamworking was used to retrieve Sears' leadership position in its merchandizing organization:

- *Sears Canada and Andersen Consulting.* In 1993, Sears Canada and Andersen Consulting entered into a partnership to turn around the troubled retailer's merchandising organization, which had just posted net losses of $91 million (Can.) the previous year. Dramatic results were realized in less than eight months after project kick-off. By focusing on quality and value, this chapter outlines how the team actually exceeded its aggressive targets so quickly. The project was awarded Andersen Consulting's 1995 Worldwide Quality-Value-Success Leadership Award.

The real, yet inventive and innovative stories of corporate and team renewal in the fourteen organizations are told in these pages by teams of experienced academic writers collaborating with some of the people who made quality improvement happen. We would like to thank both the writers and the companies for their willingness to share tools, experiences and insights so that others may benefit from them. We should also like to thank the NSQT based in Salisbury, Ruth McCurry and David Barker at Cassell, and the book's designer and copy editor, Kenneth Burnley.

Lesley Munro-Faure, Richard Teare and Eberhard E. Scheuing
May, 1998

Part 1

THE MICHELIN EXCELLENCE
AWARD FOR IMPROVEMENT TEAMS

One

GLAXO WELLCOME

'Saying goodbye to a friend'
while implementing reduced cost assembly

ROGER J. CALLAN
AND
JANET COBURN

One

GLAXO WELLCOME

'Saying goodbye to a friend'
while implementing reduced cost assembly

INTRODUCTION TO THE ORGANIZATION

Glaxo Wellcome, employing 7,500 people, has six manufacturing plants in the UK. The 63-acre Barnard Castle site is a major manufacturing centre where 'active' ingredients are converted into a wide range of medicines.

Products include ampoules, syringes, vials, inhaled liquids, ointments and creams. These forms of medicines are used to treat a variety of conditions including hay fever, ulcers, migraine, nausea, eczema and asthma. More than 80 per cent of the factory's output is exported to over 100 countries.

The Quality Improvement Programme

The vision of the Barnard Castle factory is that of all Glaxo Wellcome operations, which is 'To be the supplier of choice'. The key goal to achieve this is 'To involve all staff to achieve continuous and individual job satisfaction'.

The company introduced five-year business plans in the early 1990s which are regularly reviewed to reflect changing business goals. They attempt to manage continuous improvement consistently across all areas of the company. A combination of diagnosis and the focused application of proven tools and techniques is employed, together with ongoing support and benchmarked measurements of effectiveness. This benchmarking is against other companies in general and pharmaceutical companies in particular, as well as inter-site (for example, Dartford against Barnard Castle). In addition, benchmarking is employed between departments (within Barnard Castle) to compare, for example, order set-up times, order line clearance times, reject levels, customer service levels and line efficiencies.

The first edition of the Business Plan was published in 1993. This was developed by fifty managers using SWOT analysis, looking at internal strengths and weaknesses and external opportunities and threats. This plan provided management with a clear picture of what they needed to achieve and

- Commitment to satisfying customer requirements.
- Attracting and retaining the best people.
- Adhering to all quality policies and the principles of good manufacturing practice.
- Meeting all regulatory requirements.
- Adopting the performance standard of 'Do it right first time'.
- Adopting error prevention as the system of quality, understanding and using appropriate technology.
- Developing consistent and approved suppliers.
- Developing and implementing a programme to achieve continuous improvement in quality.
- Continuously pursuing the policies and practices of a total quality organization.

Figure 1.1: Quality policy, Glaxo Wellcome

broadly how they intended to achieve it. The nine elements of the policy which support the plan are shown in Figure 1.1.

The Business Plan, overlaid with the quality policy, was broken down into a series of operational plans for each product stream and support area. Each plan identified the strategic direction and operating principles and goals. Targets were set for each year of the plan to include new developments in terms of production levels, staffing, quality, health, and environment.

The initial success of problem-solving teams and quality circles in these areas led to a focus on waste elimination in the organization. This process can be described as:

- Targeted at providing each team with a process by which they can identify and eliminate wasteful activities.
- The goal being to establish a habit of continuous improvement, focused on providing ever-improving levels of service and productivity.
- Waste being defined as any activity or expense that does not contribute to helping to improve service to the customer.

The means of implementing the waste elimination process is indicated in the flowchart of team activities (Figure 1.2).

The willing participation of employees in improvement teams is indicated by 50 per cent participation of all employees in 1993, which had increased to 90 per cent by 1996. These improvement teams run their own weekly meetings and call on resources and support from their team managers. These initiatives rest with the team members rather than with their managers. A

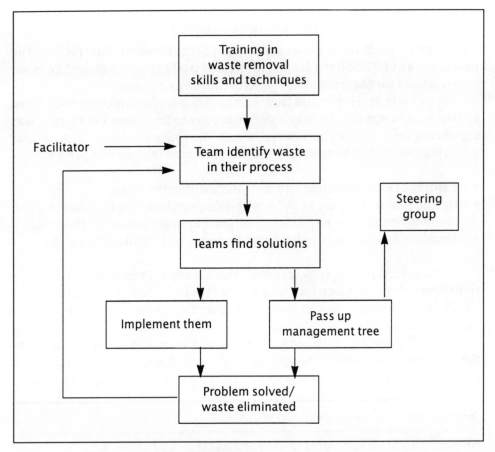

Figure 1.2: Waste elimination flowchart

team consists of all those line operators involved in a project, together with support staff and any specialists who need to be involved. A weekly one-hour team meeting is held which may cover more than one improvement project, as they overlap to form a continuous cycle. The one-hour meeting is allowed from the time schedule each week. Teams running a continuous improvement project are normally on the same shift pattern. An alternative shift pattern is available to allow for one-hour meetings with opposite shifts. The normal shift pattern incorporates a twenty-minute 'hand-over' when some inter-team discussion can take place. Individual team members have been trained to apply techniques such as statistical process control (SPC), total productive maintenance (TPM), overall equipment effectiveness (OEE), Pareto analysis (PA) and measles charts (MC), which are used willingly and enthusiastically to drive improvements.

THE ZOVIRAX PROJECT

The project is set in the Topicals department of the Barnard Castle facility. The new line was to be utilized for the filling and packaging of tubes of Zovirax, which is used for the treatment of a virus known as herpes.

Zovirax was developed and launched by Wellcome, who merged with Glaxo in March 1995. One of the major opportunities to flow from the merger was significant cost efficiencies as a result of consolidation. Three major principles were applied as part of the integration of the two companies:

- Centres of excellence and specialization within the group.
- Optimization of the use of skills, technology and existing facilities to allow manufacturing to be more closely aligned to the needs of the business.
- Simplification of the supply chain to provide competitive advantage.

A manufacturing review decided that Zovirax production should be transferred from the Dartford site to the Topicals department at Barnard Castle. A key objective was *to move the line and operation at the same time as reducing costs.*

The self-directed continuous improvement team was formed to address the problem. The team consisted of multi-skilled members who had been trained in many of the techniques employed for continuous improvement.

Team member	Team role
Ian Henderson	Department co-ordinator and team leader
Janet Coburn	Continuous improvement co-ordinator and team facilitator
Margaret Wood	Department trainer/assessor: extra trainer
Jean Pybus	Department trainer/assessor: extra trainer
David Allinson	Process operator
Andrew Albury	Process operator
Susan Harper	Process operator
Karen Fielden	Process operator
Carol Latcham	Process operator
Julie Walters	Class 1 operator

Table 1.1: Zovirax line improvement members

The team considers that fun, humour and recognition are important elements of their initiatives. Celebration days are held where all teams present their improvements to the rest of the department and guests. Managers are encouraged to attend the continuous improvement meetings.

The teams' belief in their purpose has encouraged them to make presentations outside the company, to such organizations as Boots, Nottingham; Vandenburgh Foods, Essex; Betts tube manufacturing, and

South-West Durham Hospital. The team who accepted the Zovirax line problem, were, therefore, experienced, skilled and confident.

DEVELOPMENT OF IDEAS

The development of ideas for instituting the new line at no additional cost began with a brainstorming session by the team. The outcome is as follows:

- Review pack size and packaging.
- Train all line members in process control (IPC) checks.
- Staff to do IPC checks.
- Review existing equipment.
- Use conveyor for filtrona.
- Improve scheduling of materials.
- Prepare line in advance for filling.
- Train team members for flexibility.
- Include engineers as part of the team.
- Improve documentation.
- Use larger capacity hoppers for cartons and leaflets.
- Change the structure of the line.
- Use one supervisor to run two lines.
- Review the need for line clearance.
- Staff to take pallets off line.
- Staff to do second line clearance checks.

The team reviewed the findings using a cause and effect (fishbone) diagram to analyse the main areas on which to focus their efforts. As the problem was the development of a new line, the members had limited experience of the packaging materials and the methods used to run the line. It was agreed that the focus would be on manpower as the best way of reducing costs until the new line was operational and the staff were confident about their work. Further initiatives could then be considered regarding machinery alternatives (see Figure 1.3). The other ideas were filed for future improvements once the line was operational.

It was at this discussion stage that the team first considered the idea of reducing existing members of operators on the lines to staff the new Zovirax line.

REVIEW OF EXISTING LINE OPERATIONS

A review of the operation of the existing lines in the Topicals department identified the numbers and types of jobs on each line (see Table 2). There were three other lines, two of which operated on a double-day shift system: 6 a.m. to 2 p.m. and 2 p.m. to 10 p.m.

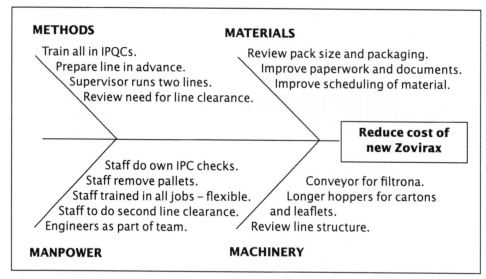

Figure 1.3: Fishbone diagram to reduce costs of Zovirax line

Line no.	81 (early)	81 (late)	82 (early)	82 (late)	86
Staff	7	7	7	7	6
	Filler	Filler	Filler	Filler	Filler
	Cartonner	Cartonner	Cartonner	Cartonner	Paddler
	Collator	Collator	Collator	Collator	IPQC
	Filtrona	Filtron	Filtrona	Filtrona	Cartonner
	(IPQC)	(IPQC)	(IPQC)	(IPQC)	
	Class 1	Class 1	Class 1	Class 1	Collator
	Serviceman	Serviceman	Serviceman	Serviceman	Class 1
	Trainer	Trainer	Trainer	Trainer	

Table 1.2: Staff numbers and roles on lines in Topicals department prior to introduction of Zovirax

It was agreed by the team that the initial investigation and implementation of change should concentrate on line 86 which was a relatively slow line with fewer staff compared to the others.

A multi-activity chart was developed to indicate each staff activity at particular times so that optimum use could be made of available time (Figure 1.4).

Following the analysis of the multiple activity chart it was clear that the operator responsible for conical paddling was only required for 50 per cent of the time. The 'paddling of the product' is an operation designed to prevent air from entering the filling system. During the filling process, the cream or ointment is drawn from the conical vessel through pipes connected to the filling machine, where it is filled into tubes. A conical vessel has a capacity of 500kg of product. When the amount of cream in the conical vessel falls below

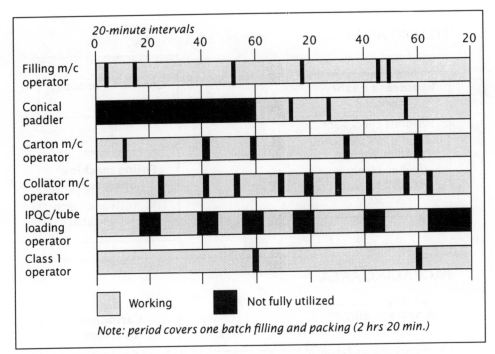

Figure 1.4: Staff multi-activity chart of line 86 in Topicals department

50 per cent of capacity, it is possible for air to be drawn into the system unless it is 'paddled' by folding the cream with a paddle. If air enters the filling system it results in high levels of rejects due to below standard weights. Previous attempts to automate the paddling process had been unsuccessful. The team decided that an operator was needed to 'paddle the product' once the conical vessel was half empty. Figure 1.5 shows a simple representation of the line process prior to reorganization.

A further review of the multi-activity chart indicated that it would be possible for the In Process Quality Control (IPQC) operator to pick up the duties of the conical paddler, provided that other members of the team could carry out their own regular IPQC checks to ensure that they were in control of the process. The IPQC operator would move from the packaging area to the filling room. These planned moves resulted in a major modification of the process quality control and process security control documentation. These documents are the monitoring framework, not only of the quality of the product but the security of purity and content of these highly sensitive medicinal products.

Batches of products can only be released to the market with the approval of the quality assurance department, whose representatives were invited to meetings of the team. The proposals were outlined and it was agreed that handwritten proposals could be used for a trial period.

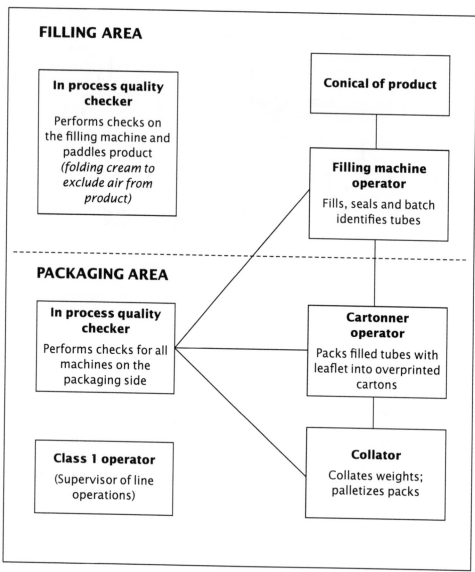

Figure 1.5: Line process prior to reorganization

TRAINING

The period in which these developments were taking place was one of high demand and production. The need to release staff for the new Zovirax line, coupled with the need for staff training for the reorganized line, was stretching resources.

The team and operations managers were invited to a meeting so that their support could be enlisted. They offered help in the form of two operators who were experienced in IPQC testing and would train the team in these duties. It was considered to be essential that these changes were implemented smoothly, not only for the maintenance of quality, but also to boost the morale of the staff who were being asked to take on extra tasks. A four-week trial was planned which was successfully completed by week three. One operator would be released from line 86 to staff the new Zovirax line. A representation of the line process after reorganization can be seen in Figure 1.6.

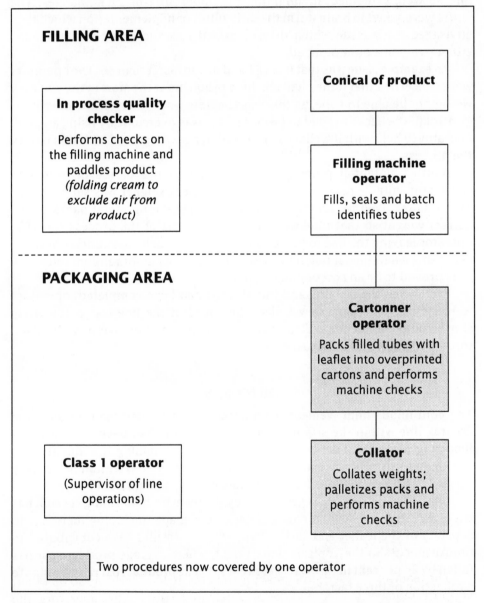

Figure 1.6: Line after reorganization: two procedures now covered by one operator

IMPLEMENTATION OF THE APPROACH TO OTHER LINES

The next stage was to standardize this approach on lines 81 and 82 also. Management were keen for the plan to succeed and allocated trainers for the task. These lines had slightly different ways of operating and, as it was difficult to persuade people to change the way they worked, the improvement team treated each shift as a different case. The modifications implemented on line 86 were explained, highlighting the importance of such changes. The shifts were asked to brainstorm the difficulties of implementation which they envisaged. Each issue which they identified was addressed and problems either overcome or minimized.

An example issue was that lines 81 and 82 ran faster than 86. The operators were concerned that if they had machine problems at the start of the run they would not be able to cope, as this was the time when many of the In Process Control (IPC) checks needed to be done. This was overcome by using an extra operator to help with IPC checks until confidence was gained with this part of the process.

Another potential problem was the inexperience of the operators in setting up suitable packs to ensure that the checkweigher was set correctly. This was resolved by asking the engineers to make up metal packs to the correct weight so that time was saved at the start of the process run. The operator leaving the line to move to Zovirax was usually a volunteer because of it being a new line. If not, names were placed in a hat for random selection. This proved to be an acceptable solution.

Even when the training and initial trials had been completed, operators were slower with some new tasks. The speed of the line was deliberately slowed until confidence and competence had grown, thus enabling the speed through the line to be increased.

OUTCOMES

The continuous improvement team assembled a trained team to staff the Zovirax line within the stipulated time-frame. This had been done without incurring any additional payroll costs, while maintaining line quality and health and safety performance. There had been no deterioration in delivery service deadlines, while employee morale had been maintained.

The original list of ideas generated by the team brainstorming session has been revisited and several changes have been made, including increases in capacity of the leaflet and carton hoppers. The results have contributed to improvements in the Topicals department, where average product cost has fallen by 26 per cent in the past three years. These product cost reductions are a reflection of three factors:

- An ability to absorb new business without incremental cost increases.
- Real cost reductions in materials, labour and infrastructure (£117,000 each year).
- Fully flexible teams.

THE LESSON TO BE LEARNED IS 'GOOD COMMUNICATIONS COUNT'

The most difficult issue faced by the team was to persuade line members to accept the proposed changes. The teams were reluctant to lose a team member as this meant more work for the remaining members.

The continuous improvement team developed a presentation to help 'sell' their idea to their colleagues. The *team* made the presentation, not their manager, as this indicated their commitment and enthusiasm. The presentations were made to individual lines and shifts, amending the content as the process of change developed. The focus of the content was *why* changes were needed and *how* other lines or shifts had overcome their problems.

Progress was recorded on the continuous improvement project's notice board. Minutes of each meeting were posted, together with the implementation plan. The team manager was invited to each meeting so that he could contribute to the planning and implementation process. The staff on each line who were included in the project were asked to complete a questionnaire. This looked for feedback on the performance of the continuous improvement team – how well or badly they had communicated and how well or badly the training and implementation had been handled.

In general, the results were positive, but some comments have given the team indicators of where they can further improve their performance.

The initiatives have already had an impact on other areas of the business. Another department at Barnard Castle is planning a new line to increase capacity. They have been monitoring the Zovirax initiative closely and intend to encourage a continuous improvement team to generate staff for a new line from existing staff resources.

GLOSSARY

Filtrona

A machine which automatically unloads empty aluminium tubes from the supplier's outer boxes. The tubes are loaded onto a conveyor in the correct orientation for supply to a cream/ointment filling machine.

In Process Control Checks

Quality checks carried out routinely throughout the process by the machine operators. These checks are recorded on check sheets and provide documented evidence of all checks performed during filling and packaging.

Line clearance

The process of removing all components (cartons, leaflets, tubes etc.), product (cream/ointment) and paperwork from the production line at the end of a production order. This clearance ensures that all orders are segregated during the packaging process.

Measles charts

Diagrams created by marking a diagram/chart showing the places where incidents have occurred or defects have been found. This technique has been used to identify recurring document errors on batch documentation.

Operational equipment effectiveness

A system that combines availability, quality and efficiency of production line. By using these three measures the line staff can review the live performance or note any issues.

Pareto analysis

A technique used as an interpretation tool in determining the relative frequency or importance of different problems, and for focusing on vital issues by ranking problems and causes in terms of significance. All operators are trained in this and other continuous improvement techniques.

Product stream

The functions/activities associated with receipt of customer orders, the process of converting packaging components and raw materials into finished products and the despatch of these products to the customer. These activities and supporting functions (e.g. engineers, quality, human resources etc.) report to one manager, the product stream leader.

Two

DENSO MANUFACTURING UK

Improvement through teamwork

THE PIONEERS:
MALCOLM MUNRO-FAURE
AND
DAVID ATKINSON

PROJECT 60:
JOHN BICHENO
AND
DAVID ATKINSON

Two

DENSO MANUFACTURING UK

Improvement through teamwork

Denso Manufacturing UK Limited was set up on a greenfield site in Telford in 1990 as a joint venture between Denso of Japan and Magneti-Marelli of Italy. With a turnover of £92 million, it is growing at the rate of £20 million per year – supplying evaporators, condensers, heaters and air-conditioning units for customers including Toyota, Audi, Jaguar, Land Rover and Volvo. Denso is committed to becoming the leading manufacturer of these components in Europe and, to achieve this, the management team have identified an opportunity to create a competitive advantage by maintaining current levels of delivered quality while driving down costs.

The factory is designed to maximize efficiency, using process flow principles to minimize movement on the lines, and a very visible approach to monitoring quality and productivity performance. Denso is committed to implementing best-practice working methods and has approval to ISO9002, ISO14001 and Investors in People. It has also received several supplier awards from major car manufacturers and the British Safety Sword of Honour.

The company also places great emphasis on involving their 900 employees, called associates, in teams to improve performance, creating three main types of team to address different problems:

- *Project Teams* – these are management-led and directed, cross-functional teams set up to address defined problems involving more than one function. Project teams are responsible for resolving individual problems and hold regular meetings with local managers to review progress and remove obstacles. In addition to resolving the problem, the teams are responsible for communicating with all employees affected, to stimulate their involvement in the problem-solving process and to gain their support. To demonstrate support and commitment, Denso's Managing Director attends these meetings at three-monthly intervals. Once the problem has been resolved, the team tasked with its investigation is disbanded.

- TIE working groups – these are cross-functional groups set up to improve the efficiency of production lines by eliminating waste and inefficiencies. These teams are inter-departmental, management led and their role is to focus primarily on productivity improvement. They have a typical duration of four to six months and, unlike Quality Circles, are disbanded once the project aim has been achieved.
- Quality Circles – these are groups from the same line or department who meet to address problems which affect their normal working activities. These teams meet to investigate problems selected by the team themselves. They are self-directed and concerned with problems which affect their ability to work effectively. Problems are tackled one at a time and once one problem has been resolved the team does not disband but moves on to tackle the next problem.

Denso introduced their first Quality Circles in 1993 and, perhaps surprisingly, do not consider that their principal objective is to resolve problems on the line. Denso considers that the fundamental objectives of the teams are to promote teamworking, provide an opportunity for the personal development of participants and to improve the working environment for associates. The fact that the teams also resolve problems on the line is important, but it is not the sole driving force behind them.

The company now has a total of thirty-three Quality Circles which involve 270 associates – some 36 per cent of the workforce. This represents a substantial commitment to the development of their people and to involving associates in the continuous improvement of processes for which they are responsible. Indeed, the programme has grown to such an extent that it has now become part of the annual planning cycle with:

- A timetable for the formation and registration of Quality Circles and the presentation of results.
- A time plan for Quality Circle activities during the year.
- A performance monitoring programme for Quality Circle activities.
- Quality training for circle leaders.
- An annual Director's award for the Denso UK Quality Circle which demonstrates the best effort.
- On-site and European competitions to identify Quality Circles which have achieved the most significant improvements in performance.

Quality Circles form at the start of each year and meet over a six- or twelve-month period, after which they make a presentation to the Managing Director. Participation is voluntary and teams usually meet for an hour every second week, either during the normal working week or in overtime if necessary. A Quality Circle Committee meets once or twice each year to review Circle activities over the previous period and to make plans for the next.

The remainder of this chapter focuses on the achievements of two of these teams:

- 'The Pioneers' are a Quality Circle team which was chosen from over fifty initial entries as one of the winners of the NSQT's Michelin Excellence Award 1997.
- 'Project 60' are a project team which were one of the eight teams selected as finalists of the NSQT's Michelin Excellence Award 1997.

'THE PIONEERS' – THE HEATER 3 QUALITY CIRCLE

'The Pioneers' are a Quality Circle formed by the twenty-two associates working on the Heater 3 line. This is one of the newest lines at the plant and produces heater and air-conditioning units for Jaguar and Audi cars. The line formed their first Quality Circle in January 1995 and during their first year they chose to investigate packing damage. In January 1996 they formed a new Quality Circle with seven members to tackle another set of problems, retaining their original name, 'The Pioneers'.

Problem-solving methodology

The Deming Plan/Do/Check/Action Cycle
The activities of Quality Circles at Denso are carefully structured to help associates to achieve results which help to improve the performance of the line, while allowing them to retain ownership over the selection, investigation and resolution of problems.

Denso apply an eight-stage programme which guides the activities of Circles from the initial selection of the problem through to the presentation of the project to the Managing Director. This programme provides a powerful method through which to apply the Deming, or Plan/Do/Check/Action Cycle to the resolution of problems in the workplace, and it is illustrated in Figure 2.1.

This programme forms the basis for Quality Circle activities and is used to drive the activity reports produced after each meeting (see Figure 2.2). These reports provide a structure to guide the activities of the team, and they enable supervisors and managers to support and monitor the progress of teams working in their areas.

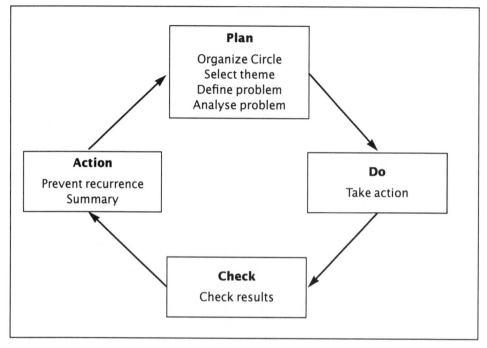

Figure 2.1: The Plan/Do/Check/Action Cycle

The training programme

Denso recognize that the key to the success of their problem-solving teams is the ability of team members to work together to agree the selection of a specific problem to tackle, to analyse the problem, find its root cause and to implement effective countermeasures. To do this, groups need to understand a range of problem-solving techniques and how the tools link together to provide a simple, powerful method for investigating and resolving problems.

To help associates develop the necessary skills, the company schedules a training programme for newly elected Quality Circle leaders. With two half-day sessions followed by a series of six one-hour sessions over a three-month period, this programme introduces associates to different problem-solving and quality tools, and provides guidance on preparing reports and how successful teams have tackled problems in the past.

The company also ensures that Quality Circles have access to advice and support from specialist on-site teams when they request it. During the course of the Pioneers' work, for example, they were supported by colleagues from production engineering, quality assurance, product engineering, production control, industrial engineering, maintenance, their supervisors and fellow line associates.

CIRCLE NAME:	PIONEERS		SECTION:	ITR ;
CIRCLE THEME:	BROKEN CASES/MOULDING DEFECTS		SHIFT:	DAYS
DATE / TIME:	4/4/9?	2-2.30pm	SECRETARY:	ELAINE MARTIN

DETAILS OF DISCUSSION David & Ruth have produced the temporary jig, we examined this and then as a group did in line trials. It was suggested that extending the case support under the evaporator dash would help. We agreed to use the jig on line once the modifications have been made.

We reviewed the data on the coal tar packing. The thickness of the packing is greater than the case gap. This in turn is causing the associates to press down hard breaking the drain holes. Our measles graph showed this to be main concern area.

At this point we reviewed our progress and due to the small number of Audi units involved we decided to concentrate our efforts on the Jaguar unit.

We reviewed our assignments and used brainstorming techniques for each problem.

Craig has asked TIE to do an analysis on the bridge and we will re-design this stage around an off line free standing rack and table. David Reese will draw up the line and racking so we can see if we can eliminate some racking or reorganise the line. PEN have vided us with a process flow & David Atkinson will do comparison times for line balance to confirm our countermeasure line balance is OK. We believe the unit is damaged as it is turned so our line balance must reduce the number of times the unit is turned.

CIRCLE MEMBERS	ASSIGNMENTS	DUE DATE
David Reese	Redesign Racking - New Driver Balancers	21/3/96
Elaine Martin	Monitor damage - measles graph/minutes	
Angela Reese	Re-write manuals	
Craig Hodgetts	Bridge Damage - C/Measures - Removal	
Paul Yates	Screw Driver striking unit	
Richard Lent	Repair Trolleys	
Tony Martin	Re-write manuals	
David Atkinson (Guest)	Entering/exiting booth	

No OF ATTENDANCE	7	LENGTH OF MEETING	1 1/2 hr	TOTAL QC CIRCLE HOURS	61 1/2
NEXT MEETING	11/4/9?	TIME	5-6	PLACE	MR 4

ACTIVITY STATUS BAR (PLEASE COMPLETE CIRCLE WHEN ACTIVITY IS IN PROGRESS)

ORGANISE CIRCLE	SELECT THEME	DEFINE SITUATION	ANALYSE SITUATION	TAKE ACTION	CHECK RESULTS	PREVENT RECURRENCE	PREPARE SUMMARY
●	●	●	●	●	○	○	○

PLAN — DO — CHECK — ACTION

	CHECKED	COMMENTS
TEAM LEADER	R Groome	Well done
SUPERVISOR	G. Lairford	Still keep the records for Audi up to date
MANAGER OR ASS/ MGR	A. Maxwell	Some good thinking there especially turning of the unit

Figure 2.2: Quality Circle meeting progress sheet

It is this painstaking attention to detail in the analysis of problems, and the continual search for solutions and better ways to do things, which underpin the achievements of the Quality Circles and other team activities at Denso.

Setting objectives for the team

When the Pioneers formed their circle for 1996, their first action was to agree their objectives for the Circle. In line with the company's view of Quality Circles, they defined their objectives in terms which were far wider than the resolution of a specific problem. By making the exercise contribute to the development of the individual team members, Denso benefits from the enthusiasm that members bring to the task of improving their working conditions. The specific objectives identified by the team include:

- Improving team-working skills. The members all work together on the same line and they felt that the Circle activities could help improve how they work together.
- Increasing their understanding of Quality Control. Starting out with very little knowledge of QC methods, members undertook training and home studying to enable them to apply the techniques in practice.
- Creating an atmosphere where all associates feel comfortable using QC tools. After Circle meetings the members each took a turn to do a short presentation to their line associates, explaining their plans, assistance needed, actions to be taken and results achieved.
- Improving the quality of their working life. They wanted to enjoy the Quality Circle and accomplish something to benefit all the associates on the line.

These objectives mirror the company's overall objectives for the Quality Circle programme – which are to promote teamworking, improve performance, help in the personal development of individual team members and improve working conditions.

The Quality Circle life cycle

The six-month life of a typical Quality Circle can be divided into three elements. The first couple of months are spent doing some preliminary analysis of the problems facing the team. This allows the team to identify potential problems and to select one of these as the theme for the Circle's intensive problem-solving activities.

Once the theme has been identified, the next stage involves analysing the problem and identifying potential countermeasures. The third stage involves implementing the countermeasures and ensuring that they really do eliminate the problem concerned. The Pioneers devised a 14-point programme based on the Deming cycle to guide their activities (see Figure 2.3).

The Deming Cycle-Stage	The Pioneers' 14-point programme
Plan	Investigate line defect history
	Choose a theme
	Define the problem
	Brainstorm possible causes
	Analyse the problem
	Investigate the cause
	Run trials for countermeasures
Do	Do the countermeasures
Check	Check the results
	Modify countermeasures
	Recheck the results
Action	Standardize
	Consider the next theme
	Presentation

Figure 2.3: The Pioneers' 14-point programme

Selecting the theme

The Pioneers started by analysing their line's monthly evaluation reports – looking at the safety, cost, delivery and quality of output. When looking at the incidence of defects, the team used three main sources of data:

- In-process defects – those found by manufacturing.
- Inspection defects – those found by QA.
- Customer complaints – those defects found by customers.

Using a simple grid they found that they achieved company targets in all areas except for *in-process defects*. For instance, 11.5 per cent from one group of units had some form of in-process defect, many of which had to be removed and re-worked; this all cost time and money.

Combining the information on *in-process* and *inspection* defects over a five-month period, they created a Pareto diagram (Figure 2.4), which shows that the most frequent defects on the line were repairs, loose screws and missing parts.

A preliminary investigation into each of these problems enabled the team to choose a theme which would cut the number of in-process defects – helping to achieve company targets and remove a source of frustration for associates:

- The problem of loose screws was already the theme for another Quality Circle, and so the team decided not to investigate this area further.

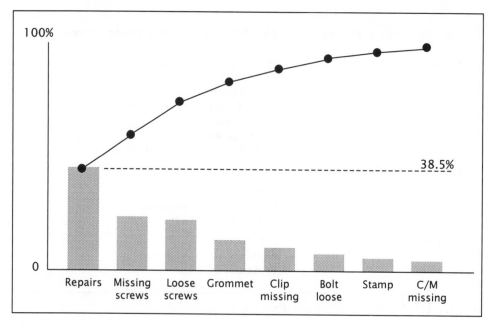

Figure 2.4: Choosing a theme: in-process defect analysis

- The team found that there was no pattern to the incidence of missing parts. Parts could be missed for a number of reasons, and at any stage in the production process. Knowing that new auto-feed machines would be installed later in the year, and that this might cut the number of parts which were missed, the team chose not to look into this problem.
- The team found that repairs to units represented the biggest category of in-process faults and that the number of units requiring repair was increasing. The team felt confident that they could find some solutions to the repair problem in the timescale available to the Circle, and so they analyzed the causes of repairs over a two-week period. Finding that case damage accounted for 57.1 per cent of all repairs, the team voted to tackle this problem as their theme for 1996. Reviewing the company's targets for the year, they calculated that they would have to reduce the incidence of case damage by 60 per cent in order to hit the company target for reducing in-process defects by 30 per cent during 1996. So this was the target they set.

Defining the problem

Having chosen their theme, the team set about ensuring that they fully understood the causes of case damage. Brainstorming the question 'What causes case damage?' the team created a fishbone diagram to provide a structure relating potential causes to the problem of case damage. At the end of their meeting, the team placed the fishbone diagram in the hot corner – by

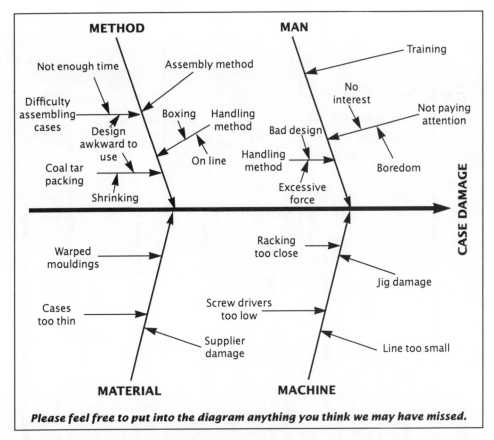

Figure 2.5: The Pioneers' fishbone diagram

the coffee machine – in order to gather ideas from all the associates working on the line (see Figure 2.5).

Analysing the problem

Having identified a number of potential causes for case damage, the team created a Cause and Effect Sheet (Figure 2.6) to manage the process of analysing and designing countermeasures for each of them. Each Circle member was tasked with investigating a potential cause, assessing whether or not it contributed to the problem, and designing a potential countermeasure if appropriate. Team members reported the status of their investigations at each Circle meeting. This information, and details of any proposed counter-measures was recorded on the Cause and Effect Sheet.

Team members employed a number of Quality tools in their search to find the root causes of case damage, the principal ones being as follows.

	POTENTIAL CAUSE	COUNTERMEASURE	RESULT X O Δ
MAN	TRAINING	Rewrite training manual to improve understanding.	
		Introduce repair procedure	O
	NO INTEREST	Not a cause for actual case damage	X
	NOT PAYING ATTENTION	Not a cause for actual case damage	X
	BOREDOM	Not a cause for actual case damage – possibly rotate jobs	X
	BAD DESIGN	Each part plays a role in the unit	X
	HANDLING METHOD	Introduce assembly jigs to improve handling	
		Extend rubber on repair trolley to returns and bench	O
	EXCESSIVE FORCE	Introduce assembly jig to counter this major cause of breakages	O
MACHINE	RACKING TO CLOSE	Racking which was too close to the line did cause damage to units.	O
		Remove unwanted racks by rebalancing the line	O
	SCREW DRIVERS TOO LOW	Some drivers were striking units	
	JIG DAMAGE	If used correctly – not a factor	X
	LINE TOO SMALL	Rebalance the line - reduce packing	O
MAT-ERIAL	SUPPLIER DAMAGE	Introduce dividers into the packaging for some plastic parts	O
	CASES TOO THIN	100% correct to drawing	X
	WARPED MOULDINGS	Not a factor unless stage 1	X
METHOD	SHRINKAGE	Not a factor in case damage	X
	COAL TAR PACKING	Major reason cases will not fit together – possible redesign of material	O
	DESIGN AWKWARD TO USE	As bad design	X
	DIFFICULTY ASSEMBLING CASES	As bad design	X
	NOT ENOUGH TIME	Rebalance line to equal out each stage's work	O
	ASSY METHOD	As for training – introduce assembly jig	O
	BOXING	Not a factor as new boxing was introduced to replace temporary boxing in use	X
	HANDLING METHOD	Reduce over line bridges	O
	ON LINE	Reduce packing	O

Key: X = Not a cause; O = Actual cause; Δ = Countermeasure implemented

Figure 2.6: Cause and Effect Sheet

Data analysis and check sheets
In order to monitor which activity on the line caused the case damage, the team designed check sheets so that associates could indicate the stage in the production process where they spotted units which had suffered case damage. This survey indicated that damaged cases were principally found at stages 5, 6, 11 and 12. This meant that the team could focus on the reasons for damage occurring at or before each of these stages.

Measles charts
The team also produced a large measles chart – essentially a large drawing of the unit – where associates could indicate, using spots, the location of any damage on cases. Again, each associate on the line was asked to mark damage as they discovered it. Transcribing the information from the measles charts onto a bar chart pinpointed the principal locations on the case where damage was suffered (see Figure 2.7). These were:

- Drain plate on the lower case.
- Evaporator dash case.
- The main case which fits over the evaporator dash case.

From this data, the team decided to look at the causes of damage to the lower case. This damage was principally discovered at stage 5 on the production line. The next step was to find out what was causing the damage.

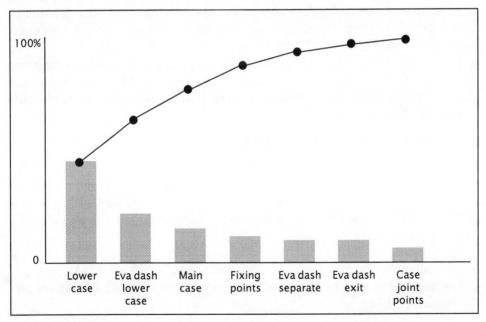

Figure 2.7: The location of case damage (information from measles graph)

Video-recording the process at problem areas
Using a video camera to record the activities at stage 5, the team found that the coal tar tape, used to reduce expansion valve noise, was too thick and so excessive force was needed to put the case together. It was this force which was the principal cause of lower case damage on units.

Taking action – introducing immediate and long-term countermeasures

Having identified that the coal tar tape was a significant potential cause of damaged casings, the team enlisted help from TIE and product engineering to identify possible solutions to the problem. They found that they could use pre-formed expansion valve packing as an alternative to coal tar tape. This had the advantage that it could compress as the case was being joined together, and it offered other real benefits:

- It provided complete coverage with no gaps.
- It was very quick for associates to apply.
- It was much cleaner for associates to use.

The pre-formed packing seemed to offer a long-term solution, but it would have to be approved by major customers before implementation. In order to improve performance now, the team had to find an immediate counter-measure.

So, the team looked in detail at the method of assembly at stage 5. This led them to consider using a jig to support the unit while the lower case was being fitted. They designed a trial jig which proved to be an immediate success – instantly reducing the number of damaged cases. This is clearly shown on the graph (Figure 2.8), which shows the incidence of in-process defects over the life of the Quality Circle. The installed jig had to support the unit in the correct places in order to prevent damage occurring. It also had to be compatible with existing and new product lines.

The problem with bridges on the line

The team's check sheets also showed that case damage arose at many of the stages where units were lifted onto a bridge to enable associates to work on them. They found that units were damaged when the case knocked against the bridge and designed three specific countermeasures to eliminate this as a cause of damage:

- Initially the team countered this problem by rebalancing the line, removing two over line bridges and building a side table and rack for off-line assemblies.

- The second countermeasure involved looking into the design of the cross line bridges. Placing packing onto the side of the bridge absorbed the shock of impact and reduced the incidence of damaged cases.
- The long-term measure to counter this problem has involved attaching an electric eye to the bridge. If a light beam is broken, the line automatically stops and the Andon sounds and so prevents the unit from striking the bridge. This countermeasure has proved so successful that it has been introduced onto all assembly lines.

The impact of each of these countermeasures is graphically illustrated in Figure 2.8 which records the results achieved by the Pioneers over the life of the Quality Circle.

Check results

The team's QC activity commenced in January 1996. During the course of their work they introduced six measures to reduce the incidence of damage to parts assembled on their line. The principal countermeasures were:

- Substituting the use of pre-formed packing for coal-tar tape to reduce the pressure on cases during assembly, save time and ensure a better product quality.
- Introducing an assembly jig to reduce the pressure on the lower case and drain holes.
- Rebalancing the line to reduce the number of over-line bridges and remove unwanted packing that could catch on the unit.
- Introducing auto stop sensors on the bridge to detect approaching units and stop the line if the unit is likely to strike the bridge.

The cumulative effect of these measures, introduced over a five-month period in 1996, has been to reduce the incidence of case defects by 86 per cent and is illustrated graphically in Figure 2.8. The introduction of the assembly jig has had the most dramatic impact on results, but each of the countermeasures has helped contribute to reduce case damage.

Prepare summary

The team completed the project in 1996, having logged a total of 116½ hours. To conclude, they asked four questions:

How effective have we been?
Many of the countermeasures that the team has developed have been standardized throughout manufacturing: the new packing and assembly jigs being the main two.

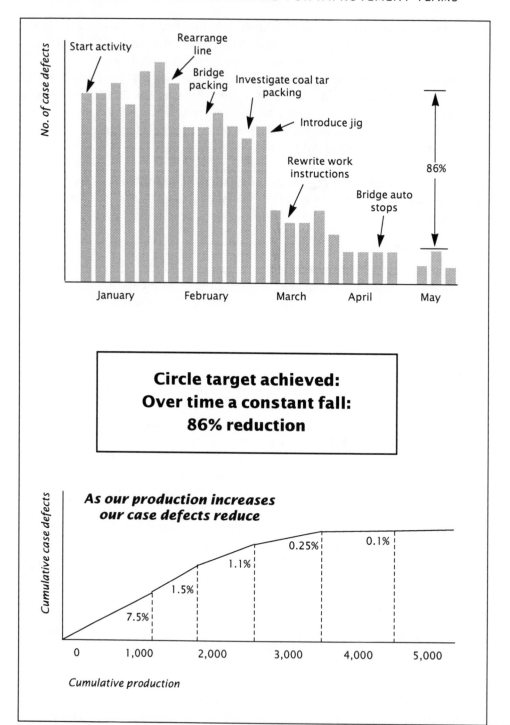

Figure 2.8: Results achieved by the Pioneers

What have we actually achieved?
The team have developed a number of successful countermeasures which are all running to schedule and which have led to an 86 per cent reduction in case damage.

What have we learned?
Team members have all learned valuable lessons in seven key areas over the six month period:

- Using the Plan/Do/Check/Action cycle.
- Teamworking.
- Investigation techniques.
- The tools of Quality Control.
- Problem-solving.
- Implementing countermeasures.
- Presenting results.

Who do we have to thank?
Everyone who helped us, including the line associates.

The team has also thought up a slogan which they would like to see used throughout manufacturing: **'It's better to build it right than put it right'.**

By combining the drive for performance improvement with a drive to achieve personal and teamwork development, the team has succeeded in meeting all its goals. It is now moving on to tackle some of the other problem areas on the line.

PROJECT 60

'Project 60' has been concerned with evaporator production. Project 60 was so named with the aim of achieving a reduction in scrap to a maximum scrap of 60 units per day. An evaporator is part of an air conditioning unit which cools the air. It fits behind the dashboard of a car and is normally never seen by the driver. In appearance, it looks like a small car radiator or the back of a refrigerator. It has 'fins' of corrugated metal which serve the purpose of dissipating heat. However, the evaporator units are small, a typical unit being approximately 250mm square. The units have close tolerances, and must be absolutely watertight. A unit comprises about forty plates and twenty fins, with an inlet and an outlet pipe.

The evaporator line process is shown in Figure 2.9. The seven stages are (1) press; (2) core crimp; (3) degrease; (4) core assembly; (5) vacuum braze; (6) leak test; (7) surface treat.

During 1994 and 1995 Denso experienced a very rapid volume increase, as

33

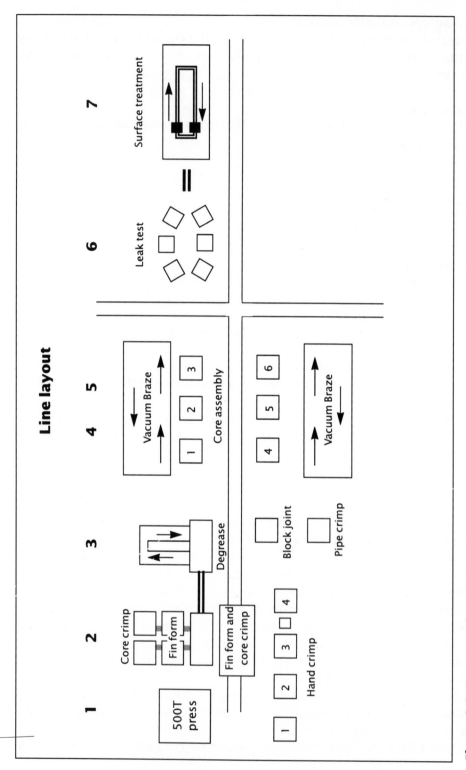

Figure 2.9: Evaporator line process

demand more than doubled. This meant employing new staff and starting a night shift. With the rapid increase in new staff, and with tight tolerance and safety requirements, the scrap rate increased, reaching around 200 units per day in mid-1995. High scrap means more production to replace the lost units which adds to the already fast-growing demands. Project 60 aimed to reverse this vicious circle, the aim being a reduction in the scrap rate to sixty units per day by December 1995. An initial investigation revealed that of the 200 scrap units per day, irreparable leakage represented the biggest cause of failure so the additional aim was to more than halve the overall leakage rate to 3 per cent. The project organization as described earlier was established with members from manufacturing, production engineering, and total industrial engineering. A regular series of meetings was established.

The team began with data gathering and a Pareto analysis of the daily scrap record. A two-dimensional fault table of the twenty-four types of evaporator and the forty-five scrap reasons lead to a broad categorization of process-related problems (brazing and surface treatment), and operator-related (slippage, dents and damage, and others). These five areas were each again Pareto prioritized, and specific responsibilities and target dates for the resolution of each established by the project team. The schedule reflected the Plan/Do/Check/Action cycle.

Since the start of Project 60, the PDCA cycle has progressed through three revolutions. What is reported in the sections following are three examples of sub-projects that have been tackled, but it must be stressed that many more took place, both process-related and operator-related. The common thread through each of the examples is that careful analysis of the problem and controlled experimentation led to dramatic improvements.

Example 1: Fin slippage

Fin slippage is a condition when a fin protrudes from the side of an evaporator. Fins are corrugated metal sheets which are compressed and inserted between the plates of an evaporator. If they protrude beyond the side of the evaporator, excess condensation may appear which can result in droplets of water being blown into the car through the air conditioning unit. Evaporators with protruding fins have to be scrapped.

The analysis began with a measles chart showing the most common locations of protruding fins. The fins are delicate, high tolerance heat dissipation protrusions, susceptible to damage and requiring exacting manufacture to maintain the correct distance between fins. The end plates (or sides of the evaporator) were revealed as the most common locations for faults. On the end plates, the last bank of fins has to be compressed into a length some 12mm shorter than in other areas, so this made sense. The team brainstormed possible solutions, eventually asking the 'obvious' question of whether it would be possible to use a smaller number of fins for the end plates.

This proposal had to be checked and tested by QA, but was approved. This innovation resulted in an 80 per cent reduction in scrap due to fin slippage. The only technique used was brainstorming, but this followed a systematic analysis leading to the root cause of the problem.

'Trial and error' or experimentation is also important, especially the support of management to allow the team to undertake trials.

Example 2: Pipe voids

An evaporator has an inlet and an outlet pipe, which must be secured in place. These pipes are brazed onto the evaporator, and are held by a pipe clip. During the brazing process, there was a tendency for 'voids' to be created. A void simply means that the pipe is not squarely held against the evaporator, but instead is located at an angle with a void created in the angle. The consequence of a void is a weak point resulting in a leak, either immediately or during service.

An important part of this sub-project was realizing that it was the clips holding the pipes together too tightly during the brazing process, that was causing the problem. The clip has to therefore perform a balancing act between holding the pipes in place, but not so tightly as to cause deformation during brazing. This realization was again brought out by brainstorming and detailed observation.

Once the problem became clear, solutions could be attempted. Again, trial and error was adopted with the support of management. The solution process went through several iterations. Shopfloor associates made several suggestions, eventually leading to that shown in Figure 2.10.

Willingness to pursue theory through trial and error once again proved effective. The results speak for themselves – from a 33 per cent defect rate in September 1996 to a 1.7 per cent defect rate in February 1997.

Example 3: Evaporator leakage

The third example concerns a leakage study sub-project. It will be appreciated that leakage cannot be tolerated from an evaporator, so each evaporator is subject to stringent tests. Leaks can occur through very small holes which, due to the length of pipe in a small space, is difficult to detect. The problem was approached in a Pareto-type fashion. First the evaporator type having the highest leakage rate was identified. Then, the types of defect on the evaporator were classified, and the highest-occurring defect became the subject of the next sub-project.

The highest frequency leakage problem concerned block joints. A block joint holds two of the evaporator pipes together. It was not easy to determine the source of the fault, and several theories were put forward. By cutting up some defective evaporators and examining the joints under the microscope, it was discovered that a void was present. The presence of the void meant that the two sides of the evaporator tank were not parallel, causing a weakness and

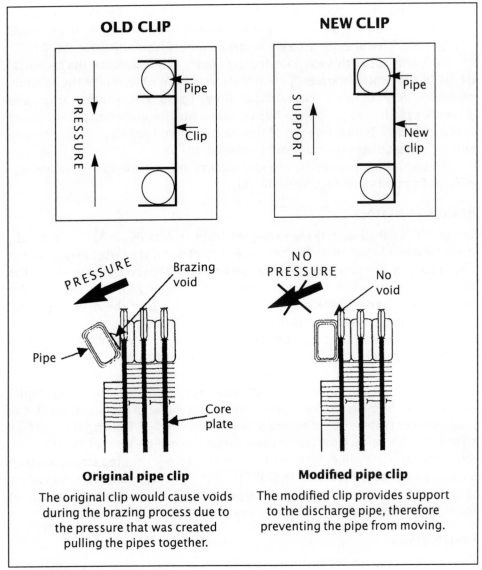

Figure 2.10: Changes in pipe clip to reduce voids

eventual leaks. This discovery was the important breakthrough, achieved by a willingness to hear opinions, hypothesize, and investigate in fine detail.

Once the effect was known, the causes could be investigated. Once again, associate experience, suggestions, and detailed investigation were used. Two possible causes were identified. First, the team found that it was difficult to consistently locate the block joint squarely onto the tanks during assembly. Second, the final check and adjustment required high levels of associate skill.

Now a range of solutions could be explored. The eventual solution required manufacturing engineering involvement and associate innovation. The manufacturing change made was to design a support jig to help keep the block joint square. The associate innovation was to design a support jig which required a far lower degree of associate skill to make the necessary adjustments.

The point about this exercise for the reader is not so much the technical detail, but the spirit of investigation and innovation which made the solution possible. Very detailed microscopic investigations, involving time and patience as well as support, may be necessary. Also, tapping into the shopfloor associate's detailed knowledge of the process would not have been possible without a high degree of trust and co-operation.

The implementation of the two measures resulted in a reduction of leakage defects from this source to virtually nil.

Project 60 history

We have described only three examples from Project 60. In fact, many sub-projects took place. However, the entire project was not a series of haphazard mini-projects, but proceeded from a top-down data based analysis, where the principal causes were identified, measured, categorized, and targeted for improvement. The whole project was co-ordinated by the overall project team, including presentations to the managing director.

The three examples described come from one Deming PDCA cycle which had specific targets in terms of time and achievement. In fact, the project went through four iterations, as shown in Figure 2.11.

The effect of all the sub-projects has been dramatic. The team implemented countermeasures on a progressive step-by-step basis against all the main problem categories of slippage, dents and damage, brazing, and surface treatment. The effects of the countermeasures can be seen in Figure 2.12. Since the start of Project 60 there has been an 80 per cent reduction in scrap and an 88 per cent reduction in leakage. The project group has achieved its target of fewer than sixty scrap units per day. It has now set a new target of forty scrap units per day, and has been renamed 'Project 40'.

Conclusions

Project 60 was a large co-ordinated project involving many sub-projects, but all targeted at one focused area. The success of the project was due to the organization of the project, using clear data-based targets, based on factual analysis of the problem which enabled it to be successfully broken down into sub-projects. The role of several departments – manufacturing, production engineering, total industrial engineering, and plant engineering – was crucial. So too was the willing co-operation of the shopfloor associates. The willingness of the management to permit trial and error experimentation, involving cost and time, was also important. Finally, the reporting arrangements whereby the Managing Director attended the three monthly report-back meetings, gave the project a sense of urgency and importance.

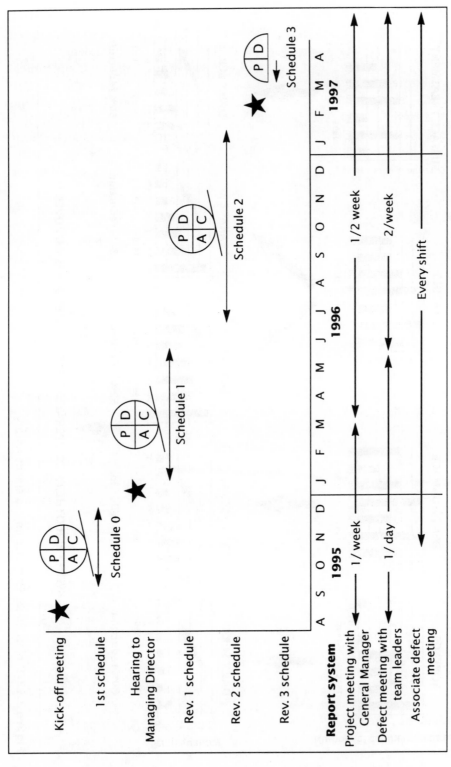

Figure 2.11: Project 60 schedule

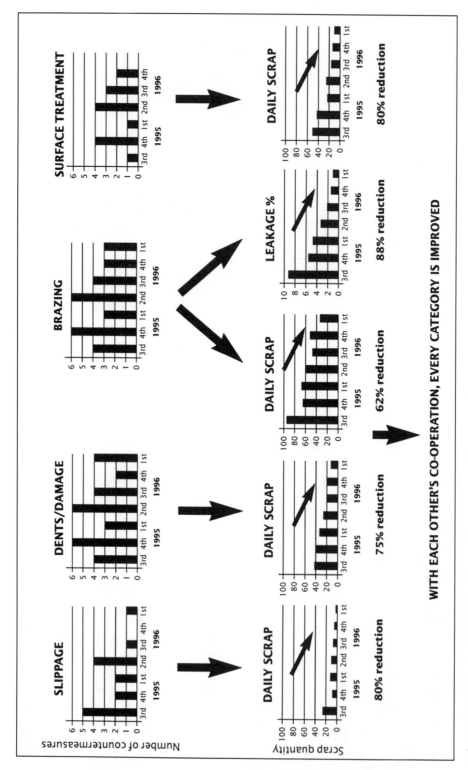

Figure 2.12: Project 60 performance improvement history

Three

RHP PRECISION BEARINGS

Mission Impossible:
zero tolerance of defects and reworkings

CONRAD LASHLEY,
PAUL NEWTON
AND
DON WATT

Three

RHP PRECISION BEARINGS

Mission Impossible:
zero tolerance of defects and reworkings

INTRODUCTION TO THE ORGANIZATION

RHP Precision Bearings is a specialist division of NSK-RHP Bearings which produces precision bearings. The manufacturing process involves high precision processes which had been producing reworkings averaging 20 per cent of output. Plans to increase output showed that reworkings would constitute a considerable proportion of the total increase in the production capacity. A teamworking project involving all the relevant production operators was established and they identified the potential causes of the problem. Targets were introduced and via close monitoring of output, reworkings were all but eliminated from the production output.

INTRODUCTION

RHP Precision Bearings produces high precision ball bearings suitable for either high accuracy or high speed running. The parent company, NSK-RHP Bearings, aims to be the world leader in bearing manufacture, and is committed to processes of continuous development and employee involvement. RHP Precision Bearings supplies new and replacement bearings which are used exclusively in the machine tool industry. It has an annual sales turnover of £14 million, of which 85 per cent is from export business. The division employs 208 people. Initiatives involving the implementation of NVQs, plans to be recognized as an 'Investor in People', and the use of the Business Excellence Model as a benchmark for improving performance have all been taken as steps in working towards the parent company's objectives.

Two departments within the division – Machine Shop and Assembly – work two-shift patterns. Both departments had introduced teamworking and quality improvement processes based on the work teams. As a part of the company's commitment to quality improvement through Total Quality

Management and training and development, the manufacturing departments were supported by a Total Quality Facilitator and a six-strong full-time training team.

Manufacture of precision bearings involves a high degree of accuracy as the bearings are 'preloaded' – set precisely against inner and outer rings to guarantee running accuracy and speed. The subsequent performance of bearings is affected by the size of the 'preload' step – built into the rings. The rings have to be ground with a high degree of accuracy to a tolerance of approximately 5 microns. The tolerance of the interface (the preload step) is about one-tenth of the thickness of a human hair.

The processes involve a high degree of physical handling and are largely dependent on manual skills. Prior to the initiative being reported here, the manufacture of the 'preload and rotary facing process' involved assessing the amount of grinding required to achieve the desired preload step. This was done on a special bearing fixture. The rings were ground and then passed on for checking. Material which was assessed as being within the manufacturing tolerances was sent for assembly and wash. However, approximately 20 per cent of the bearings were found to be outside the tolerance at the checking stage.

The preload and rotary facing process had been a cause of concern for some time as it represented a limiting factor in the output because of the restrictions on the number of bearings that could pass through the checking process. In particular the number of 'reworkings' represented considerable extra effort. Analysis of output between January 1994 and January 1996 showed that reworkings occasionally dropped towards 15 per cent per day and occasionally peaked at nearly 25 per cent. Given the average reworkings of 20 per cent, a production level of 3,000 units per day would result in some 600 having to be rectified. Furthermore, production was due to increase to 4,000 units and on this level of rectification, 800 units would be sent back for reworking. This meant that two and a half people would be fully employed on reworking bearings.

Given the organization's objective to be the international market leader and its commitment to continuous improvement, management had a limited number of choices. They could increase overtime working, with the risks to employee stress and possible further increase in reworked product, or they could attempt to increase capacity, either through the purchase of more machinery or by putting on additional shifts. Both these solutions represented increases in costs. Finally, they could set up a team to investigate the problem and make suitable suggestions for improving the quality of output and reduce the amount of reworking needed. Immediate production costs would not be increased, and the solution addressed a key quality issue. This third option was chosen and the company set up Team 1 in March 1996, and Team 2 in April of the same year. The objective was to reduce reworked units to an average of 10 per cent by the end of the year.

ADDRESSING THE PROBLEM THROUGH TEAMS

Team 1 was set up as a cross-functional problem-solving team. It involved eight members including senior, middle and first line management, as well as operatives from the production process concerned. Apart from direct production experience, the team involved people with engineering, quality and training expertise, and in total accounted for almost 100 years work experience with the organization.

This first team spent its initial meetings identifying possible causes of the number of reworkings needed. Brainstormed suggestions included a number of causes based around equipment, materials and people problems. These were first listed on a flip-chart in random order. Later the team ranked these in priority form, as follows.

1 Work practices.
2 Training.
3 Quality of marking-up.
4 Dirty tracks.
5 Machine capability.
6 Quality of work from finish facing.
7 Datum plates.
8 Size of work.
9 Flat clocks.
10 Slave balls.
11 Lack of equipment.
12 Flats on base plate.
13 Output targets.

The suggested key causes appeared to be associated with the way people were working on the tasks, either in exercising skill or in the methods they used. This first team took the view that if the causes were largely located at the point of production and involved the immediate production team, *they* should be involved in overcoming the problems. It was essential therefore that production operators took ownership of the difficulty and solutions to the problem. Production operators had, after all, the most experience of the processes involved. Team 1 continued to be available as a technical and quality back-up but the main focus shifted to the creation of Team 2 comprising twenty-three members covering two shifts. Apart from the twenty operators from the two-shift production line, the team also comprised the two shift leaders, and the team leader who was from the training department.

Weekly team meetings, followed up by monthly update sessions, were organized in work time. Contact between members of the two shifts was initially difficult, because both teams were not formally on duty at the same

45

time. However, information was initially passed between shifts by team members coming in to work outside normal work time, and occasionally the night shift would stay on so as to be able to talk to the dayshift team. In these cases, team members were prepared to give their time to resolving the problem even after an eleven-hour shift.

Team members became self-managing in that they took ownership of the project and supervisors did not need to keep asking for results and progress reports. The group were sharing information and empowered to improve output. They accepted responsibility for the quality of the output and for improving the overall performance. As the project progressed, the skills and abilities of the team developed. Prior to the project only the supervisors and management had experience of making presentations, but as the project progressed, increasingly team members made presentations to management and outside clients. On one occasion the team made a presentation to the senior management of a Japanese client company. Subsequently the team entered several internal and external competitions which were aimed at celebrating teamwork and team development in the cause of quality and productivity improvement.

TOWARDS ZERO DEFECTS

The first meeting of Team 2 occurred in late April and they discussed the outcomes from Team 1. It was felt that a 10 per cent target for reworking was tough but, on balance, achievable, given adequate support. The team selected a team leader who would make notes and communicate information between the day and night shifts. The team also decided to consider the causes of reworkings and possible solutions suggested by the brainstorming meeting held by Team 1. The team also organized a programme of weekly meetings. These commenced in the first week of May.

Team members took ownership of the problem and were committed to doing whatever it took to overcoming difficulties. The team worked out best methods of doing jobs, examining and sharing best practice within the group. They organized their own tests, drew up quality procedures and information charts so that all members knew where to find information and so that all the team knew what they should be doing, and why. They conducted their own training sessions, and introduced information and feedback systems so that both the group and individuals were able to monitor performance, identify difficulties and take corrective action where needed. All team members were in touch with the progress of the project.

After consideration of the suggested causes, the team identified a number of actions that were needed to address the problem. First, the team recognized that different practices were being used at both the preload and rotary facings stages of the process. The team decided that standard procedures were needed, supported by trials to establish best practice. Second, the team set up an information system which presented a breakdown of the figures for the numbers of rectifications needed by individual operators. These figures were to be displayed on the notice board with a weekly/monthly graph showing progress. Eight different part-time trainers had been used over the years and it was felt that it was not surprising that individuals were using different methods. Finally, the team decided to set up a revised and more user friendly information source. It was felt that the current filing system was complicated and confusing.

By the end of the third week of Team 2 coming into being, the average number of rectifications had dropped to 16.2 per cent, the lowest so far that year. Team members felt that just being aware of the problem was helping to focus practices on more accurate methods. Within five weeks the number of rectifications had dropped to an average of 13.3 per cent – just 3.3 per cent off target and the lowest figure for approximately five years. The first individual performance figures were made available and these showed some wide disparities between the reworkings required from different operatives. The figures showed that individual performance varied between one operator where approximately 45 per cent of output had to be reworked and another operator where the amount of reworking was below 5 per cent. Most individual operators were producing between 10 and 20 per cent of reworkings.

Monthly production figures for June showed that the average had dropped to 12.6 per cent and the team introduced individual assessment procedures which would assist in identifying training needs. Individual performance results showed that there were still wide differences between individual levels of output of rectifications, but the overall level of reworkings being produced was falling across all members. Through the next few weeks competence assessments were carried out and coaching sessions organized where individual performance warranted it. By mid-July, average rectifications dropped below 10 per cent for the first time in the company's history. They had achieved what had appeared to be a tough target, five months ahead of time. The team was keen to ensure that this level could be sustained and the processes of individual assessments and coaching sessions continued.

Improvements in the production of high quality product continued and the average number of reworkings also fell. The team meeting at the beginning of August confirmed that the rate was now consistently below 10 per cent and team members were reminded of a quotation from the Engineering Department at the beginning of the project: 'You'll never get rectifications below 10 per cent!', they had been told. Team members felt that there was still plenty to sort out, and they decided to adjust the target to 5 per cent rectifications by January. The team continued the individual assessments and coaching. They felt that individual differences in work practices were largely responsible for differences in levels of reworkings needed.

The assessment of performance continued but the need for coaching sessions dropped as team members increased the consistency of work practices. All members were producing less than 10 per cent of rectifications, and some individuals were producing as low as 2 per cent. The September results showed the average rectifications at 5.4 per cent, just over the January target.

Though team performance was now consistent, there were still some variations between members and the team continued to work on ironing out the variations. In addition, the team looked at issues related to equipment. The rectification rate continued to drop so that by January (the initial target date for rectifications to be 10 per cent – revised to 5 per cent), the average rate of rectifications being produced was 1.1 per cent.

Over the space of the project time of nine months the team had reduced the total number of rectifications produced by 64,766 units. This saved some 2,619 hours of working time. Calculated on an annual basis, and allowing for extra training time, the project saved £57,465. All this had been produced without extra capital investment. The savings had been generated through the team and the time and effort involved in self-managing their performance. In addition, these savings were not just historical, as the procedures introduced would continue to reap benefits. The project has in effect yielded a 19 per cent increase in productivity by reducing the average number of reworkings down to 1 per cent.

MISSION IMPOSSIBLE

Using traditional, directive approaches to managing the production process for these bearings had, on average, produced 20 per cent of the output which required to be reworked. Managers and engineers were convinced that a high level of reworkings was a natural outcome of the production of these items. Indeed the initial target set represented a reduction by half of usual levels of reworkings over a nine-month period, the revised target of 5 per cent seemed to be a 'mission impossible'. Yet by teamworking and tapping into the expertise and knowledge of the operators actually doing the job, the impossible mission was not only achieved – it was further reduced. This case study provides a valuable insight into what can be achieved when organizations tap the talents of teams.

Figure 3.1 shows the levels of reworkings over recent years and indicates the dramatic reduction produced through the period of the project. The organization gained by increased output without increased costs; indeed, as was shown above, there were considerable savings in costs. Quality and reliability improved and the organization was better placed to meet its service quality obligations to clients. The whole process of production was streamlined as the level of reworkings dropped to such a low point there was

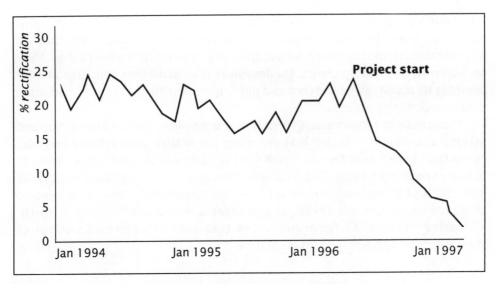

Figure 3.1: Preload rectification levels from January 1994

no longer a need to undertake the component checking stage. This released a further three people for other tasks within the plant.

Apart from these direct gains in increased productivity, quality and reductions in costs, the company gained from the impact on employee morale and commitment. The team took ownership and responsibility for improving the quality of the outputs. By working as one project team over the whole process, operators at different stages recognized the impact their work had on others and developed a team spirit across the whole process. Through the development of a shared vision of the process at every stage, employees became more flexible. With the mutual support gained through teamworking, building a shared understanding of what was needed and by being actively involved in identifying problems and resolving them, all team members grew in confidence.

Testimony from operators involved in the tasks confirms this point. 'It made me feel more confident', a preload operator said of the project. Another preload operator said, 'Time was taken to hear our views on our job as a group which made us feel like a team. We have saved money on man hours and rectifies, and this made us feel more confident.' The importance of being asked for views and suggestions was also confirmed by one of the rotary facing operators, 'I felt involved by being asked our opinion and asked if we had any ideas. We were informed every week and at the end of the month, and shown nice clear graphs and charts.' Analysis of these and other comments gathered from the operators involved in the team suggests that being informed about both expectations and outcomes were important ingredients in gaining their support. Similarly the support given both by the team and the organization through training were also vital.

The team's experiences are now used as a model for the rest of the company. For employees the team's experiences show what they can contribute to organizational performance when they are given the opportunity. Most importantly for management, the lesson is that managers can gain greater benefits by involving employees and participating with operatives in defining and overcoming problems.

Essentially the approach is to empower employees to make decisions and to encourage them to accept responsibility for quality, productivity and cost reduction. In this case the approach used a quality circle technique set up to solve a specific problem. The trick with this approach is not only to tap into the employees' enthusiasm to resolve the specific problem, it is also to continue to sustain the levels of enthusiasm and commitment generated. Ultimately the benefit for managers is that they can increase control of operations by appearing to let go of it.

Four

BRITANNIA AIRWAYS

Wombats recharge their batteries through continuous improvement

Nigel Hemmington
AND
Nigel Williams

Four

BRITANNIA AIRWAYS

Wombats recharge their batteries through continuous improvement

Introduction

Britannia Airways has made a clear commitment to improving quality through teamworking by the establishment of a company-wide Continuous Improvement Programme. The programme, facilitated by the Continuous Improvement Team, seeks to encourage groups of staff at all levels to take responsibility for identifying, analysing and solving their own work-related problems. The company's commitment to quality through continuous improvement is reflected in its mission: 'To be the world's best holiday airline' and by its focus on 'continuous improvement and teamwork'. This chapter reports one particular project in the Engineering and Maintenance Division concerned with improving the efficiency of aircraft battery servicing.

Britannia Airways is part of the Thomson Travel Group which also includes Thomson Tour Operations, the UK's largest tour operator; Lunn Poly, the UK's largest chain of travel agents; and The Holiday Cottages Group which specializes in self-catering holidays in the UK and Europe. Britannia is the world's largest charter airline and Britain's second-largest airline carrying over eight million passengers to more than 100 destinations worldwide.

The company was founded in 1962 by Ted Langton, owner of the tour operator Universal Sky Tours. Then known as Euravia and based at Luton Airport, the new airline operated three Lockheed Constellation aircraft bought from the Israeli airline El Al. In 1964 the company was renamed Britannia Airways and in 1965 became part of the International Thomson Organisation (now the Thomson Corporation). The company has a reputation for innovation in its field; it was the first airline to offer its holiday passengers hot meals, it was the first European operator of the Boeing 737-200, it was the first UK holiday airline to offer passengers free inflight entertainment, and it pioneered charter flights from the UK to Australia. The 1990s have seen

Britannia continue to modernize its fleet and further expand its route network, and in 1997 the company formed a Germany-based subsidiary company, Britannia Airways GmbH, which operates flights for German tour operators.

The Continuous Improvement Programme

The Continuous Improvement Programme was introduced in 1990 by the Technical Director in charge of the Engineering and Maintenance Division, one of seven divisions within the company, the others being: Flight Safety, Sales, Personnel, Systems, Marketing, and Operations and Aircrew. He recognized the fact that employees are experts in their own area of work and sought to draw on this expertise to improve quality and efficiency. This participative approach to quality improvement was also encouraged by the introduction of European standards of operational auditing that were being applied to the UK airline industry at about this time. This initiative required companies to establish operating standards, the development of which provided the focus for employee involvement (Lashley, 1997).

Since 1990 there have been many Continuous Improvement projects in the Engineering and Maintenance Division, and the success of the programme has been such that it was extended to include the rest of the company in 1995. Although it now has a company-wide remit the Continuous Improvement Department is still located in the Engineering and Maintenance Division.

The Continuous Improvement Department supports Continuous Improvement Teams in a number of ways. It provides training through a series of modules, it provides documentation and process support, it provides advisers to facilitate the work of the team, and it co-ordinates Continuous Improvement projects. In response to its wider remit in 1995, the Continuous Improvement Department reviewed its processes and support documentation and as a result introduced a number of important new features. These included the publication of *The Essential Guide to Continuous Improvement*, the development of a project book to act as a framework for the work of teams and the introduction of the 'three meeting structure' (described below) for implementation of the process. In many ways these developments reflect a continuous improvement approach being adopted by the Continuous Improvement Department itself!

Continuous Improvement projects can be initiated by either employees who identify an area for investigation within their own area of work, or by managers who might request the establishment of a team to address a problem that they have identified. In all cases, however, membership of teams is voluntary. Teams of about four to eight people within the area being investigated would come together to meet for one hour per week in company time. Each team is supported by two other groups: the Continuous Improvement Department who provide process support and allocate a

CI Teams

Solve work-related
problems . . . by
selecting best solutions

Support Teams

Support and commit to
team projects. Approve
implementation plans

CI Department

Develop and deliver CI
modules, advise/support
CI teams

Figure 4.1: The tripartite approach to Continuous Improvement

Continuous Improvement Adviser to the team; and a Support Team made up
of more senior staff who can advise, assess and authorize proposals that the
team brings forward.

The approach to Continuous Improvement

Britannia's tripartite approach to Continuous Improvement, based on the CI
Team, the Support Team and the CI Department, is shown in Figure 4.1. The
actual process of Continuous Improvement at Britannia is based on a five-
stage problem-solving process shown in Figure 4.2. This problem-solving
process provides the structure for the project book which teams use as a
framework for their activity and a record of their progress. The project book
is used as a guide to take the team through the process, for training purposes,
to set and review team agendas, to keep records, to track progress, for team
reviews, to log team minutes and to act as a team project report. At the end of
each of the five problem-solving steps there is a review of progress with the
Support Team who can, if necessary, provide authorization for further
progress.

Facilitation by the Continuous Improvement Adviser is achieved through
the 'three meeting structure', as shown in Figure 4.3. This approach is
designed to ensure that the team leader, rather than the Adviser, is always the
focal point of the team. Before a team meeting takes place, the Adviser and the
team leader meet to set objectives for the meeting, to discuss the agenda and
to clarify the tools and techniques to be used. The team then meets with the
team leader as the focal point and the Adviser observing. Sometimes the
Adviser will act as a member of the team to bring a fresh, non-expert view to
the problem. After the meeting the team leader and the Adviser meet again to

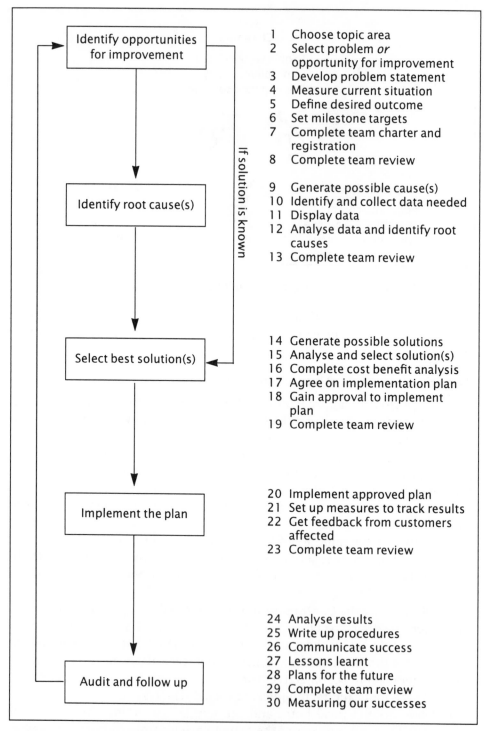

Figure 4.2: The five-stage problem-solving process

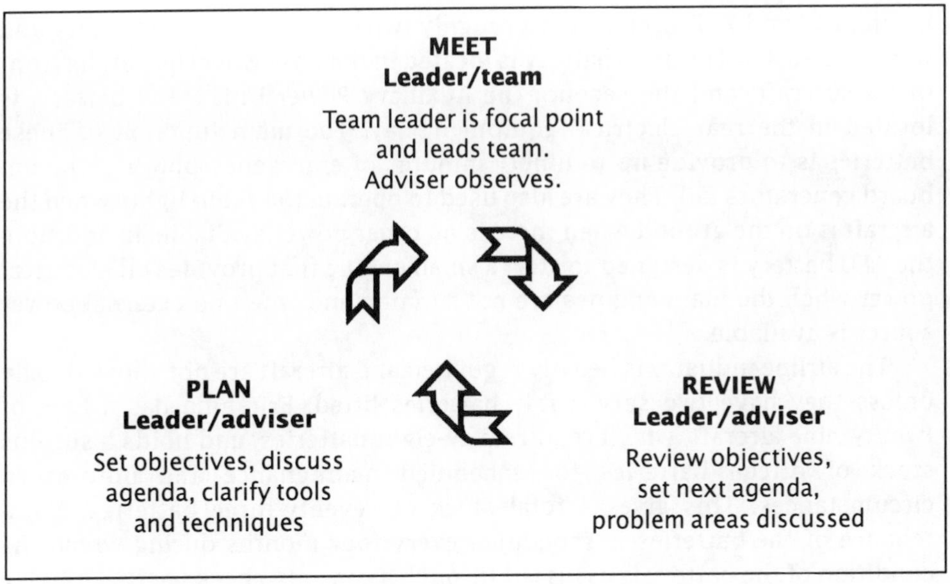

MEET
Leader/team

Team leader is focal point
and leads team.
Adviser observes.

PLAN
Leader/adviser

Set objectives, discuss
agenda, clarify tools
and techniques

REVIEW
Leader/adviser

Review objectives,
set next agenda,
problem areas discussed

Figure 4.3: The three-meeting structure

review the objectives, discuss problem areas, agree an action plan and set the agenda for the next meeting. This process takes place at each of the five stages of the problem-solving process.

PART 2: THE WOMBATS' PROJECT

The Wombats

The Wombats is a Continuous Improvement Team made up of technicians from the Avionics Workshop at Luton Airport. The Avionics Workshop deals with the maintenance and overhaul of all electrical items that are fitted to aircraft. This includes a wide variety of components, including galley equipment for the provision of hot meals, the inflight entertainment system which includes audio and video equipment, navigational equipment, lighting equipment and flight data recorders ('Black Box').

The Wombats is an experienced Continuous Improvement Team. They were formed in July 1993 and are currently one of thirty-four CI Teams operating in Britannia Airways. They have successfully completed five projects over the last four years, including investigations into emergency battery packs, monitor boxes, hangar signage and extractor fans. At the time of publication they have already embarked on their sixth project!

The problem

This project is concerned with the maintenance and overhaul of aircraft batteries. There are two batteries fitted to each of the company's fleet of

Boeing 757 and 767 aircraft, each roughly twice the size of a car battery and weighing 96 lbs. The main battery is located in the nose wheel bay at the front of the aircraft; and the second, the Auxiliary Power Unit (APU) battery, is located in the rear electrical equipment bay. The main function of these batteries is to provide up to ninety minutes of emergency power if the on-board generators fail. They are also used to operate the cabin lights when the aircraft is on the ground when there is no other power available. In addition, the APU battery is designed to start a small engine that provides all electrical power when the main engines are not running and when no external power source is available.

The airline industry is heavily regulated and aircraft are not allowed to fly unless they have two serviceable batteries fitted. Britannia has a fleet of twenty-nine aircraft, which require fifty-eight batteries, and holds a surplus stock of fifteen batteries for scheduled maintenance and unforeseen circumstances. This gives a total stock of seventy-three batteries. Maintenance of the batteries is scheduled every four months during which the condition of the battery is assessed through a capacity check.

The team's problem stemmed from the fact that although there is a surplus stock of fifteen batteries there were still insufficient serviceable batteries available to meet the maintenance requirements. Information from the battery history cards indicated that batteries were being removed from the aircraft up to one and half months before the maintenance interval had expired. Therefore, some batteries were only on the aircraft for two and a half months, as opposed to four months, before they were removed for scheduled maintenance. From this preliminary investigation, the team developed their problem statement as: 'poor utilization of aircraft batteries'.

Further investigation revealed that this had the following implications for the Avionics Workshop:

- A very high turnover of batteries through the workshop.
- The existing battery charger could not cope with the volume of batteries coming through the workshop.
- The workshop was frequently running to a zero stock of batteries.
- Significant amounts of additional paperwork.

Measuring and defining the problem

The team then set about investigating the current situation in more detail. They started by establishing exactly how much battery life was being wasted through poor utilization. This information was obtained from the battery history cards which record the individual life history of each battery. The history cards are updated at every visit to the workshop and record the following information:

- The date the battery was removed from the aircraft.
- The aircraft it came from.
- The work carried out on the battery.
- The capacity check due date (the maximum period before the next scheduled capacity check).

Ideally, to maximize utilization of batteries, they should be removed from the aircraft as close to the capacity check due date as possible. Using the data from the history cards for the period July 1994 to March 1995, it was established that the total battery life wasted was 2,405 days. This is the equivalent of 16 per cent of the available battery life. Indeed, some batteries were being removed up to five weeks early; this wastes a quarter of their lives. This is despite the fact that the Civil Aviation Authority (CAA) have granted a concession that allows batteries to be submitted for maintenance late (up to 10 per cent of the battery life). From this analysis of the problem, the team generated a desired outcome statement as follows: 'to maximize main aircraft and APU battery utilization'.

Analysis of root causes

Having measured and defined the problem, the team held two brainstorming sessions to explore the root causes of the problem. In the first the team produced a bubble diagram identifying the departments involved in the battery maintenance programme – the workshop's suppliers and the customers in battery maintenance.

In the second session the team produced a cause and effect diagram (Figure 4.4) which identified all the possible causes of the problem and acted as the basis of the subsequent data-gathering process. The cause and effect diagram identified two areas as the probable root causes: planning and the maintenance schedule. The Planning Department was contributing to the problem because it was not scheduling battery removal close enough to the capacity check due date. The maintenance schedule was also a contributory factor because of the limited four-month life.

The two root causes were investigated further. The four-month battery life between capacity check due dates is written into Britannia's maintenance schedule and is determined by the battery manufacturer (SAFT), the CAA and Britannia's Schedules Committee.

Although the background to the four-month limitation on battery life was quite clear, the situation with the Planning Department needed closer examination. The function of the Planning Department is to control and co-ordinate the use and maintenance of batteries. They raise the necessary paperwork and arrange to have batteries removed from aircraft when their capacity check due dates are reached. This requires the Planning Department to schedule battery removal to coincide with the nearest aircraft hangar check.

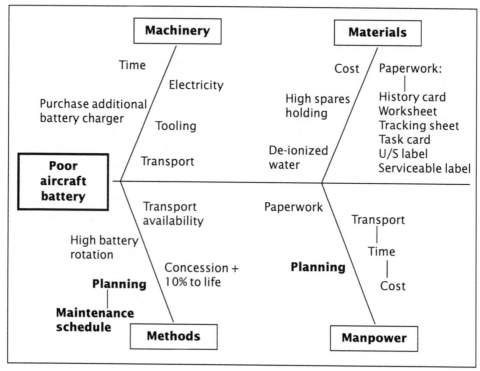

Figure 4.4: Cause and effect diagram

Although batteries could be removed at any of the company's outstations, in practice they were usually scheduled to be removed by the main workshop at Luton Airport. Despite the 10 per cent leeway allowed by the schedule, the need to coincide with hangar checks meant that batteries were almost always removed early, and frequently well before the capacity check due date.

The team then investigated the reasons why more battery changes were not performed at outstations in other airports. If this could be done it would provide a greater number of opportunities for battery changes and therefore the possibility of changes closer to the capacity check due date. Their investigation revealed two reasons for the infrequency of battery changes at outstations. First, the battery change takes approximately an hour, and with the aircraft on the ground for no longer than an hour between flights there is insufficient time for the engineers to deal with all the pre-flight checks and change the batteries. Second, changing the batteries is a very awkward process, particularly changing the main battery which is located high in the nose of the aircraft and requires the engineer to use a set of steps and a hoist to manoeuvre the batteries in and out of the confined space. It was clear that the engineers at the outstations would prefer not to change more batteries and as the Avionic Workshop sees these engineers as one of their main customers it was decided that any solution should also consider their needs.

Potential solutions

The next stage of the problem-solving process was to generate potential solutions, analyse them and then on the basis of the analysis select the most suitable solution. To generate potential solutions the team conducted another brainstorming session and came up with four possible alternatives:

- Removal of batteries nearer the capacity check due date.
- More removals of batteries at the workshop outstations.
- Purchase more batteries.
- Extending the capacity check due date.

Each of these alternatives was then examined within the context of the team's analysis of the problem and its implications for other stakeholder departments. Removal of batteries nearer the capacity check due date had already been discussed with the Planning Department and it was clear that the need to co-ordinate changes with hangar visits was the limiting factor which could not be circumvented without other radical changes.

The possibility of more battery removals at outstations had also been investigated as part of the preliminary research. As discussed earlier, the limited time between flights, the need for hoists and the difficulty of removing batteries makes this an unlikely alternative and the managers and engineers at these outstations made it clear that they did not favour this option. The third alternative of purchasing more batteries was seen as feeding the problem rather than curing it and would incur substantial costs with each new battery costing £3,500.

Through a process of elimination, therefore, the team settled on the fourth alternative: extending the capacity check due date. Having agreed to look at this solution more closely, the team produced a solution effect diagram as shown in Figure 4.5. This analysis identified a number of significant benefits associated with this solution:

- It would reduce the frequency of capacity checks and therefore reduce the demands on both the Avionics Workshop and other departments involved in the process.
- It would increase the availability of batteries for capacity checks and for spares.
- It would reduce the movement of batteries between Luton and the outstations, again increasing the availability of batteries.
- It would remove the need for an additional battery charger.
- It would remove the need to purchase additional batteries for backup.
- It should extend the life of each battery because of the reduction in the frequency of discharging and recharging associated with battery maintenance.

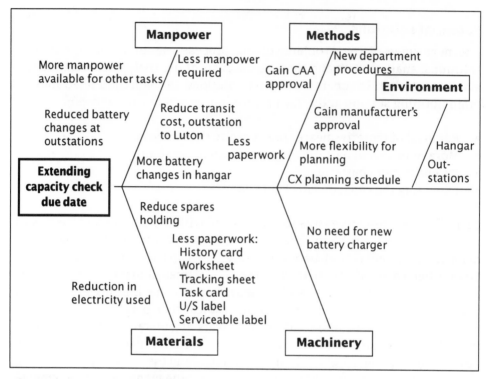

Figure 4.5: Solution effect diagram

However, analysis using the solution effect diagram clearly revealed that the critical aspect of this solution was the need to obtain approval for extending the capacity due date from the battery manufacturers (SAFT), the CAA and the Britannia Schedules Committee.

The next stage was to carry out a cost-benefit analysis of the preferred solution. This analysis indicated that the only cost of implementation was the one-off cost of the CI Team's time. The benefits included a saving of 800 engineer hours per year in the Avionics Workshop alone. This would help Avionics to improve their service in other areas, including reduced turnaround times of other components. Direct financial savings would arise from the fact that an additional battery charger would no longer be required (saving £4,300), and that additional new batteries would not be necessary, saving £3,500 per battery.

Implementation

Having agreed on a solution to address the battery utilization problem, the team drew up an implementation plan in the form of a milestones chart. The critical aspects of this implementation plan were to conduct a trial to test the proposition that the capacity check due date could be extended without compromising performance and safety, and to gain approval from the three key bodies: the battery manufacturer (SAFT), Britannia's Schedules Committee, and the Civil Aviation Authority.

The team started by contacting SAFT, the manufacturer, for their recommendations on extending the maintenance interval for the batteries. They had no objection to extending the maintenance interval as long as certain key criteria were met. These were that the operating conditions for the battery remained the same, that the capacity check was at least 107 per cent and that the amount of de-ionized water added during maintenance should not exceed 50ml. The final condition was a critical test; if the water added exceeded 50ml it would not be feasible to continue with the project.

In order to meet SAFT's criteria, the team monitored the average quantity of de-ionized water added to a random sample of fifteen batteries over a period of a month. The results of this trial were that the smallest quantity of de-ionized water added was 0ml and the largest amount was 28ml; the majority were between 5ml and 15ml. All the results were below SAFT's critical threshold of 50ml.

Armed with this information the team moved on to present their proposals to Britannia's Schedules Committee. The Schedules Committee is a group of key personnel from a wide range of engineering departments across the company. It includes representatives from planning, reliability, airworthiness, technical support and the local Civil Aviation Authority surveyor. The function of the committee is to review proposed amendments to Britannia's maintenance schedule and to either recommend or reject their implementation. The team presented their proposal, along with the supporting data that they had gathered from the history cards, information from SAFT and the results of the trial that they had carried out to meet the SAFT criteria. The committee gave provisional acceptance of the proposal subject to CAA approval.

The team then presented their proposal and the findings of their research including the de-ionized water usage and the capacity check pass figures to the Civil Aviation Authority. The CAA approved the proposal on a two-year trial basis and imposed a number of conditions:

- That on five randomly selected batteries the initial capacity check figures should be recorded showing the state of charge of the battery and the quantity of de-ionized water added to each cell.
- That the history cards be amended so that the initial capacity check could be recorded.
- There would no longer be any 10 per cent concession for late maintenance.
- That all cell replacements be recorded.

It was also a requirement that this information should be reported to the CAA every six months.

With approvals from SAFT, Britannia's Schedules Committee and the CAA, the team could now move towards implementation in terms of the maintenance schedule. In line with the maintenance schedule amendments there also had to be revisions of procedures in the Avionics Workshop, planning schedules and the technical records department. This required considerable co-ordination between departments and it was at this stage that the team were able to draw on their manager's support in pursuing departments to complete the necessary changes. Once the procedures were in place a date for implementation was set in consultation with the other departments involved. The date agreed was 1st June 1996.

PART 3: THE OUTCOMES AND IMPLICATIONS OF THE PROJECT

The results

Before the team could start to measure the results of the trial period they had to wait for all the batteries to complete their first workshop visit under the new maintenance schedule. By December 1996 the team were able to generate their first report and measure the effectiveness of the new schedule.

Ideally each battery should use its full life of six months. In practice, however, there were still constraints in terms of planning and aircraft utilization and most batteries were actually being removed between five and six months after the last capacity check. Nevertheless, this was still a significant improvement in battery utilization and, on average, using the new maintenance schedule led to a gain of fifty-one days use per battery – previously batteries had been removed an average of twenty days early; they were now being removed an average thirty-one days after the four-month interval. This led to a reduction in planned battery changes from 292 in 1995 to 146 in 1996 with the same number of operating aircraft.

Additionally, there were direct financial savings arising from the fact that an additional battery charger was no longer required, saving £4,300, and that additional backup batteries would no longer be necessary, saving £3,500 per battery. There was also the benefit of saving time in the Avionics Workshop; this was projected to be a saving of 800 hours per year.

Customer feedback

An important aspect of the Britannia Continuous Improvement Programme is the involvement of internal and external customers in the problem-solving process. The team's customers had already been consulted in the initial stages of the project and were represented in the Support Team. Having implemented the new maintenance schedule the team needed to monitor how the changes had affected the satisfaction of their customers. Being aware of the limitations and impersonal nature of survey-based approaches the team decided to contact their customers personally through one-to-one discussions, through focus groups and by telephone. The feedback from the four departments who are their main customers was as follows:

- *Base maintenance* – interestingly, because of shift patterns and seasonal maintenance, this group had not noted any significant changes in the frequency of scheduled battery changes.
- *Planning* – this group felt that they now had greater control and could achieve improved planning of battery maintenance because the two-month extension fits the maintenance schedule better.
- *Material services* – this department noted that they now have more batteries available for scheduled maintenance and that, to date, they had had no requests to purchase additional batteries.
- *Outstation maintenance* – this department are now able to allocate more time to rectifying cabin defects because they no longer have to carry out scheduled battery changes.

Audit and communication

At the time of writing, the team are still conducting the two-year trial and providing six monthly reports to the Civil Aviation Authority. They are also carrying out the audit and follow-up process using data gathered from the new format battery history cards.

An important part of the follow-up is the communication of the results of the project. The publication of findings is a way to share the team's experience, both positive and negative, so that other operations within the company may also benefit. The team has put together an information pack, circulated the minutes of all its meetings to its customers, it has made a presentation to the support team members and delivered an awareness presentation to senior management and key personnel within the company.

Communication to those outside the company has taken place through the team's entry for the Michelin Award 1997 and the publication of this chapter. There is, however, a degree of commercial sensitivity about the findings of the project inasmuch as other airlines have not yet succeeded in extending their battery maintenance schedules.

The Wombats

As discussed earlier, the Wombats are an experienced Continuous Improvement Team. They have worked together for four years, they are experienced in the CI process and they have successfully completed five CI projects. The ethos of Continuous Quality Improvement seems to be embedded in their work, and they have already started their next project; it seems that they are now a self-perpetuating CI team. Their new project is concerned with the entertainment equipment on aircraft, specifically the 'inflated prices of approved spares for inflight entertainment equipment', the desired outcome of the project being 'to be able to use commercial spares on inflight videos and monitors which will reduce turnaround times and cost'.

Discussion with the Wombats revealed the benefits that encourage them to participate in the CI Programme; these include a feeling of being valued by the company, greater commitment and improved motivation. It is interesting that although they recognize that their CI projects save the company money, the primary motivation for the team is that the projects 'help us in our work' and that they 'make working practices better'. They recognize the wider benefits of increased access to people in other departments and they feel that they 'understand the business better' as a result. They also have a better and more effective relationship with management; as they say, 'they listen to you', and 'you can actually talk to them'. At a more fundamental level, they recognize that participation in the CI programme has changed the way that they think about their work, that they are more open-minded about change, and that they are always thinking about how 'we might be able to improve that'. This all helps improve morale, and members of the team stated that they 'feel quite appreciated' as a result.

This project and the experience of the Wombats as a CI team demonstrate the benefits of Britannia's Continuous Improvement Programme. In enabling, encouraging and supporting teams to take ownership of the quality improvement process the company benefits from the experience and detailed knowledge of those actually involved in organizational activities. The fact that there are now thirty-two CI teams working on forty-three projects in Britannia and that in 1995 the programme was extended across the whole company clearly demonstrates the success of the Continuous Improvement Programme.

GLOSSARY

APU

Auxiliary Power Unit – the unit that supplies electrical power to the aircraft whilst on the ground.

CAA

Civil Aviation Authority – the governing body for the civil aviation authority in the UK.

Capacity check

The capacity check tests the ability of the battery to meet the requirement to provide power for a minimum amount of time.

CI

Continuous Improvement.

CI programme

Continuous Improvement Programme – the team-orientated approach to solving work-related problems at Britannia Airways.

CI Team

Continuous Improvement Team – a group of staff that solves work-related problems through teamwork and the CI Programme.

De-ionized water

Distilled water added to battery cells to maintain the required electrolyte level.

Outstations

Maintenance facilities away from the main hangar maintenance facilities at Luton.

SAFT

Battery manufacturers.

Schedules Committee

A group of Britannia personnel who liaise with the CAA to approve maintenance scedules.

Support Team

Group of key managers with interest in the project and authority to approve proposals.

BIBLIOGRAPHY

Continuous Improvement Department (1997), *The Essential Guide to Continuous Improvement*, Britannia Airways.

Lashley, C. (1997), 'Who needs ashtrays? Continuous inprovement at Britannia Engineering and Maintenance', in Teare, R., Scheuing, E. E., Atkinson, C. and Westwood, C., *Teamworking and Quality Improvement*, Cassell, pp. 39–49.

Five

NSK BEARINGS EUROPE

Double Sided Designers and 'No Sweat Again'

Roger K. Armstrong
AND
David Davies

*The authors wish to thank
Kevin Nicholson, NSK TQ Facilitator
and Kenneth Kemp, NSK Team Leader,
for their assistance in compiling this chapter.*

Five

NSK BEARINGS EUROPE

Double Sided Designers and 'No Sweat Again'

THE COMPANY

NSK Bearings Europe was established in the UK in 1975, to supply Europe with 'popular' metric sizes of single row, deep groove, ball bearings. NSK was the first Japanese-owned company to have a manufacturing plant in the North East of England, in Peterlee, Co. Durham. From the initial five sizes of ball bearings, the company now produces a range of forty-seven sizes, of which there are many variants.

During the 1980s, NSK Bearings Europe started the production of wheel hub bearings and now the company supplies this product to many of the major European car manufacturers. The company's stated aim to achieve localization of resources, materials and product has necessitated building a satellite forging plant and also a steel ball plant, which is a joint venture between NSK and AKS (the world leader in precision ball manufacturing), both plants being conveniently located in Peterlee. NSK, whose head office is in Tokyo, Japan, is a truly global organization, having manufacturing plants and sales offices throughout the world.

The Peterlee plant is typical of manufacturing plants in the engineering industry. The flow production system receives from suppliers materials which are soft machined, heat treated, ground, assembled, inspected, packed and despatched to customers, including Nissan, Rover, Bosch and Meile. The plant has a long history of securing quality improvements, being past winners of the Michelin Excellence Award, and a culture of continuous improvement is the norm. Internal quality proposals and communications bear the legend, 'Beyond Product Quality: *Everything we do, we do in a quality way*'. This culture is often stimulated by management directives; the one most pertinent for the project we are about to consider is the message to 'reduce costs'. This chapter features two improvement teams whose investigations led to significant performance improvements for NSK.

71

PART 1: THE DOUBLE SIDED DESIGNERS

Introduction

The 'Double Sided Designers', a team of four, had to demonstrate significant soft machining productivity improvements of bearing outer races. This improvement had to contribute to a 'localization' of product policy designed to increase the local content of production and services, whilst having to import steel tube – the raw material of manufacture – from Japan. This project was originally based upon a false premise that a local supplier of '608 series' production material could be found; but for this, a most valuable opportunity for improvement would have been overlooked.

The two-year project, which experienced many challenging setbacks, proved to be successful on all objective measures, resulting in total savings of £350,000 per year for 608 and 6000 bearing sizes.

Concern had been expressed by management of a lack of competitiveness in the small-size bearing market when compared with competitor companies and sister overseas plants. There was a need to identify the true cost of producing a small bearing; this in turn would help generate a costing model which could be used to accurately cost all bearing sizes. In particular they wished to identify production improvements to reduce the cost of producing the small 608 bearings. Each of the main production processes, i.e. soft machining, grinding and assembly, were tasked with reducing manufacturing costs of the 608 bearing series within their own process. The small-project group, which was set up in the soft machining area where they perform the initial machining of the steel raw material and are the focus of this chapter, was selected to provide the skills required and to represent all groups affected by the project. Their average age was 38, yet they had accumulated sixty-nine years' service between them.

Selecting a theme

The 608 series bearings are an assembly of an inner and outer race, caging ball bearings. The group brainstormed, which resulted in a focus on outer ring soft machining as a key issue if productivity was to improve. 88 per cent of monthly production was in-house at Peterlee, though to meet customer demand for the final product, they had to import 12 per cent machined soft outer rings direct from Japan. This had the effect of increasing the component and product cost and reducing local content of the finished bearings, contrary to the declared aim of the company – a theme we shall return to later in the chapter.

The current situation was that the six multi-spindle lathes were producing one part per 360° indexation of the machine. The raw material is held secure in each rotating spindle of the lathe, which are then indexed through 360°, stopping at six fixed tooling stations, which cut and form the steel prior to separating the finished outer rings from the raw material.

Having taken as their aim to improve outer race machining capability, the group used brainstorming to produce a comprehensive, seventy-item Cause and Effect (Ishikawa) diagram, identifying the likely variables, using the four-m approach: materials, machines, manpower and methods. The team's analysis led to a focus on four key items: plant expansion; improved machining efficiency; reduce machining cycle time; increase machining production rate. Of the four items, the latter proved to be the most significant when taking into consideration the management directive to reduce costs; the degree of difficulty of change and implementation; the investment required in time and finance; and the effect it was likely to have on reducing production costs while maintaining or improving quality. This led the group to select their theme and objectives.

- *Theme:* The reduction of 608 bearing production costs by increasing machining capacity of outer races.
- *Objectives:* The introduction of two parts (soft outer rings) per 360° index operation on six multi-spindle lathes; increase the output of the 608 bearing outer rings machines, reducing machine capacity from five to three machines; remove the need to import machined outer rings from Japan.

Problems and potential for added value

The production of two races per index on a six-spindle machine was first considered at Peterlee in 1985 and rejected due to limitations imposed by the production materials (solid bar). The time required to drill the solid bar determines the cycle time of the machine. The additional depth of drilling required when producing two races per index extends the machine cycle time. The extended cycle time eliminated most of the benefits of producing two races per index.

The production of two races per index from a six-spindle machine (all of which use solid bar) was therefore considered to be impractical. However, the group quickly identified that if they could use tube rather than solid bar, they could eliminate the slow speeds and feeds employed in drilling. A boring process could be used with tube material, which is able to operate at far higher speeds and feeds than a drill. Therefore, they perceived that two races per index could be produced from tube without extending the cycle time. The change of production material from solid bar to tube was essential to the project. It was necessary to consider the material cost in detail, as this represents approximately 50 per cent of the value of the finished ring. The 608 bearing is a relatively small product, and the group noted that small diameter tube material is difficult to produce to the required accuracy. This resulted in the material price (£/tonne) increasing as the size reduces. Also, tube material is approximately twice the price per tonne of solid bar. So how could there be a pay-off?

The production of bearing races from solid bar wastes large volumes of material. The quantity of races produced from a tonne of solid bar will be less than that produced from a tonne of tube. The percentage of material wastage increases with the material diameter.

This potential pay-off was strengthened when the group considered tooling costs. The use of solid bar requires the bore of the ring to be drilled out. The large diameter drills are expensive. The throwaway tip boring bars used in machining tube material are relatively inexpensive and unaffected by bore size.

The production costs for each material type had to be calculated against the above criteria to determine which was the most cost-effective production material for each bearing race. In general there is a critical diameter below which solid bar is the most cost-effective material. The sizes above the critical diameter are most economically produced from tube.

The 608 bearing size was first introduced to Peterlee in 1985. From 1985 to 1990 the 608 outer race was produced from Japanese tube material. A review of the production material selection carried out in 1990 found that the 608 outer race could, with equal cost-effectiveness, be produced from tube or solid bar material. The 608 outer race changed to solid bar to comply with company policy of localization, as the solid bar could be obtained from a local supplier.

Investigating the possibility of changing the 608 to tube material revealed that the main local supplier of tube material was quoting a price considerably more than envisaged. Given the small diameter of the 608 tube and its difficulty in manufacture, coupled with the relatively small quantity required by the Peterlee plant, meant it did not justify the supplier's effort required to produce this tube cost-effectively. However, Sanyo Steel, of Japan, produce 608 tube for other NSK factories and therefore already have the manufacturing ability. The larger volumes required to supply the NSK group improved the price over that offered by local suppliers. The introduction of Sanyo steel as supplier for the 608 bearing size would result in a loss of £444/month compared with solid bar and would also reduce the local content of the finished product. The benefits of the production of two races per index had to support the above losses in order for the project to proceed.

In summary, projected cost savings could be achieved given:

- The 608 outer race was at that time produced on five 32MRA-6 multi-spindle lathes each producing 3.2K items per shift. Monthly capacity 961K.
- The introduction of two rings per index was expected to increase the output of the 608 outer race machines to 5.4K items per shift. The increased capacity would allow three machines to produce the monthly requirement for 608 outer races. The other two machines would then become available for other work.

- Peterlee plant did not have enough turning capacity to supply the plant's requirement for bearing races. In order to support production, races are currently imported from Japan. The two machines freed by this project could be used to reduce the requirement for imported races by 399K items per month. This reduction represents a cost saving of £18,492 per month.

This projected cost saving would easily justify the additional costs incurred by changing the material to Sanyo tube steel (£444/month).

The main objection to the material change was the company policy of increasing the local content of the product. The proposal would involve changing from a local supplier to a Japanese supplier. The objections were overcome by the following arguments:

- The quantity of raw material purchased from Japan may have increased, but the quantity of turned races imported will have reduced. The net effect will therefore be an increase in the locally added value of the product.
- An extensive survey was carried out in an attempt to find a local supplier of 608 outer race tube material at realistic prices, without success.

The viability of changing from solid to tube material depended on the ability to produce two races per index. The project group therefore had to prove the process was capable of producing two races per index.

Trials to prove viability of two races per index

The production of two races per index from six spindles had never been tested at Peterlee. Whilst the group were very confident that the necessary tooling layout could be developed, the possibility of unforeseen problems always existed. Trials had to be carried out to confirm their ability to produce two races per index before a change of production material could be proposed. These trials were carried out on the 6000 bearing size which is already produced from tube material and is on occasion produced on a six-spindle machine (one ring per index).

The group, now named the Double Sided Designers, set about demonstrating the feasibility of producing the 6000 outer races, for which tube material was already available, at a rate of two parts per machine index. An important consideration in their planning was to ensure that the operator workload on the six-spindle test machine was no greater than that of the operator on the eight-spindle machine (the standard machine for the production of two races per machine index). If this trial proved to be successful it would give the group confidence to recommend that the six-spindle machines producing the 608 outer race could be converted to machining tube to produce two parts per index. The group investigated the immediate problem of how to compress the tooling layout from an

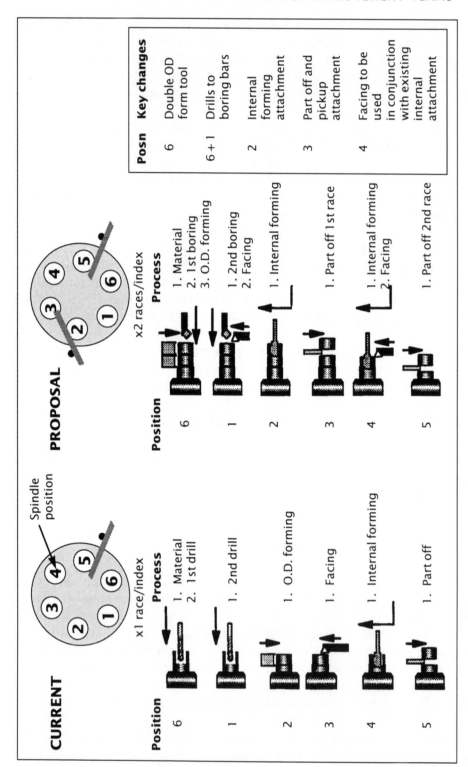

Figure 5.1: 6000 outer race tooling layout

eight-spindle machine, so that it would fit on the smaller six-spindle machine. Three options were considered, one of which resulted in the layout shown in Figure 5.1. In this figure the proposed layout is compared with the traditional solid bar, drilling process, producing only one race per machine index.

The machine, with new tooling layout, was then trialled by the group using the company's standard machine shop pass-off procedure:

- Ten parts per spindle were manufactured and 100 per cent inspected for all items.
- The machine was operated under controlled conditions for eight hours, with a sample production check at regular intervals.

The machine passed the tests without difficulty and was handed over to the shop floor for operation trials. Operators monitored the machine's progress towards production targets every hour during each eight-hour production shift, and noted a number of operational problems. These related to a lack of cutting oil reaching the cutting tool, leading to tool failure; the need to install a cut-off failure safety device, to avoid serious damage to the following tooling station; other problems related to the relative difficulty found when making tool adjustments on the machine.

In conclusion, the first objective of the trial was achieved: two races per index were produced upon the six-spindle machine. Unfortunately, the second objective was not achieved, as the machine proved difficult to operate, the operator's and setter's workload being greater than when operating on an eight-spindle machine. However, the good news was that the problems were clearly identifiable and could be corrected. The project was approved to proceed to the next stage (Figure 5.2).

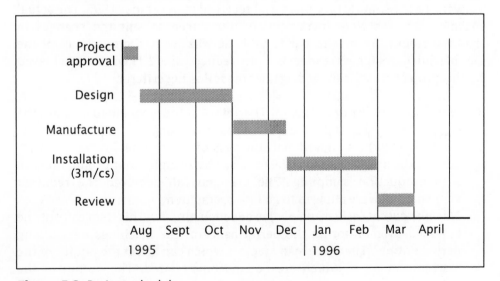

Figure 5.2: Project schedule

The ultimate aim of the project was production of 608 outer race (including the change to tube) on condition that the following items were actioned:

- A cut off failure safety device be fitted.
- The boring adjustment method be redesigned.
- The first position facing holder be redesigned due to poor access.
- The fourth position facing holder be redesigned due to poor access and difficult adjustment.

The latter three items to be actioned were all tool setting problems, brought about by a lack of space in the tooling zone on the six-spindle machines. Many countermeasures were explored and the decision was taken to introduce a Block Tool System; this would permit accurate tool setting to be carried out off the machine.

The cut-off failure warning device is a switch located after the first race cut-off. If the race is not cut off then the uncut part contacts the switch during machine index. The switch then stops the machine when the index is complete. The basic tooling layout and method of control was the same as used during the 6000 trial on the outer race, as outlined in Figure 5.1. The new block tooling was trialled, and proved to be highly effective, reducing the average setting time to one-third of the original methods.

Production results

The encouraging machine trials resulted in the group submitting a project capital request in September 1995. The necessary parts were ordered, to convert the six-spindle machines, and received in December 1995. The actual machine changes were incrementally introduced to suit the changes in material stocks, from solid bar to tube. So what were the outcomes of the Double Sided Designers' endeavours to 'reduce costs'? The results achieved by this project must be judged against the following criteria:

1. *Production quality and stability.* The ability of the machine to produce the component to size and to hold the sizes over a long period of operation is confirmed by the standard machine pass-off procedure, i.e. the ten parts per spindle production sample, followed by an eight-hour production run with production sampling. The machines all achieved the required standard and were allowed to go into production.
2. *Machine output (achievement of production targets).* This item can only be assessed by monitoring the performance of the machines over a long period of time. There are many factors which can affect the output of the machine, many of which are not machine-related. The output of the machines was reviewed over a period of six months and the average shift

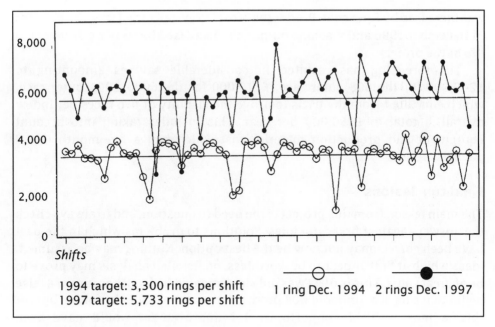

Figure 5.3: Output increase from one to two rings/index

output calculated. The targeted shift output was set at 5,400 parts per shift and average shift output over the six-month period was 5,388 parts per shift. The machines were therefore judged to be achieving the required production targets. In order to better quantify the production gain resulting from the introduction of two parts per index, the outputs of one machine were compared for the periods of December 1995 (one part per index) and December 1996 (two parts per index) and are illustrated in Figure 5.3.

3. *Machine operability and safety.* The modifications using block tooling principles introduced as a result of the problems encountered during the 6000 bearing outer race production were judged to have solved the tool changing problems, whilst avoiding any increased workload for the setter/operators.

4. *The achievement of project objective.* The main objective of the project was to reduce the number of machines required to meet the plant's 608 bearing outer races production schedules. This objective has been achieved. Two of the five original 608 machines have now been set changed to produce another bearing size, namely bearing 6000/6001, and the plant's requirement for imported parts has been reduced by 399,000 items per month, which represents a cost saving of £18,492 per month.

The three machines producing the 608 reached productivity of 96 per cent of target in March 1996. At a subsequent review of the project the original target was increased by 8 per cent. Productivity to the revised target was 124 per cent in December 1996 and machine output had increased by 73 per cent over the life of the project.

The foregoing has resulted in considerable savings amounting to £240,000 for the 608 outer race, £110,000 for the 6000/6001 outer race, which emanated from the trials to prove the viability of two races per index: overall, a total of £350,000 per year. This includes taking into account equipment and production material cost which had a five-month initial payback period.

Final conclusions

The main lesson from this project is the need to question, and to always check the answers against first principles. Solutions to problems which in the past have been correct may not now be the best option. Nothing may be assumed. Ideas which at first appear to be worthless, on detailed analysis may prove to be of great value. This project was only investigated in detail because of a false belief that a local supplier of 608 production material could be found; but for this, a most valuable opportunity for improvement would have been overlooked.

The 6000 bearing trials were at the time viewed as nothing more than a six-month delay, but in retrospect proved to be of great value. They allowed the group to demonstrate their intentions to the machine operators in a most effective manner. The operators were able to become involved while the project was still at the experimental stage when major changes were still possible. The feedback received at this stage contributed greatly to the final success of the project.

The group is now looking at future developments. The limitations of the drilling process prevent the production of two components per index from six spindles being expanded to any other bearing sizes. Investigations into new type of drill are in progress but as yet have found no solution to the problem. The current direction of future development therefore is looking to answer the question: 'If two parts per index can be produced from six spindles, then could three parts per index be produced on an eight-spindle machine?' The search for continuous improvement is ongoing.

PART 2: 'NO SWEAT – AGAIN'

Introduction

The project was located in NSK Bearings Ltd, Peterlee, County Durham, an engineering company whose Japanese origins go back to 1916 and the start of the bearing industry in that country. The company as a whole is a major player in the field of bearing products, machine tool parts and products for the automotive industries.

The Peterlee plant was in fact the first Japanese investment in engineering in the United Kingdom and started in 1976. Since that time expansion has occurred into production of an extensive range of bearings. Some twelve million bearings are produced monthly with over one hundred different types available to customers.

The products are manufactured by associates who operate highly sophisticated automatic cutting lathes. Solid metal is drilled out to high specifications in a series of stages, resulting in a tooled steel ring or bearing case which will house the finished bearing.

The machine shop at Peterlee has approximately sixty multi-spindle lathes which can produce in excess of twelve million bearing 'rings' per month. In spite of the volume of production, the accent is very much on quality. The metal rings are heat treated to a specific hardness and ground to very fine tolerances, then assembled with balls, cages and grease, and are then sealed, inspected and noise tested. A final inspection is made before they are packed and shipped to customers in Europe and around the world, including Nissan, Rover, Bosch, Miele and many other leading manufacturing companies.

The 'No Sweat Again' team of five had been in existence previously as a company-supported small-project group within the company's machine shop. The problem selected by the team was to reduce the number of tooled metal rings which were lost during the manufacturing process. The problem initially was that chutes, blocked by the excess metal cuttings called swarf, were causing the rings to fall from the machine into the waste system, which itself produced further problems. Planning and team activity took place between January 1996 and January 1997 and the team followed a logical process to set out their targets and tasks which looked like the following activity plan shown in Figure 5.4.

Key activities and targets

The team set itself a business and production-related task: to reduce the number of dropped rings which were lost in the manufacturing process. This fact and the associated costs of recovering lost production was generating significant costs for the company. It was thought that a series of countermeasures could produce significant gains. The team were well aware, as were management, that cost reduction and competitiveness in global marketplaces go hand in hand and that continuous improvement in productivity cannot simply be handed down to production associates on the shop floor. Earning such productivity through teamwork was uppermost in everybody's mind.

Key processes and procedures

A Group Activity Registration and Monitor Sheet was drawn up which took a series of activities and plotted who was responsible for key activities and charted progress on a time schedule. The activities covered the range of activities from planning, to analysis and evaluation of results shown in Figure 5.4:

- Planning.
- Investigating present conditions.
- Analysing results.
- Deciding targets.
- Implementing countermeasures (solutions).
- Confirming results.
- Evaluation.
- Making results 'standard'.

Over the time period of the project – twelve months – fourteen dedicated team meetings were held. The focus of these meetings ranged from the intensely technical to the intensely reflective. It was clear that the team recognized the need to have clear objectives and to subject these to the scrutiny of technical experts skilled in the manufacturing processes. The bearings have to be produced to specifications involving tolerances of thousandths of centimetres. On the other hand, the team had to work as a team for each other and for commonly-held and agreed goals. The team had in fact been involved previously as individuals in fourteen small project groups, eight of which had been winners of plant awards from the company. The 'No Sweat Again' team adopted the name they had used for a previously successful project and thought success would help breed success. The team worked within departmental guidelines and aimed to reduce departmental costs, improve the use of materials in the manufacturing process, create a better service to customers and improve the working environment.

Putting the show on the road

The first team-meeting brainstormed the problems and themes where improvements could be made. Seven themes were listed; criteria for selecting a theme were agreed and a 1 to 10 points scoring theme adopted. The team speculated on the identity of their most significant problem and after deliberation between group members and some outside managerial advice, decided to use a weighted points selection system. The highest score was for reducing the number of dropped rings within the tooling zone. Cutting this waste would reduce costs, increase the efficiency of materials usage and

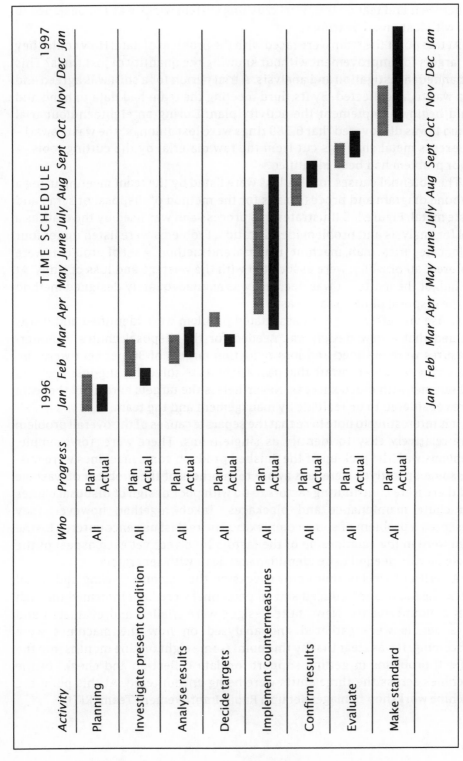

Figure 5.4: Activity plan

reduce wear and tear on the swarf crushing system which was not designed to deal with lost metal bearing rings!

At this point the team were faced with the problem of data. How could they set targets for improvement without knowing the quantity of lost rings? This demanded investigation and analysis. A trial period for a shift was agreed and data was to be collected. By its third meeting the team had data to hand and could begin to implement the activity plan. During an eighteen-hour trial period it was discovered that 6,589 rings were lost amongst the waste swarf – the excess metal shavings cut from the raw material by the cutting tools. A major problem had been identified.

The potential causes for this loss were listed by the team meeting using a fishbone diagram and process maps for the method of disposal of scrap and waste metal. Figure 5.5 illustrates this process and was used by the team as a tool for analysis and problem identification. Problems were listed under four major categories: man, machine, material and method. A set of problems were explored, all of which were associated with the wastage and loss of rings. At the hub of the matter, it was decided, was an inadequately designed method for the disposal of necessary waste.

Cause and effect for each associated problem were identified and it was decided that a new design was needed for the disposal chutes. Counter-measures were outlined and loss reduction targets of 30 per cent were set, though the team were aware that past attempts to solve the ring-loss problem had not met with much success. Nevertheless the targets agreed by the team were considered to be realistic by management and the team.

It is interesting to note here that the separate causes of the overall problem were relatively easy to identify as single items. There were, for example, problems with the pick-up of the finished product, some machines were mis-set, some operatives were less aware than others of the problem of wastage and there were contributing factors to do with poor design of disposal chutes and chute maintenance and blockages. Taken together, however, they presented a problem of some complexity. The real issues encountered by the team were in the *relationship* of the factors involved; yet each aspect of the whole picture needed to be identified and dealt with separately.

A series of weekly four-point checks on the machines, using additional check sheets, was introduced and all personnel were kept informed through shift announcements. New chute designs were trialled and evaluated and more details were gathered and analysed on how the machines were performing. It was clear that by this point (some eight or nine months into the project) problems in getting support for data collection and checks of the machines across the three shifts were being encountered. At this point the machine workshop manager set up a Rapid Improvement Team (RIT).

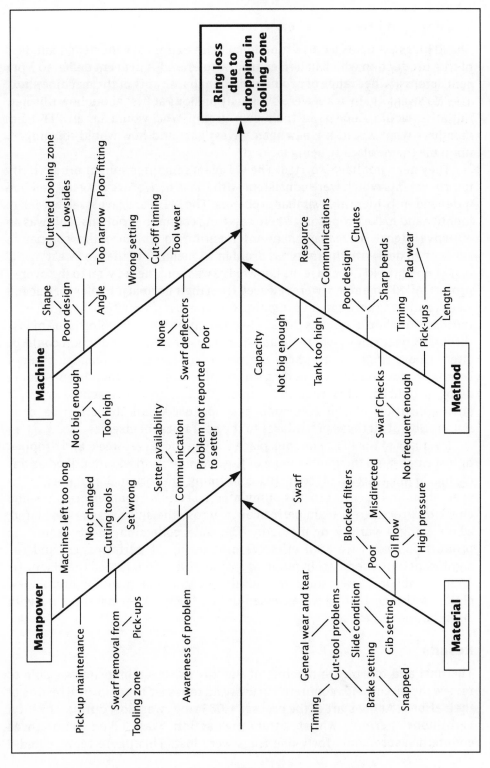

Figure 5.5: Investigate present condition

The Rapid Improvement Team

The RIT was set up as a cross-functional team to improve the deficit and loss of ring production which had risen from a 'tolerated' 4 per cent deficit to 7 per cent across a wider range of production than that simply of the machine shop. The 'No Sweat Again' team were obviously anxious at first about how this new initiative would impact on their own group. Who would be an RIT team member? What would the new team investigate and how would this impact upon the theme already being tackled?

They need not have worried. The RIT team's findings sought productivity improvements which were consistent with those of 'No Sweat Again' and had independently identified similar problems. The RIT team gave itself a week to identify and make proposals to help solve the common problems. This was an effective signal of management intervention to enhance the company's capacity to deal with the ring-loss problem. A member of the 'No Sweat Again' team joined the RIT because his knowledge was considered vital to the overall project. All RIT members were released from their normal job roles for one full week to allow a thorough investigation into the lost production. In addition to the machine shop diagnosis this RIT team identified an intriguing issue of loss through 'ghost rings', where no apparent cause for lost production could be cited. Ghost rings occur where the machine production quantity counter counts production and where for a variety of reasons no actual ring pieces are being produced. This required a modification to the machine itself, a standardization of the collection systems used and the effective communication of all these procedures to the operators themselves.

Meetings of the RIT team took place daily in the target week, and dropped or lost rings from the tooling zone of the machine shop was identified as one of the highest areas of concern, confirming the original diagnosis. The evaluation and review process stimulated a series of countermeasures and checking procedures; team performance across the shifts was re-evaluated, again using a variety of methods. The data collection sheets issued to production teams were an effective monitoring of performance, and the significant improvements in reducing loss and waste confirmed the diagnosis of the problem. New countermeasures involving the manufacture of new chutes and their testing were carried out by the work teams; this time with success, and hugely so!

Results

The final and fourteenth meeting of the 'No Sweat Again' team was able to review the three major countermeasures and to assess the empirical results of their efforts. At the start of the process 1,065 rings were lost during a twenty-eight-hour period, whilst after the action was taken with three countermeasures only forty-one rings were lost. This figure represented a

96.2 per cent reduction in waste. In addition, excessive downtime of the machines was eliminated. The team was able, of course, to quantify all of these results alongside those for improved machine efficiency.

The costs of implementing the improvements turned out to be in excess of £22,000, whilst the pay-back period was twenty-eight working days. However, the net savings to the company were to be nothing short of remarkable. Some 2,143,540 rings per year were saved with consequent reduction of wear and tear on the machinery which handles waste. This translated into a financial saving of over £98,000 which, with £95,000 saved by reduction in machine downtime, amounted to an annual saving of over £193,000.

In summary, a major cost saving was achieved alongside an effective system of accountability for the production of key components in the company's business. The original target of a 30 per cent decrease in loss of product was exceeded threefold with a 92.6 per cent decrease. The results for the shopfloor morale and their management were equal to those of the annual financial saving, though they are less easily quantified.

Some conclusions
The 'No Sweat Again' team were at one level addressing a wholly concrete set of problems and issues which impacted on their own toolroom practice and experience. They found, however, that there was no solution or special section

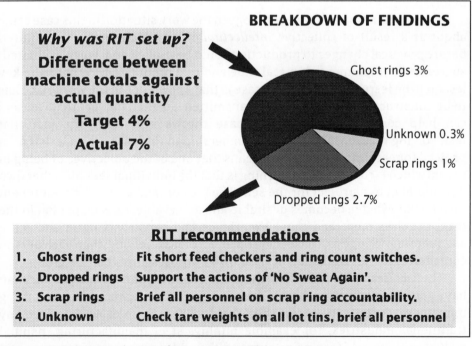

Figure 5.6: Posting the Rapid Improvement Team targets

of the company whose purpose or function it was to resolve *their* problem. In taking a team ownership of their working problem, they were also taking on the problem of formulating new knowledge about their own manufacturing process. Within the enterprise they were in fact creating a learning culture, or rather, creating a cell within the culture of the firm. The preformulated or 'foundational' knowledge (see Bouffee, 1995) each individual had, as well as that of the management, was insufficient for the technical and organizational development required to solve the ring problem. The skill and knowledge embodied in the team had to be applied, and once applied, continuously renewed as the problems became ever more complex and new demands came to the fore. New ideas and knowledge were being created and individual and collective learning took place as a by-product of the daily work activities of the associates. The workplace became an opportunity for learning and creating knowledge; admittedly this was practical and applied knowledge, but it involved reflection, evaluation and re-assessment at sophisticated levels of problem-solving and abstraction. Here we have an example of organizational change achieved by a group of individuals who collectively helped shape and determine organizational behaviour. The individuals in the 'No Sweat Again' team were convinced of the need to change, rather than the other way around. We can see some of the principles of action learning applied to what Drew and Smith (1995) have referred to as 'focus, will and capability' of the organization to address and exploit change, though in this case the impetus came from below.

The introduction of new technology in the work situation in this case came about as a result of collective *intellectual* effort which itself was required before practical changes to production could be trialled and, when evaluated, successfully implemented in real time and real production. Perhaps the key lesson to be learned from the NSK case is that knowledge in the workplace has to be constructed rather than just transmitted. Further, the fact that workers can help construct a knowledge base throws into relief the fact that task-solving relationships – team membership in this case – is an 'existential project' for each individual. This means that one of the objectives of being in a team which is committed to learning is that the individual sees his or her own development as a project for the self. The idea of 'self' and self-development through knowledge becomes desirable and achievable. As each person in the team acquires more and more experience and constructs more and more adequate knowledge as a base for the project of task-solving, then each person contributes to the realization of their own purposes as part of the group.

There is clearly evidence here that action learning and learning at work can have a significant basis in the group experience. The presence of teamworking in many work contexts (historically the dominant form of work in so many traditional industries, for example mining, steel manufacturing, fishing) makes work-based learning relevant to the wider concerns of learning and teaching. One issue that arises in respect of such learning in the workplace is that of how such collaborative learning can be effectively supported and developed. There is also the question: where there are collaborative group activities in the workplace, how can we design and implement methods for assessing and reflecting the contributions of learners both as individuals and as members of a team? There is also, as Brown (1995) points out, a major new role associated with the support and development of collaborative learning which is now required of middle managers (Kriegesmann *et al.,* 1995). The 'No Sweat Again' team became a self-regulating team for much of their existence and were able to be creative in respect of technical and organizational improvement. This required the management to seriously 'empower' the team and to delegate responsibility in what for many firms would involve a culture shift of seismic proportions.

From an educational or learning perspective the work context enables the worker-learner to actively construct knowledge. The opportunity for task-solving in terms of action and reflection or interpretation constitutes a major opportunity and condition for learning. Introducing change and improvement in the work context is not a question of introducing and transmitting knowledge but rather a question of identifying the contexts in which the required knowledge can be built up and applied. It is perhaps a truism that organizations will use new systems only if it pays them to do so (Sherman, 1995). It is true that cost recovery and cost reduction was a major concern in this case and, from an employer's point of view, sooner or later the loss of production and competitiveness would have engendered an incentive to replace unproductive processes and their workers. However, the 'No Sweat Again' team did not employ their skills in repetitive and predictable ways. Rather they were able to raise the level of efficiency of their workplace through a process of thinking commitment. This was not simply in the interests of the employer, but if the team themselves are to be believed, it was beneficial to them in terms of job security, recognition and self-awareness of their own value.

The 'No Sweat Again' team had surely learned to identify the learning conditions afforded by the company. Team formation, problem identification, testing, trialling, reviewing, evaluating, critical reflection, documentation skills and application of interpersonal and communication skills were all demonstrated in full measure. These are surely the building blocks of knowledge-building activity. The goal-directed and functional activity of the team produced valid knowledge in both a technical sense (better productive processes and procedures) and in the sense that employees developed the capacity to formulate new understanding based on specific work-related experiences. The task formulation and task-solving demonstrated by the team also constructed an environment which threw up more and more diversified goal-directed activities. The small project has led on to a future orientation ring accountability and to evaluate the mysterious problem of ghost rings!

So in conclusion we need to draw the lessons from the construction of techniques at work which allow us to see the knowledge-creating processes at work. With the creation of new techniques at work, new and more complex understandings can arise and reveal knowledge not only of the external, real world of work processes but also of ourselves as active and self-conscious agents in that process. There are benefits to both employer and employee in this. Companies are able to offer an enriched and diversified working environment for a more knowledgeable and committed workforce. This can be expected to have payback for productivity, efficiency, employee satisfaction and hopefully for profits. Those companies that aspire to be 'learning organizations' (see Teare *et al.*, 1997) can take a step towards that goal. For the individuals concerned, as action learning and problem-solving evolve as part of individual experience, there can be little doubt that the benefits accrue to those who learn. Furthermore, those who learn how to learn, and apply learning to the transformation of tasks in hand, learn also how to transform their own prospects and themselves.

REFERENCES

Bouffee, K. A. (1995) *Collaborative Learning: Higher Education, Interdependence and the Authority of Knowledge*, Baltimore and London, Johns Hopkins University Press.

Brown, A. (1995) *Thematic Review of the Recognition, Assessment and Accreditation of Work-based Learning in Europe*, University of Surrey, November 1995.

Drew, S. and Smith, P. (1995) 'The learning organisation: 'change proofing' and strategy', *The Learning Organisation*, 2, I. pp. 4–14.

Kriegesmann, B., Reuther, U. and Kühne, H. (1995) Report – *Creation of a Network of Training Projects in the European Automobile Industry and Related Sectors*, Germany, Bochum, University of Bochum.

Sherman, B. (1995) 'The end of work as we know it?', *New Statesman & Society*, 27 October 1995, pp. 27–30.

Teare, R., Ingram, H., Scheuing, E. and Armistead, C. 'Organisational teamworking frameworks: evidence from UK and US-based firms', *International Journal of Service Industry Management*, Vol. 8 No. 5, 1997

Six

KENNAMETAL HERTEL LTD

Continuous improvement to reduce waste
and add value throughout the business

GERALD BARLOW,
JOHN SPARROW
AND
COLIN BENEFER

Six

KENNAMETAL HERTEL LTD

Continuous improvement to reduce waste and add value throughout the business

INTRODUCTION

Kennametal Hertel Ltd is a division of Kennametal Inc. (USA) and controlled through its European headquarters located in Fürth, Germany. During the fiscal year for 1996 the Kennametal group had world sales in excess of $1 billion, and is pursuing an aggressive sales growth programme aimed at doubling this figure by the year 2000. This will be achieved through expansion of existing structures and acquisition.

In 1994 Kennametal Inc. acquired a controlling share of Hertel AG, and so created the European organization of Kennametal Hertel AG, to include the former Kennametal Ltd. The UK operations are based at Kingswinford in the West Midlands and a Scottish Office in East Kilbride. The main activities in the UK involve design and manufacture of:

- Cutting tools.
- Tool holders.
- Tooling systems.

for the global metalworking industry. These are supported by:

- Direct field sales force.
- Customer service centre.
- Distribution warehouse.

Kennametal employs around 7,300 people worldwide, including 300 in the UK.

The UK company has a quality management system which complies with BS EN ISO 9001:1994, and is currently certified by BSI QA within the registered Firms Scheme, and the registered Stockists scheme.

The company announced its intention of commencing a continuous improvement scheme in late 1994 as a part of the group's 'Vision 2000' programme, and in January 1995 the programme began.

The continuous improvement scheme was aimed at reducing waste and adding value throughout the business. Six quality teams were established, in two project areas: 'specials' and 'credits'. The 'special's' team's tasks were aimed at improving delivery times for non-standard products and maximizing business opportunities, clearly focused on the sales growth targets for the year 2000. The 'credits' team's tasks were to focus on reducing credit note issues, resulting from customer complaints, so adding value to the organization's operations. This area was broken down into two distinct sections: credit notes issued through errors in order entry, and those credit notes issued as a result of pricing errors. The second of these tasks fell to the VAT (Value Added Team) group to fulfil.

THE QUALITY TEAMS

The teams were voluntary, initially with eight members each, and drawn from a cross-section of the UK organization's departments (Figure 6.1). They represented a full range of employment positions, from management, supervision to clerical and shop floor. The Value Added Team members were initially drawn from all areas, as can be seen in Table 6.1.

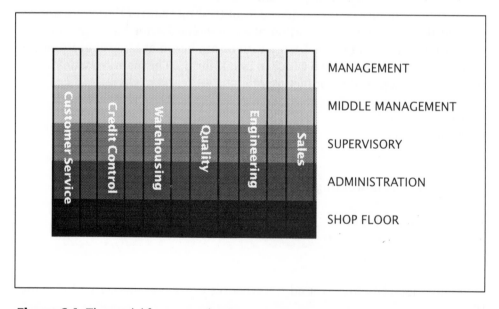

Figure 6.1: The model for team selection

Name	Department	Team role	Member at 1 April 1997
Dave Beardsmore	Applications Engineering	Secretary/Deputy Leader	Yes
Dave Bridgens	Field Sales	Team Leader	Left team
Simon Eason	Quality Assurance	Data Cruncher	Yes
Alva Gutteridge	Warehouse	Time-keeper	Yes
Julie Hipkiss	Customer Service	Deputy Team Teader	Left team
Derek Pargeter	Warehouse	Scribe	Left team
Terry Wood	Credit Control	Data Collator	Yes
Sarah Baker	Customer Services	Team Member	Yes/new

Table 6.1: Value Added Team members

TRAINING FOR QUALITY

In early 1995, the teams' membership was established, and plans were made to run a series of training programmes in quality awareness and appropriate quality techniques. An external consultant was enlisted, who then went on to act as adviser, and continues to do so. The purpose of the training was to teach people how to approach and undertake their future tasks. To this end, techniques and tools were introduced to enable the teams to identify problems, operate as an effective team, and provide methods for problem-solving. The first stage of the training was to develop awareness and commitment, and create self-managed action teams (see Table 6.2).

Year commencement	Process	Commitment
Stage 1: Jan. 1995	Team creation	Voluntary; 1 hour a week or fortnightly group meeting two hours.
Feb. 1995	Team training	Four day courses (work-based time).
1995	Problem identification Brainstorming Pareto, cause and effect	Group meeting – group facilitator.
1995	Data collection	Data sort and collection; 3–4 month process collation, data crunching.

Table 6.2: Training programme Stage 1

By this stage two members had left, Dave due to commitment with field sales work and customers, and Derek to join another group which he felt he was more suited to. Julie was elected to Team Leader and Simon as Deputy Leader.

Year commencement	Process	Commitment
Stage 2: Data Analysis		
May 1995	Data analysis was undertaken. Methods used: Pareto, histograms, matrix analysis.	All credits notes issued due to billing errors, were now analysed and their results considered (July 1994–April 1995). Problem areas were identified.
June 1995	Potential problems identified.	
Summer 1995	Possible solutions decided upon.	Areas: Discount structures – full revision. Full customer discount structure review (1,200 accounts).
October 1995	Implementation of chosen process and results taken and analysed.	Sales office admin. procedures implementation – new discount structure – all items entered into system. Operators introduced to the new systems.
December 1995 ongoing	The benefits measured.	December 1995 no credit notes issued due to pricing errors.

Table 6.3: Training programme Stage 2

This initial process was essential to convert individual enthusiasm into group awareness and commitment, and led to the next stage of training (Table 6.3) where the groups were introduced to classic problem-solving techniques, and how to:

* Identify and focus on the problem.
* Analyse the problem.
* Identify and collect appropriate data.
* Develop a set of solutions.
* Identify the most appropriate solutions.
* Create an implementation plan.
* Implement and measure the process.

THE EARLY DAYS

The initial data collection involved investigating and analyzing all credit notes over a ten-month period. This proved time-consuming and tedious, but the data provided the following facts:

1 143 customers complained (11 per cent of the active customer base) between July 1994 and April 1995.

2   1,288 credit notes were raised (21 per cent of the total invoices issued) within the group's specific sector.

3   A cost survey suggested an annual cost to the company of £53,748 for this sector alone.

The team thus proposed that resolving the problems caused by credit notes issued due to pricing errors would bring the following possible benefits:

- More reliable sales figures, affecting forecasting and commissions.
- Fewer queries.
- Improved customer relations.
- More effective use of resources.
- Improved company cash flow.
- Reduction in service complaints (improved quality system).
- Retention of customers, and selection of Kennametal as first choice;

and revealing tangible causes of complaints, which were coming from the following areas:

- Group's accounts.
- Discount system errors.
- Price.
- Sales office administration – standard product.
- Sales office administration – special product.
- External sales.

The tools and techniques the team had learned now showed their value, with Pareto analysis clearly identifying two of these causes as the major areas:

- group accounts;
- discount system errors.

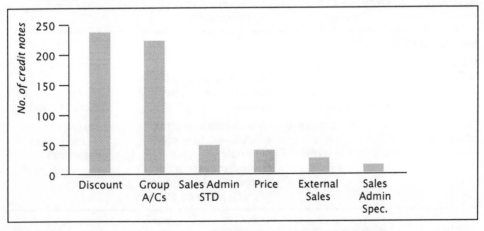

Figure 6.2: Analysis of credit notes by reason, January to April 1995

The team worked on collating more data and gaining support from senior management, with a vested interest. Eventually they gained full management approval to overhaul the customer database and discount structures.

The first stage was to examine all sales areas, which are split into the following segments, all with key geographical sectors:

- Automotive.
- Aerospace.
- General Engineering – North.
- General Engineering – South.

The geographic sectors were already established within the company organization.

The team tackled the discount system, reviewing them segment by segment, commencing with General Engineering North. This process identified a series of issues related to the process of customer orders. This included areas where internal sales staff relied on manual lists or memory for the discount structure, as they lacked confidence in the data available on the computer.

The team concluded that the way ahead was to request all sales engineers to review the entire discount structures for all customers. Initially this met with management and sales force resistance, due mainly to the time required for this exercise, and the commercially sensitive nature of some of the data. However, the team persisted, and eventually secured approval for the whole programme. From the findings it was discovered that 12.5 per cent of all customer discount structures required amendment. With the final stage a pricing audit identified over 850 items not priced within the current computer system.

Stage 1 Innocence	Stage 2 Awakening	Stage 3 Commitment and Implementation	Stage 4 World Class
Invoice failure			
Pricing	Failure identified.	Use of I.T. Errors reduced by 50%.	Zero errors.
	Customer order acknowledgment.	New standard invoicing system.	Zero errors. No credit notes.
Discount structure	Too many discounts available, not all within IT system.	New discount structure established. New special over-riding process – fewer discounts in the system. Cut in number of credit notes by 455.	Zero error. No credit notes by Jan 1996.

Table 6.4: The four stages of quality: examples.

The group now felt confident in designing a new, simpler discount structure, which included the following controls being introduced:

- Confirmation of all orders to all customers, and written acknowledgment of the order and actual prices to be charged to all incorrectly priced orders.
- New procedures for order with special discounts.
- A system to ensure all new items were priced and entered into the system.
- Price maintenance and an updated process, to ensure all new items are entered on the system.

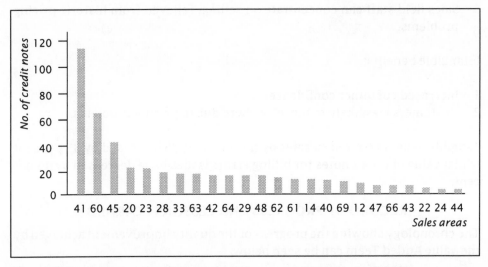

Figure 6.3: Analysis of credit notes by sales area, January to April 1995

RESULTS

December 1995 saw the company have its first month where no credit notes were issued due to discount errors. No further credit notes for either discount errors or pricing errors have been issued since January 1996. By the establishment of systems and processes to overcome the problems identified through pricing and discount structures, Kennametal Hertel UK's Value Added Team were able to show how the group's work had been successful, and could bring company-wide benefits. This has enabled them to go on and investigate other more complex areas, such as group accounts.

THE BENEFITS

Tangible:

1   Reduction in customer complaints.
2   Customer service departments deal with fewer queries and are now able to concentrate on customer requirements and orders.
3   More reliable sales records, for the company and sales staff (commissions are now more accurate figures).
4   Better use of resources, reduced paper-work, time and postage.
5   Sales field staff can concentrate on selling, relieved from historic pricing problems.

Intangible benefits:

1   Increased customer confidence.
2   Customers less likely to buy elsewhere due to pricing problems.

Tangible benefits have seen sales by the end of 1996 increased by 35 per cent whilst value of credit notes for billing errors issues have decreased by 45 per cent.

RECORD OF PROGRESS AND LESSONS LEARNED

The chronology showing the progress of the quality improvement achieved by the Value Added Team can be seen below.

1994
December   Vision 2000 programme launched.

1995
January   Six quality teams established.
                VAT team task is established.
February   Training programme for teams.
March   Second stage of training.
April   First stage of analysis established.
July   Two key issues identified.
August   Only one of the problems to be continued with.
October   Solutions proposed and changes introduced.
                Problem area 2 investigated.
November   Area 2 – issues and solutions identified.
December   First time in five years no credit notes due to discount errors.

1996

January	Second month of zero credit notes (discount errors). Zero credit notes caused by pricing errors.
February	Team commence next stage on standard inventory.
March	First issue of company quality information paper *The Improver.*
April	Zero credit notes continue in both initial areas. Analysis of standard inventory continues. New discount structure (two pages from initial twelve pages) is approved by management. 963 standard product prices have been installed.
June	Sixth consecutive month of zero credit notes in both areas. Current analysis proving more time-consuming and difficult to achieve full details. Discount form designed for use on Microsoft Access for reps' lap tops.
September	Sales admin/external sales credit notes still not improving despite implementation of Stage 1 procedures – next stage of analysis to be continued. Eight and nine months of zero credits notes on areas 1 and 2.
November	Commence collection of data regarding group discounts. Eleven months of zero discounts for discount errors and ten for pricing errors.
December	One full year without one credit note caused by discount errors. Current data collection and analysis into group accounts and sales office administration on standard products.

These achievements have been brought about through a planned process of quality, and a step-by-step approach to achieve it:

- Training (full and professional training).
- Data collection and analysis (painstaking and boring analysis of all data).
- Problem-solving (not assumptions based on individual ideas).
- Implementation (team, getting the staff themselves to believe in the implementation by practical operations).

During the process of introducing these practices, a number of noticeable changes occurred in the system and procedures. In common with many quality improvement activities the standardization and formalization of processes was necessary. In addition the culture of the organization also began to change. The original company background was one of a sales-based culture with quality regarded as part of the product, not the service. A large percentage of the workforce was based around selling, or providing the products required to support the sales staff. Errors in the process, such as discounts or prices, were accepted, and credit notes were issued to correct these errors. The process of getting the service right first time was not seen as a source of competitive advantage. Working through the analysis and detailed problem-solving procedure permitted the team to gain an understanding of the reasons behind the current situation. This allowed the design and implementation of the new systems and processes. Working step by step and through slow implementation and change, the thinking and culture of all those involved at Kennametal Hertel Ltd was gradually changing, with the results visible to all in the early months of 1996.

An excellent start having been made to the quality process by the Value Added Team and all the other teams, nevertheless there is always the feeling in any workforce that they could have done better. There is still much more for the team to do. But, the key lessons learned so far by Kennametal Hertel Ltd can be successfully summarized as:

- *The process must be voluntary* – there is no point in forcing people to join, or stay in a team that they feel unable to contribute to.
- *It's hard work, though enjoyable* – at all levels and throughout the workforce any quality improvement programme can easily be seen as following one of its principal tools, the Pareto principle: 80 per cent hard work and perspiration to 20 per cent inspiration.
- *Training is essential* – the initial temptation is to rush in and assume you know the answer, without training. The team probably would not even have found the real problems without the training.
- *Everything takes longer than you first think or plan* – no matter how detailed you plan a project it takes far longer: two to three times if this example is to be considered.
- *Publicity is essential* – once the programme has begun, do not stop, do not lose interest or sight of the goals; to encourage this you need to tell people – tell everyone.
- *Tell the people why they have to undergo change* – quality processes may be obvious to the people who have discovered the new solution, but it is not instinctive to the workforce. People need to be educated in how to approach a task that they may have been undertaking in one way for years. Training and education are a continuous process.
- *Getting the 'buy-in' of the people involved in the change* – once the staff involved feel part of the process, its success is much easier.
- *Persistence pays off* – never accept 'No' when you are certain that you have identified a problem and potential solution.
- *Good data analysis is essential* – no matter how hard or long it takes.
- *When you've fixed it, it must be monitored to stay fixed* – never expect the first implementation to stay as planned on its own.

- *Recognize the work and the successes* – say 'Thank you' as often and as publicly as possible; it works. This goes for team members as well as management.

ISSUES FOR THE FUTURE

The programme of the Value Added Team has been seen to be successful, not only with the direct aims of reducing credit notes, but also in that staff have seen their peers solving problems which originally were considered as a normal part of their business, or which were too large to even be considered, let alone solved. The team has continued with its aim set out by the group in its own mission statement:

MISSION STATEMENT:

To eliminate credits and improve the quality of customer care.

The next stage, having successfully provided and implemented solutions to the problems of credit notes caused by discount system errors, and pricing errors, is to return to the outstanding issues – group accounts, external sales, sales office administration. Having proved themselves, the team can now return to issues originally considered by management as perhaps too sensitive, or complex.

CONCLUSIONS

Kennametal Hertel Ltd's continuous improvement scheme has undoubtedly been successful; not just the Value Added Team. The quality initiative has been successful in making changes in procedures, communication, behaviour and attitudes towards quality in the service sector of the organization. The programme has now become embedded in the Vision 2000 programme and accepted at all levels of the organization, and has altered the approach towards change. The quality initiative actually started in Kennametal Ltd with the process to acquire BS EN ISO 9001:1994, but has now become a general part of the company's whole operations, not just production and warehouse systems. The process has encouraged other teams to become established and has helped ensure that the process of continuous quality improvement has become embedded within the company's culture.

Part 2

THE VARITYPERKINS
EUROPEAN QUALITY AWARD

Seven

CASE UNITED KINGDOM LIMITED

*A transformation to a world class
centre of excellence*

JACKIE BRANDER BROWN
AND
ALISON KING

Seven

CASE UK LTD

A transformation to a world class centre of excellence

INTRODUCTION

Case United Kingdom Limited (Case) is part of the Case Corporation, a multinational manufacturing/marketing organization which operates from fifteen sites worldwide – eight of which are in Europe – and which has been producing a comprehensive range of agricultural and construction machinery equipment for some 150 years. Case employs more than 2,000 people, over 500 of whom work at the company's 110-acre Wheatley Hall Road site in Doncaster, where they assemble more than 12,000 tractors every year, of which 85 per cent are destined for export. These tractors, moreover, are widely considered to be among the most technically advanced in the world – as are the manufacturing facilities at Doncaster which produce them, and which now comprise the Corporation's World Class Centre for Excellence for tractor assembly in Europe.

The outlook for Case, though, has not always been so bright. In fact, the late 1980s and early 1990s was a period of great uncertainty for Case. Indeed, their achievement in being named as the 1997 winners of the VarityPerkins European Quality Award is all the more remarkable given that, as was noted in *The European,* it '. . . represented a complete turnaround from the situation little more than three years ago . . .', when the outlook for Case seemed particularly bleak. For it was in early 1994 that the Corporation announced that, in order to address an excess of manufacturing capacity within the worldwide organization, they intended to implement a substantial restructuring programme. At best it was thought that this restructuring would necessitate redundancies at Case – while, as one manager noted, '. . . no one dared to contemplate the worst-case scenario'. Yet, everyone at the Doncaster site knew that the plant had real potential, and that with the proper investment and support they believed they could achieve great things. Fortunately this was a belief which the Corporation's executives shared, and in the detailed restructuring plans which followed it was announced that Case's Wheatley Hall Road site was to become the Corporation's European Centre for Excellence for tractor assembly operations. This exciting announcement, however, also left Case with something of a 'mountain' to climb if it was to successfully transform itself into a world-class facility, and this chapter sets out to describe how they rose to meet the challenge – a 'journey' which began in December 1994.

CASE'S QUALITY JOURNEY: FIRST STEPS

The scale of the challenge which faced Case soon became very evident as they visited a number of 'high achievers' in motor vehicle manufacturing – including Nissan and Toyota in the UK, and Chrysler in the US. As a result of such visits it became apparent that Case was, as one manager put it, '. . . in danger of being left behind at base camp'. Consequently, to meet the demands of transforming the Doncaster plant into a Centre of Excellence, many changes were planned. These included the closure of the foundry at the Wheatley Hall Road site, the outsourcing of its machining operations to an affiliate plant in France, and also the sale or joint venture of Case's Carr Hill operation – also located in Doncaster – by the end of 1998. It also crucially involved the implementation of a plan known as 'Future II/Team Doncaster', which was to comprise both an enormous amount of input from the Case workforce as well as a £10 million investment in the reworking of the entire assembly process.

FUTURE II: TRANSFORMING THE ASSEMBLY FACILITIES

Future II consisted of a detailed plan specifically designed to meet the Case board of directors' challenge to transform the Doncaster site into a world-class assembly facility. This transformation plan, which was designed around four key criteria – as described in Figure 7.1 – of Process, Logistics, Systems and, most important of all, People, entailed an extensive rebuilding programme, to be achieved in five main phases – Transmission and Engine Dress, Hot Test, Wash and Paint, Cab Assembly/Sub-assembly, and Main Line Assembly. This commenced in December 1994, when the existing buildings which housed the plant's fabrication shop, transmission line and assembly line were joined. Subsequent developments have further simplified and re-routed the production line to provide greater flexibility and on-line facilities.

A critical factor to the success in meeting the challenge and completing the transformation was the total support of the Case workforce and their trade unions. Indeed, Case took the view that none of the planned rebuilding would be achieved in the time-scale proposed unless 'their' people worked together to make things happen. To this end, Case developed the aim of fostering a culture of teamworking and team spirit – an aim that initially took form through 'Team Doncaster'.

PROCESS:
the creation of a continuous
assembly track with on-line leak and
transmission testing, selective automation and
a new paint facility that improves quality
and conforms to emission regulations.

LOGISTICS:
sequenced material deliveries
direct to the production line, partnership sourcing
and an optimum 100 suppliers.

SYSTEMS:
factory-wide data, daily MRP runs,
real-time product tracking and
dynamic line sequencing.

PEOPLE:
an empowered workforce, operating
simultaneous engineering in focused business units
and using self-directed work groups.

Figure 7.1: Future II Strategic Criteria

TEAM DONCASTER: TRANSFORMING THE 'PEOPLE'

Establishing the teams

Team Doncaster involved placing seventy volunteers from all levels within manufacturing into one of five fully empowered working teams, which mirrored the five previously noted key assembly/plant installation phases. Importantly, each team was able to bring to bear a wide range of skills and expertise, comprising as they did 'members' who specialized in such fields as process engineering, layout and materials handling, production, safety, plant engineering, material logistics and quality. Each team was assigned a sponsor, whose primary role was to manage the team process, which included arranging and leading team meetings, ensuring their team developed a plan and that their goals were met, liaising with other team leaders, and also making available – within agreed budgetary limits – any resources, equipment or training that the team identified as being necessary to achieve their aims and objectives.

Developing teamworking skills

In order to foster effective teamworking, the teams took part in a three-day outdoor team-building course, which Case had specifically developed with the assistance of the Lindley Training Centre in Castleton, Yorkshire. This team-building course particularly focused on working towards common goals and the sharing of resources, and included a range of tasks, some of which were physical, while others required creative thinking and/or logical analysis. For example, one exercise involved the building of a raft, which required the teams to compile a list of parts and to assess the optimum build method – all of this reflecting the 'bill of materials' process used at Case. Another short exercise, meanwhile, incorporated a profit-linked time element, which particularly served to reinforce the message that working as a cohesive unit produces results. From the start the teams could clearly see that what they were learning and experiencing had a very real and very useful application for their day-to-day work, and by the end of the three-day event the wider benefits were very obvious to everyone: confidence was high, people were motivated, and there was a genuine and tangible respect for fellow team members. In addition to this team-building course, each team member was also offered the opportunity to further develop their team skills through a series of one-day workshops, which covered such topics as problem-solving tools and techniques.

Team objectives

The teams' objectives were clear:

- to review and amend the plant layout;
- to oversee the capital projects in their respective areas;
- to critique and buy-off the new facility;
- to develop process information, training and manning requirements in their areas of responsibility;
- to develop their tasks and timing objectives.

A major challenge facing the teams was not just the making of wholesale changes to the plant and its layout – an undertaking the scale of which would usually necessitate a 'shut-down' of anything between four and eight weeks – but at the same time to introduce a new MX30 tractor range, and so set the foundation for future new products. The MX30 range, whilst generating a considerable amount of excitement throughout Case, also represented 'unexplored territory' for the plant: with models ranging between 110 and 135 horsepower, it is not only by far the biggest tractor ever built at Doncaster, but it is also the most sophisticated and technologically advanced. Consequently, the introduction of the MX30 tractor would not only require the introduction of new processes, but also that Case's 'people' would need to acquire knowledge of new technologies and systems, and achieve competencies in a whole new range of skills.

Team-working 'outcomes'

The fact that the five teams were involved from day one, contributing to the planning and improvement process, and that they were given the responsibility to put their ideas into action, enthused and motivated the workforce who became eager to commit themselves fully to the cause. Indeed, some extremely 'tangible' benefits of teamworking were becoming very apparent: the teams were working as cohesive units with everyone under-standing their role and responsibilities; individual members had an increased awareness of what other people do within the company, and what their jobs entail; they had a better appreciation of the challenges being faced; and they had trust and confidence in their team-mates' skills and judgement.

The effectiveness of this team-working concept also extended beyond the five teams that formed the backbone of Team Doncaster. For example, the members of the Cab Assembly team worked with the company which was contracted to design, manufacture and install the new Cab Assembly line. The Cab Assembly team met regularly with the contractor's team to ensure that a system was developed which would meet key operational objectives. By pooling their resources in this way, their expertise and their experience enabled potential problem areas to be ironed out at an early stage of development.

Ultimately, the success of Team Doncaster became very clear as *all* the five phases of the Future II rebuilding project were not only achieved on time, but also within budget. Even more remarkable is that, while this rebuilding was taking place, the production of the plant's existing product lines not only continued, but also the introduction of the new MX30 tractor was successfully implemented – all of this being achieved without the loss of a single day's production. Moreover, the overwhelming feeling was that Team Doncaster had broken down barriers. The people at Case had developed immense ownership and pride in their work, as well as a considerable and genuine interest in the performance of the company – indeed, many of the employees are now shareholders in the company, and can monitor the performance of their shares on a daily basis on a large overhead display at the plant. With this outstanding team spirit, motivation and commitment, there was a growing belief that no challenge would be too great for Case! However, to ensure this, it was felt that a new, fundamental work culture also needed to be developed – a change that has started to be addressed at Case through 'Project Breakthrough'.

PROJECT BREAKTHROUGH: TRANSFORMING THE CULTURE

Project Breakthrough, which is being piloted in Zone 1 – the start of the tractor assembly line – also extends to related sub-assemblies, internal disciplines, affiliates and suppliers. It was introduced not only to complement the facility changes and new product development programmes at Case, but also to complement the plant's traditional methods of training by bringing employees together in teams to solve real problems while actually working on the assembly line. In particular, it is intended that the Project will, through helping to create a motivated and quality-focused workforce, build a work culture able to deliver the total and consistent quality required by all of the company's new production metrics – especially 'first pass yield without repair'. Also, it is planned that Project Breakthrough will build a workforce able to embrace change on a continuous basis, thus assisting in the achievement of the 'breakthrough' to a step change in performance, which Case believes is needed to deliver the new output targets. Central to the Project are the following aims:

- To achieve a sustained employee behaviour change in support of the goal of becoming a recognized world class facility.
- To achieve a first pass yield without repair on the complete assembly line.
- To achieve zero defects per unit.
- To contribute to Case's Strategic Objectives.
- To prepare and position the workforce to plan and deliver 'back-to-back' launches to schedule.

The upshot thus far of Project Breakthrough is that the company is tapping into the potential that every employee at Case has to offer, rather than just a select few – indeed, it could be said that the company is investing in its future through its people. An example of this 'investment' can be seen in the development of the MX30 tractor, when Case invested in a new purpose-built, fully equipped product development area. Using this facility, assembly employees were given the opportunity of familiarizing themselves with the new tractor range and the new technologies and build methods it entailed, so that when the production of the MX30 was actually implemented, everyone on the line knew the tractors inside out, resulting in a smooth, problem-free launch. As one manager observed, '. . . there is no substitute for good preparation and teamwork'.

While the programme still has some barriers to overcome before an overall evaluation exercise can be undertaken, and the project extended further throughout Case, it is believed that significant progress with regard to improved cross-functional communications and team participation in problem-solving has already occurred through the Project.

COMMUNICATION

It was established at an early stage in Case's transformation process that their communication systems and methods would be fundamental to the success of their teamwork initiatives. Indeed, it is considered essential that *all* Case employees understand the strategic direction in which the company is going – and moreover, how they as individuals can contribute to the success of the company.

Communications Plan

Communication at Case is carried out through a 'Communications Plan', which comprises a range of initiatives and tools designed to communicate with employees at all levels. This is achieved through such means as plant manager/management meetings, team briefings, house journals, notice boards and 'Town Hall' meetings. At these latter meetings, which are twice yearly, the plant General Manager explains what the company is trying to achieve by sharing the Business Plan – key extracts of which are shown in Figures 7.2 and 7.3 – with *all* Case's employees.

1997 CASE BUSINESS PLAN
Doncaster Plant

VISION STATEMENT
To be recognized as a customer-driven/quality-led world class 'Centre of Excellence' for tractor assembly.

MISSION STATEMENT
To be a customer-driven manufacturer of agricultural equipment by meeting and exceeding the expectations and needs of all internal and external customers in regard to:

Quality
Through our commitment to excellence and customer service.

Delivery
Through improving flexibility and material flow.

Cost
Through systematic elimination of non-value-added activity and improved plant operating efficiency.

We will fully utilize and involve all our employees to harness their commitment to excellence in everything we do, to secure a long-term and prosperous future for our organization.

Figure 7.2: 1997 Case Business Plan: Doncaster Plant Vision and Mission Statements

CASE CORPORATION

Mission

Lead the industry by providing our agricultural and construction equipment customers around the world with superior product and services that maximize their productivity and success

Strategic imperatives

Customer focus	Superior products	Outstanding dealers	Cost leadership	Speed	Real partnerships
Key drivers	*Key drivers*	*Key drivers*	*Key drivers*	*Key drivers*	*Key drivers*
100% customer satisfaction	Zero defects per unit	100% customer satisfaction	Annual operating profit achievement	Schedule adherence	Employee empowerment
			Rationalize facility	New product development in <3 years	Accident-free environment
			Achieve 5% cost of quality		
			100% first pass yield		

Operating principles (performance dimensions)

Delight the customer	Continuous quality improvement	Manage cycles	Open and honest environment	Empowered employees	Global perspective	Fact-based decisions	Uncompromising ethics

Figure 7.3: Linking Case's 'Key Drivers' to the Corporation's Mission, Strategic Imperatives and Operating Principles

This Business Plan outlines a strategic framework, which is then broken down into departmental targets from which objectives are set for departments and teams, and goals are set for each individual to work towards. In addition, the Plan also sets out how Case will be investing time and money in the training and development of employees to help the company achieve these goals.

TRAINING AND DEVELOPMENT

Case's Business Plan clearly identifies both the resources made available for training and developing employees, and also the managers responsible for regularly reviewing and agreeing training and development needs with each employee. Such training and development activities are clearly linked with business objectives and targets, and where appropriate are also linked to the attainment of NVQs.

Skills assessment and enhancement

More specifically, in order to support the skills and development needs of the Case people, a skills assessment and enhancement programme for all the hourly-paid employees at Case was developed and implemented from the end of 1994. This programme, which enabled skills gaps to be identified and subsequently addressed, has resulted in the significant improvement of the overall efficiency of the tractor assembly plant. The success of the programme is also evident in the achievement of prestigious Regional and National Training Awards at the end of 1996 while, having been developed around NVQ standards, it has also led to NVQ awards being attained by over 600 hourly-paid Case employees during 1996.

New product training

During 1996 more than 100 assembly operatives at Case received two days off-line training in a new dedicated training facility, with the specific purpose of ensuring that they were equipped with the necessary new product knowledge before the launch of the new MX30 series tractor in 1997. Four full-time training instructors have also been assigned to facilitate skills application on the assembly line both prior to and after the new tractor launch.

Information technology training

As new technology in computer hardware and software has been introduced, and most of Case information systems updated, a PC skills analysis was undertaken. As a result of this analysis, training needs were identified and addressed for more than 200 employees to ensure that they were equipped with the necessary skills. In this regard Case has established an effective 'external partnership' by utilizing the training services and expertise of Doncaster ITEC.

**Case United Kingdom Limited/
Sheffield Business School**

MANAGEMENT DEVELOPMENT PROGRAMME

PROGRAMME OBJECTIVE

To make a lasting difference to the effectiveness of Case through individual, team and organizational learning and development.

PROGRAMME STRUCTURE

Personal effectiveness:

Managing oneself
Interpersonal skills

Management context:

The business environment
The management task

Management functions:

Managing people
Managing information
Managing operations

Figure 7.4: Case's Management Development Programme

Training for management and supervisors

The ongoing development of management skills is considered vital to provide a strong foundation of competence for Case's future. This has again involved an external partnership – this with the Sheffield Business School – to develop a fifteen-month programme, which is outlined in Figure 7.4. Thus far more than fifty managers from cross-functional areas at Case have completed the programme, with many of them progressing further to pursue Diplomas in Management Studies, or even MBAs

Early in 1997, Case also launched a Supervisory Development Programme, which particularly developed from a belief that the enhancement of supervisory performance is a critical part of the overall behavioural change that Case is aiming for with the above-noted Project Breakthrough initiative. In particular, it has been recognized that supervisors at Case are currently lacking in certain 'softer skills' – a fact which was confirmed by a quality audit conducted by the Corporation's Director for Quality. Here again, as a result of the programme, the supervisors will have the opportunity to attain an NVQ in recognition of the completion of the programme.

Quality 'rallies'

For the past four years, Case Doncaster has held an event known as the 'Mini Quality Rally', the aim of which is to encourage teams working on improvement projects at the plant to present their team's achievements in innovative ways. A special panel of judges select a winning team(s) who then go forward to represent Case Doncaster at the Corporation's European and Worldwide Quality Rallies. Through such events other employees at Case can see for themselves the benefits that can be achieved through training, teamwork, commitment and involvement.

As an example, at the plant's 1997 Mini Quality Rally – which was entitled 'Take the World by Storm' – one of the winning teams undertook a study of the reasons why the Carr Hill site at Doncaster had been labelled as having the second-worst environmental improvement history of all the plants within the worldwide corporation. The team set about targeting those areas which required immediate attention and their efforts led to the installation of a new liquid waste evaporator, the replacement of some cooling towers and the repair of all underground pipe leakages. These activities, which again involved external partnerships with some of Case's key suppliers, not only resulted in a much improved plant environment, but also a massive saving of £70,000.

Other training and development activities

In addition to the above-noted planned training programmes, more spontaneous training requests are also met. For example, during 1996 maintenance training was identified as being required due to the installation of the planned new assembly facility. As a result of this additional training a new skills matrix was also developed for hourly-paid operatives, which combined inputs from operatives, supervisors and trainers.

1997 has also seen the introduction of selection testing of job applicants at Case. This development particularly supports the ongoing culture change process at Case, as it involves identifying potential employees who possess particular attitudes and aptitudes considered vital to the plant's continued development and success – including, for example, a willingness to receive new training and to work within teams.

DEVELOPING 'EXTERNAL' PARTNERSHIPS

As has already been noted, the benefits of teamworking at Case were not only clearly visible internally at the Doncaster site, but also extended to Case's external partnerships with, for example, the company's suppliers, and also with their customers and their environment.

Partnerships with suppliers

Good supplier partnerships were considered essential if Case were to successfully achieve their strategic objectives – particularly that of reducing lead times. In fact, in 1995 Case's average supplier lead time was fourteen weeks from order to delivery, but by the beginning of 1997 that had been more than halved to just seven weeks – with further reductions anticipated by the end of 1997. How did Case achieve this significant improvement?

The starting-point for the improvement was when Case began to look very carefully at how suppliers actually delivered parts to the plant. Case found that they were holding vast stocks of parts – often for months at a time – at their own on-site warehouse. Now, Case has no on-site materials storage facilities, but as a result of a complete re-think of Case's logistics strategy, an 'advanced vendor store' is located just one mile from the assembly facility. At the heart of this strategy 're-think' was the pursuit of a 'Just-in-Time' (JIT) delivery system, where Case's suppliers either transport parts direct to the production line for immediate use, or to the advanced vendor store to await call-off in line with the production line's build requirements.

Another partnership development with their suppliers involved Case in the introduction of Electronic Data Interchange (EDI), which enables such critical supplier information as schedule requirements, invoices and weekly consignment activity reports to be transacted electronically. A number of significant benefits are expected from this EDI, including the reduction of costs and cycle times, and the elimination of 'human' errors which can occur when paper-based data is re-typed. By mid-1997 Case was utilizing EDI with thirty-nine of their key suppliers – but their aim, not surprisingly, is to get all their suppliers linked up.

Such developments are obviously necessitating considerable changes – and investment – for Case's suppliers, and Case is helping them to identify and make these changes. For instance, Case has set up a special team to oversee 'change projects' and to help the suppliers to implement the necessary modifications. Amongst other things, for instance, this has entailed site visits around the world, providing appropriate training as well as carrying out joint development work with dedicated supplier teams.

Alongside this, Case is also working to substantially reduce its supplier base: in 1995, Case used more then 600 suppliers, which by the end of 1997 should be reduced to 248 – with the ultimate aim being to rationalize the base to just 100 companies. One of the ways this reduction is being achieved is by the delegation of certain minor sub-assembly work which the Case plant used to undertake itself – such as the tractor radiators. Previously, Case used to source the radiators, their plastic shrouds, hoses and pressings from different suppliers. Now, Case's key radiator supplier orders and fits the ancillary items and then delivers them to Case ready for the production line.

All of this may sound as if Case is demanding a great deal from their suppliers – but it is also true to say that they are offering their chosen suppliers a great deal in return: for instance, Case is prepared to offer their selected suppliers long-term contracts; also, as noted previously, Case will provide development support; and, through the introduction of such changes as EDI, Case believes their suppliers will not only improve their own competitiveness but may well be opening their doors to new markets.

Partnerships with customers

In order to meet the Corporation's strategic imperative of 'customer focus' and the operating principle of 'delighting the customer', Case has designed and established specific customer-focused groups, such as a 'Product Customer Service Centre' and the 'Customer Service Platform', to provide a direct customer 'Face of Case'. Within these groups all aspects relating to Case's products – and particularly improving delivery time, product choice and after-care support – could be raised, considered and addressed.

Partnerships with the 'environment'

Case are very aware of their wider community role, and are justifiably proud of the effort, commitment and achievement of their Environment Team. This team comprises a group of volunteers from all areas within the plant at Doncaster who have championed the site into joining the Yorkshire Wildlife Trust. This has especially involved the commissioning of studies into trees, flora and fauna on the Doncaster site with the aim of guiding preservation actions, and has involved significant levels of personal commitment by the team members.

With such open and interactive relationships, Case believes that the strength of their internal and external partnerships will go a long way to assisting them in achieving great things – both now and in the future.

PERFORMANCE MEASUREMENT

The previously noted Business Plan, which, as can be seen from Figure 7.3, supports the Corporation's Mission and Strategic Imperatives, also incorporates Case's Key Drivers underlying each of these imperatives and the related appropriate Operating Principles (Performance Dimensions). At a monthly meeting, known as the 'Operations Review', which is attended by the plant manager and the senior management group of functional heads – as illustrated in Figure 7.5 – the plant's performance is reviewed against the performance goals set and variances discussed. This resulting report is then circulated to each functional head to enable them to concentrate on their particular areas of concern.

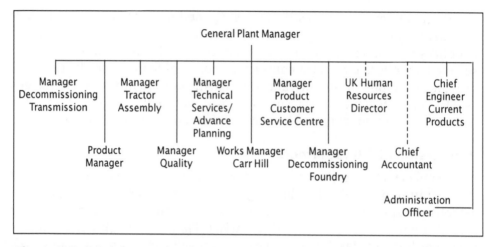

Figure 7.5: Case's Senior Manufacturing Management Group (August 1997)

Other significant performance measurement bases used include: benchmarking against other manufacturing operations within the Corporation worldwide; the Customer Satisfaction Index – a composite measure of customer satisfaction with regard both to the dealer and to the product; and a monthly quality report which, together with other key production metrics, are displayed on communication notice boards close to the assembly line. In addition, at monthly Product Performance Meetings, detailed information is made available regarding, amongst other things, customer complaints and warranty faults. Another newer performance method developed to support one of the above-noted Key Drivers – Parts Certification – is a Supplier Quality Assurance Plan, which provides the means for measuring the quality of Case's suppliers on a continuous basis. This is a vital tool for any company utilizing JIT and/or Total Quality Management (TQM) practices.

A new development in this area which has arisen from Project Breakthrough is the opportunity it presented to understand employee concerns and to determine their satisfaction levels – which was achieved through the use of a short questionnaire. This questionnaire was then repeated some months later, which enabled an assessment to be made of the progress which had been achieved through Project Breakthrough over a period of time. It is intended that the use of the questionnaire will be extended further throughout the company to be used as a measurement tool to monitor to what extent Case is achieving its 'people' goals.

TEAMWORK PRODUCES RESULTS

How has all of the preceding 'talk' about motivation, commitment, empowerment, a changing culture, partnerships and, of course, teamwork been translated into objective, measurable improvements in performance at

Case? Below, some of the key evidence about what 'quality through teamwork' has meant in tangible terms for Case is set out.

First pass yield

In 1994 the first pass yield without repair percentage for Case was recorded at just 22 per cent. By mid-1997 it had improved dramatically to 83 per cent, with the aim being that by the end of 1997 it will stand at 90 per cent.

Cost of quality

Case, in order to 'drive-down' non-value-added activities, tasked some seventy-seven teams with the elimination of scrap and wastage. It is firmly believed that by the end of 1997 the plant will have achieved its improvement target of 22 per cent compared to its 1996 figures.

Output and repairs

In 1994 the Case plant at Doncaster was turning out some forty tractors every day. Now, the output figure which is consistently being achieved is seventy-two tractors per day! Meanwhile, over the same period, Case has seen a dramatic reduction of 30 per cent in the number of repairs required to be carried out on their tractors within the warranty period.

New products

As already mentioned, Case has recently produced the new MX30 tractor range. The 'time-to-market', from concept to production, would normally be about six years for such a development – the MX30 though came to market in just three years. This achievement is even more remarkable given that, as already noted, it was achieved during a major plant refurbishment, and without the loss of a single day's production.

Other important 'milestones'

Other milestones which Case has passed along their 'journey' include: its re-recognition as an 'Investor in People' in 1996 – following its initial attainment of this standard in 1993 – reflecting the commitment of Case's people in such activities as training and development, communications and teamworking; also, as has been noted previously, in 1996 Case won prestigious regional and national training awards, while over 600 employees at the company have gained NVQ qualifications in recognition of their engineering skills; and in November 1996 a CBI award in recognition of Manufacturer's Excellence was received – reflecting the substantial production improvements made over the previous two years.

Case Doncaster is now recognized as a world class facility, and moreover is now well and truly established as the Corporation's European Centre of

Excellence for tractor assembly. It is no longer just a UK plant supplying the UK market, but rather a European plant which exports some 85 per cent of its output to the four corners of the world. Case firmly believes that none of this would have been possible without the commitment and support of *all* their people – in short, Case could not have made it to the top of their 'mountain' without *teamwork!* Through careful planning, the setting of clear objectives, and – above all – by underpinning their efforts with teamwork, Case Doncaster has achieved new heights. Indeed, today Case and its people are very much at the summit of their industry, and can look back with great satisfaction on what they have achieved along a difficult and challenging journey.

WHERE TO FROM HERE ?

Case recognizes, of course, that there will always be more journeys and more mountains to climb. Their end goal is to build an entirely new kind of organization through building a high-performance work system which will generate continuous improvements to meet constantly shifting business demands. This goal will not only take time and resources to achieve, but also determined, committed leadership from Case's management team. Project Breakthrough has begun to 'break the mould', and so move Case a long way along the road towards building that high-performance work system. It is through developments such as this that Case believes they can look forward to their future with confidence, and particularly to the successful achievement of their goal of 90 per cent of their employees working in teams by the year 2000. For whatever new challenges lie ahead, Case is in a better shape than ever to conquer them!

Eight

THE SAVOY GROUP

*Achieving excellence through
training and development*

MARGARET ERSTAD
AND
BETH AARONS

Eight

THE SAVOY GROUP

Achieving excellence through training and development

INTRODUCTION

The Savoy Group operates five-star luxury hotels, restaurants and a theatre all located within the United Kingdom. The four London-based hotels are: The Savoy (207 rooms), Claridge's (196 rooms), The Berkeley (157 rooms) and The Connaught (90 rooms). At present, the only non-London hotel is The Lygon Arms (67 rooms) in the heart of the Cotswolds. Well-known restaurants such as Simpson's-in-the-Strand provide traditional English cuisine.

Approximately one hundred years ago, the Savoy Group had its origins in the Savoy Theatre established by D'Oyly Carte of Gilbert and Sullivan fame. The theatre is still a popular venue for theatrical performances and adds a unique dimension to the Savoy Group's portfolio of businesses.

In 1995, the Savoy Group found itself with a newly appointed Group Managing Director, Ramon Pajares, and a recently formed General Management Team. One of the first initiatives of the new leadership was to develop a medium-term strategy for the Group. The strategy needed to take into account existing market conditions, the state of repair of the Group's properties, levels of occupancy, market segments, rate levels, and the training and development requirements of the approximately 2,000 employees within the Savoy Group.

The purpose of this chapter is to look at the Savoy Group's quality improvement programme and track its journey from inception in 1995 for approximately the next two years. After a short overview of the Savoy Group, the second part of the chapter will deal with how the change programme was deployed throughout the organization, and the use of quality education and training to obtain results. Methods the Savoy Group uses to measure and assess quality improvement will be discussed later in the chapter, as will some of the achievements from the change programme. The level of management commitment is also considered, as are plans for continuous quality improvement for the future of the Savoy Group. The chapter will conclude with a review of the some of the implications of the quality improvement programme for the Hotel Group.

The preparation and research required for 'Savoy 2000', as the five-year plan is called, identified areas of weakness and corresponding opportunities to improve and drive the Group into the millennium. While the Group had a well-recognized brand in the Savoy, the name had become associated with an older, very traditional concept that failed to cater for the modern-age consumer. It was apparent that the Savoy Group had stopped listening to their customers and failed to hear what they were asking for in terms of service and amenities.

Management techniques had also remained in the past and, as a consequence, the results for the Group had been failing for several years. The organization was very hierarchical and top-heavy. Money was being spent on maintaining the old and rusting property without sufficient investment being made in amenities such as air-conditioning and other modernization available at competitor properties. The 90-room Lanesborough Hotel had recently been refurbished and the 210-room Dorchester had received a £95 million facelift by the Brunei Investment Agency.

Occupancy and room rates and overall revenues were low, as was the Group's market share versus the competition. The customer base was shrinking and action was needed to stop this negative trend.

In addition to the above, The Savoy Group found it had become increasingly difficult to attract qualified and innovative staff. Turnover was high and employee morale and pride in the organization were waning. It had become more and more of a challenge to meet customer expectations with a high level of new employees, lack of training and development of staff, low employee morale and a tired product.

According to Ramon Pajares (1997), 'Customers, now more than ever, want a product beyond their expectations, at value-for-money prices, and want service delivered in double-quick time. To meet these demands from within the existing hotel industry, changes will have to be made in the way hotels are run.' At the Savoy, the decision was made that now was the time to change, for the future success of the business required investment in the hotels and the people running them. Change, brought about through the strong leadership of Mr Pajares, rallied around the common theme for all the business units of customer satisfaction. Sacrifices would have to be made in the short term to guarantee long-term growth. Indeed, with ongoing building work, occupancy levels were affected during the transition period. However, the financial results for 1997 more than speak for themselves of the soundness of this new strategy.

One of the initial steps taken was to invest in the Group's products in order to bring then up to par with the competition. Claridge's had £40 million spent on refurbishment, The Berkeley £11 million, The Savoy £18 million.

While large amounts were invested in the Savoy Group's products, it was equally important to invest in the company's human capital and with this in mind four key strategies were outlined:

- Cultural and attitudinal transformation.
- A clear vision and well-defined objectives.
- A new and improved image in the public's eyes.
- A need to work together as a team across the organization with each and every employee understanding, participating, and being involved in the change.

Another major goal for the Group running parallel with the above strategies has been to achieve 'Investors in People' for all the properties by the end of 1997.

When the Savoy 2000 team concept was created, a strong concern was how to enlist the support and contribution of individuals throughout the organization. The team should not consist only of managers at the top imposing their strategy on the rest of the Group. While management's job was to inspire staff to work towards a common goal, a team structure was sought that would engage employees at distinct levels in the change programme. As Mr Pajares explained, creating 'unity out of diversity' is an essential part of the change process.

KEY STEPS OF THE QUALITY IMPROVEMENT PROGRAMME

The quality journey

The Savoy Group worked with the expertise of a management consulting company in developing a five-year plan, 'Savoy 2000'. The birth of 'Savoy 2000' resulted in the formulation of eight key Operating Principles (Figure 8.1) which serve as the foundation of the business. The plan and its Operating Principles were launched to all staff within the Group through theatre-style presentations that reflected the dynamic nature of the Plan and represented a turning-point in the Group's strategy, as no such event involving all employees had ever been held before at the Savoy. The key to the success of the plan was seen to lie in unlocking the skills of all Savoy employees.

The organization

In order to turn 'Savoy 2000' from theory into practice and make the key Operating Principles operational, project teams were set up with members of the management team leading and co-ordinating a number of projects with representation from all parts of the organization. From the work of these project teams a number of specific programmes were identified and budget approval from the Board was obtained.

We believe in excellence

Our objective is to be universally recognized as the pre-eminent luxury hotel company in the world, offering consistently high-quality products and services – and endeavouring to improve day to day.

We anticipate customer needs.

We are passionate about exceeding the expectations of our discerning customers by anticipating and satisfying their needs and providing value for money.

We will employ the best people.

We will attract the most qualified employees regardless of race, sex or creed and retain them by creating an excellent working environment, and rewarding their achievements.

Our people are our strength.

Our greatest asset is our people. We will provide them with training and development to enable them to achieve their full potential, and to be proud to work for a hotel or restaurant within the Savoy Group.

We believe in working together.

We will create and maintain a climate of enthusiasm through teamwork, leading by example, with mutual respect and trust for each other and a sense of pride in everything we do.

We will achieve a reasonable profit.

We will achieve profits in the top 25 per cent of our direct competitor group.

Our behaviour – by example.

We will manage by example. We will deal with others as we would like them to deal with us. We believe in the importance of ethics, loyalty, and confidentiality of company information and relationships.

We are environmentally conscious.

We recognize the need to improve the environment in which we operate. Working closely with the local community and neighbours, we will actively pursue environmental initiatives.

Figure 8.1: The Savoy Group's eight operating principles

In 1996, the programmes concentrated on improving the product and altering the external image of the Savoy Group. When this work neared completion at the beginning of 1997, the focus turned towards improving customer service. Training was seen as the core to organizational change in service delivery. Thus, Intensive Instructional Techniques Training was carried out for thirty-two key people within the Group who would in turn deliver Customer Care Training for all employees within the company.

Summary of the Quality Improvement Programme and Project Teams

The Savoy Group 2000 has the following goal:

> BY THE END OF THE YEAR 2000, THE SAVOY GROUP
> WILL RE-ESTABLISH THEMSELVES AS THE PRE-
> EMINENT LUXURY HOTEL COMPANY IN THE WORLD

In order to achieve this goal, there are seven main operational areas of the business that will receive the most focus (Figure 8.2):

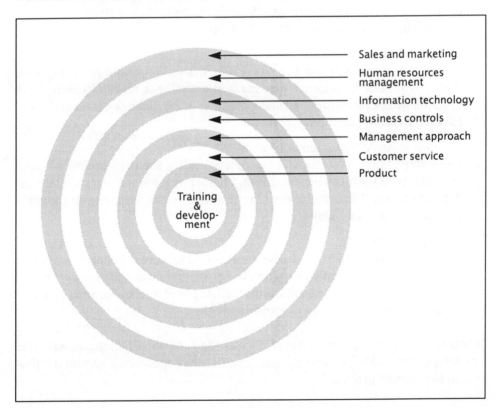

Figure 8.2: The Savoy Group's seven operational areas

1 *Buildings, bedrooms, public and staff areas*
Over the next few years, the Group will be spending millions of pounds to make their properties better than anything owned by their competitors.

2 *Customer service*
The Savoy Group's customers' needs and priorities change and, whatever their reason for coming to the Group, the Savoy Group must to learn to anticipate their needs and exceed their expectations. All the Group's employees will receive thorough and effective training in customer care, so that they can offer the highest level of service whilst improving their career prospects.

3 *Management approach*
Management will support employees by creating the best working environment, giving them everything they need to care for their customers, and ensuring their job is fulfilling and satisfying.

4 *Business controls*
The Group will do everything necessary to control their business effectively – eliminating waste and making sure the money made can be turned into a reasonable profit. The end result will be a richer company that will be able to invest more in its people.

5 *Information technology*
The Savoy Group will use the latest information technology to improve their customers' experience and make the business more efficient. New systems will be introduced to make the lives of employees easier and their customers more satisfied.

6 *Human resource management*
The Group must have the best people working for the company – and support them with the best training. The Group's personnel and training departments will develop many new initiatives to increase the employee's individual value and skills.

7 *Sales and marketing*
The Savoy Group will build the best sales and marketing department in the business. Both the employees and their customers will soon be aware that the Savoy Group is re-establishing itself as a world-class brand, offering the highest level of excellence and service.

Integral to all of the above approaches was the function of training, with the Training Centre taking on an active role rather than merely an administrative one in the change process.

The deployment of quality Improvement

Important considerations in respect to training had to be recognized. Where the Training Centre had been administering and sourcing training before the change process, a more careful look at the type of training delivered found that it was at odds with the forward-looking needs of the business. A new Group Training Manager was recruited to analyse training needs and align them with the medium-term strategy. Training was no longer an isolated area but integrated with the Company Mission Statement and 'Savoy 2000' plan.

In 1996, over one thousand staff were trained centrally, an increase of over 50 per cent on previous years. This accelerated dedication for training required a higher budget commitment from the Board, which was granted. The focus for customer service training has been for front-of-house first, then back-of-house employees.

Staff were also encouraged to participate in project teams and the Investors in People process. Each operation now holds a staff quarterly meeting inviting staff comment and questions in a relaxed and lively way.

The introduction of new uniforms in certain areas of the operation resulted in staff being asked for their comments and feedback. While this cosmetic transformation may seem superficial, it did increase staff involvement and in turn brought on new relationships within the organization and a feeling by the staff of participating and contributing to the change process.

Training was not limited only to one level of employees within the organization: senior management also participated in training programmes and team-build events which have helped to develop 'people skills', meeting skills, and performance management skills which, in turn, have encouraged supervisors and staff to contribute their ideas and impressions of the plan.

The nature of the hotel sector, with peaks and troughs in business levels, had to be taken into account when planning any training activities. This ensured a higher level of commitment from staff for the training programmes as they were not forced to undergo training when their workload was very heavy.

With approximately £75 million being invested in upgrading the properties by the end of 1997, the Group decided to put the staff at the forefront of all the restoration work; and staff dining rooms, rest areas, locker and shower rooms were upgraded prior to the rest of the building work. The concern for the welfare of staff, coupled with enhanced training and development, sent very clear messages to the employees about their position in the quality improvement programme.

Quality education and training

While training has historically been an important element at the Savoy Group, the appraisal of operational issues during 1995 resulted in a new training centre supported by a restructuring of the training department being established.

The reformulated training policy approached training from a business standpoint with training being closely linked to a benefit for the business. A training needs analysis would be carried out to identify training needs. Identification of training needs at the Savoy Group can occur through observation, questioning management and employees on how they would deal with situations, questions and errors of staff, customer complaints and mystery shopping evaluations. From the information obtained from the needs analysis, a series of key courses linked to the gaps identified were listed in a Group Training Directory that became available in February 1996. The Training Directory details the courses on offer at the operational, supervisory, and management levels. The training programme was structured to include the following range of courses:

- Induction training.
- Staff training.
- Supervisors' training.
- Managers' training.
- Executive management training.
- Statutory training.
- 'Putting People First'.
- On-job training.

A section of the Training Directory offers information on how to deal with nominations, a delegates' briefing and work required. Each course or programme is listed separately to provide practical information on who the course is suitable for, when the course should be taken, the objectives, the duration, the content, the method, and any pre-course or post-course work (Figure 8.3). To maximize the impact of training, the delegate numbers are limited to twelve per course. The training policy is backed up by documentation with pre-course briefing notes for the trainers and training records for all participants.

New starters receive a one-day induction training day when they learn about administration, terms and conditions of employment, company philosophy, standards of customer care, health and safety, and personal presentation. New inductees also have the opportunity to meet with the General Manager to discuss their individual roles, the property and the Savoy 2000 Mission Statement. Departmental training takes place over a four-week period. This training is the responsibility of the line managers and revolves around the individual's role in the department, and the functions of the department. It also reinforces the points covered in the induction day. A training plan that outlines the tasks to be trained in is explained at this time.

PUTTING PEOPLE FIRST

DELEGATES:	All staff
TIMING:	Within four weeks of starting the job and thereafter once every year.
OBJECTIVES:	To ensure the highest levels of customer service are delivered at all times. To ensure our commitment to our Mission Statement is realized. To ensure all staff understand and can demonstrate customer care in the workplace.
DURATION:	Two days.
CONTENT:	Customer care.
METHOD:	Group discussion. Syndicate work. Individual and group exercises. Video 'In the Customer's Shoes'. Role plays.
PRE-COURSE WORK:	Delegates are asked to discuss personal, good and bad service experiences.
POST-COURSE WORK:	Delegates will be given every opportunity to receive feedback in the work place from their managers.

Figure 8.3: 'Putting People First' course in the training directory

At the Savoy Group, all staff and all supervisors and managers must attend Putting People First training.

Employees are encouraged to identify courses that would be beneficial for them; if resources are not available to deliver the course internally, an employee's request is assessed in relation to the course's relevance to the business and a decision is made whether to fund the course externally.

The variety of courses offered at the Savoy Group are listed in Figure 8.4.

In addition to the above, there is a 'Customer First' series of twenty short sessions aimed at Customer Service providers. The sessions can be selected at random or run from session 1 through 20. Each Customer First session must be run by a Craft Trainer Award (CTA) or Group Training Techniques (GTT) trained trainer to ensure maximum benefit. The sessions reinforce key

STAFF TRAINING
Bars Course
Basic Wine Course
Wine & Spirit Educational Trust Course
Craft Trainer Award
Customer Care
Japanese Guest Service
Software Training
Selling Skills for Staff
Business Awareness
Awareness (for Head Office Staff)

STATUTORY TRAINING
First Aid Course
First Aid Requalification Course
Basic Food Hygiene
Intermediate Food Hygiene
Advanced Food Hygiene
Health & Safety
HAACP

SUPERVISORY TRAINING
Service Excellence
Supervisory Skills
Interpersonal Managing Skills
Performance Appraisals
Sales Skills
Time Management

EXECUTIVE MANAGEMENT TRAINING
Strategic Accounts Workshop Quality
Effective Presentation Skills
Negotiation Skills

MANAGEMENT TRAINING
Principles of Management Workshop
Staff Recruitment and Interviewing

Figure 8.4: Courses offered at the Savoy Group

Customer Service messages, and train staff how to deal with different customer contact situations.

The main forms of documentation related to training are:

1 Action Plan relating to each course taken.
2 Staff Development Form where supervisors/managers outline courses planned.
3 Central Course Training Record.
4 Personal Development Plan for individual employees.
5 Training Note Index of locally written training notes and centrally written lesson plans.
6 List of CTA trained trainers.
7 Pre-course and Post-course Briefing Notes.

In addition to the above, a variety of National Vocational Qualifications (NVQs) and other hospitality-related qualifications are sponsored by the Group in order to ensure the continuous development of staff. NVQs are offered in departments such as the kitchen, housekeeping, bars and Customer Service. The Savoy Group is a registered NVQ Centre. Assessment is an important component of training as the effectiveness of courses should be reflected in 'mystery shopper' assessments and other forms of measurement.

The systems of measurement applied

For Guest Services, formal and informal systems of measurement are used. One formal system is a regular process of 'mystery shopping'. This consists of a combination of visits and telephone calls to each property by a person unknown to the property. During their stay at the Savoy Group's properties, the 'mystery guests' experience amenities and service as a guest would and then measure actual performance against standards defined by the Group. The standards have been developed to benchmark the Savoy Group's performance against international luxury hotel companies. It is not good enough to be the best in London, or the best in the United Kingdom; to be a truly world-class organization, the best must mean the best nationally and internationally. The detailed reports are used by managers to analyse their operations and identify any areas of strength and weakness. The 'mystery shopper' reports also provide information on outstanding performance and allow the company to reward such behaviour accordingly. Positive feedback and the rewarding of employees is fundamental to developing employee loyalty, retaining employees within the organization and lifting morale.

Another formal measurement of customer satisfaction is the Guest Comment Card. By analysing and weighting the feedback, the Savoy Group has been able to identify quality gaps in service and target these areas for additional training. The response rates on the comment cards is approximately 25 per cent. The General Manager reviews and responds to each and every comment card personally. Positive and negative feedback regarding the contents of the card are then relayed to the relevant persons to ensure that any good or bad systems or processes can be noted and dealt with accordingly.

An informal means for measuring customer satisfaction is to monitor the direct contact or 'moments of truth' between customers and employees. Staff are encouraged to communicate with guests and record their interactions in departmental log books. These log books are then reviewed by the line managers and discussions take place with staff from the areas concerned to identify sources of problems and fine-tune any procedural issues immediately. Staff, in turn, are empowered to take immediate action to handle any guest requests. The Savoy Group are aware that when complaints are handled quickly and satisfactorily resolved, customer loyalty can be regained.

A formalized employee appraisal system has recently been implemented. This allows for structured two-way discussions between managers and employees where performance objectives are identified and career and personal development plans are established and documented.

Minimum standards of performance have also been established. For example, in Room Service the maximum acceptable times for the delivery of guest orders has been set: an English breakfast must be in the guest's room twenty minutes after the order is placed, and a dinner must take no longer than thirty minutes. In this case, standards have not only increased customer satisfaction but dealt with potential conflicts between waiters and chefs.

Achievements

Operational improvements from the plan have been achieved in the seven strategic areas outlined earlier.

In terms of the Savoy Group's *products*, the following upgraded features are now available at the properties:

- Air-conditioning has been installed in all the bedrooms and public areas.
- A new telephone system for guests and staff.
- The latest technology in all the bedrooms (UK and US computer sockets, fax line, dual voltage and ISDN line for video conferencing).
- A service panel.
- Stereo units in all of the bedrooms.
- The best working tools and working environment for staff.

In the area of *Customer Service*, all staff have undergone customer service training.

The new *management approach* has relayed a message of commitment and caring to the Savoy Group staff with refurbishment of staff facilities, increased training opportunities and enhanced communication as a result of the change programme and Investor in People initiative.

In relation to *business control*, Standards of Procedures Manuals have been developed in conjunction with all staff to agree Group-wide ways of working. These have been trained within the operations and are kept up-to-date as new systems are developed. These procedures have been the benchmark for assessment of staff performance.

In *human resources management*, key issues such as internal advertising, cross-group transfers, department wages structure, profit share incentive scheme, and staff handbook and induction have been developed.

Critical to the success of *sales and marketing*, an extensive Marketing Relaunch Programme has been embarked upon and new brands and images have been created through collaterals and a corporate video of the highest quality.

Information technology systems within the Savoy Group have now been standardized. This applies not only to widely-used software packages but also to the custom-designed systems such as the Savoy Information System. A yield management system, OPTIMS, was set up in April 1996 and has been used since. It is a program to capture revenue opportunities and analyse results. The yield management programme has generated overall revenue

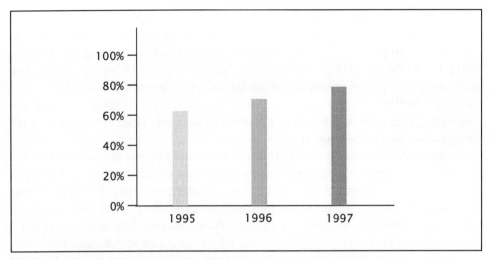

Figure 8.5: Occupancy at the Savoy Group

growth, improved customer service quality through good marketing database and targeted marketing management, and helped minimize guest turn-downs and maximize occupancy and average room rate. The system allows results to be monitored and communicated to the staff.

Lastly, a review of occupancy levels during the years 1995, 1996, and 1997 shows the extent of the turn-around of fortunes at the Savoy Group (Figure 8.5).

Management commitment and the recognition process

The Quality Improvement Programme has demonstrated a greater degree of accessibility of management to staff and to customers. The management structure is flatter in 1997 than it was in 1995, facilitating this direct contact. There is a better and more streamlined communication process. Managers have participated actively in the 'Putting People First' initiative by attending the two-day customer care course. Refurbishment was designed to enhance communication and inter-departmental co-operation. An example of this is found in the restoration of the front hall at The Savoy, where the reception, concierge and cashier counters were rebuilt in such a way as to improve communication among departments, to remove barriers to co-operation and create a working environment that is employee- and customer-friendly.

Future continuous improvement

The Savoy Group product has been updated and customer service skills training delivered to all employees, but the Group is well aware that excellence lies in the eyes of the beholder and therefore it is critical to listen to what customers are telling them.

However, the uniqueness of the Savoy Group's customer base requires special sensitivity and alternative forms of information-gathering on customers' needs rather than customer questionnaires and focus groups. Traditional focus groups are difficult to use since, in many cases, the customers are not in a position to dedicate their time to these activities and generally wish to spend their stay in anonymity. To attempt to capture the views and concerns of the customer base, the General Managers at the Group's properties hold cocktail parties where, in an informal social setting, customers can express their opinions on the hotel and the service rendered.

The Group continues to develop opportunities to enhance communication such as the staff quarterly meetings, the Annual Conference, and the various forms of employee recognition and employee incentive schemes. A more favourable pension scheme to wages-grade employees has been introduced which allows employees to join at four times throughout the year. Uniforms are provided free of charge to the employees and laundering is free. In some cases, staff are given accommodation.

The Savoy Group recognizes the importance and team-building potential of social activities within the workplace. In 1997 the company had their first-ever management dinner dance and a standardized Christmas hamper for all the staff. Plans are in place for a huge picnic next year for staff and their families. Each hotel in the Group has a social committee with numerous social activities and team sport events.

There is a well-defined and structured human resources strategy that assists in attracting, identifying, selecting, motivating, training and rewarding the best staff in the hotel sector. There is a Group Human Resources Director with a Personnel Department in each hotel. A number of human resources issues that have been dealt with positively are:

- Internal advertising and recruitment.
- Cross-Group transfers.
- Department wages structure.
- Profit-share incentive scheme.
- Senior management incentive scheme.
- Staff handbook and induction.

In May 1997, the first hotel of the Group, The Lygon Arms, achieved Investors in People (IIP) status. With the completion of the restoration work at the other hotels, all the properties are currently enveloped in the IIP process.

In order to ensure the development of a cadre of highly qualified managers, a new Graduate Training Programme was started in September 1997 to complement the existing post-A-level five-year scheme currently in place. The Graduate Training Programme introduces graduates to the hotel industry and the work of the Group in achieving superior quality.

IMPLICATIONS OF THE QUALITY IMPROVEMENT PROGRAMME

The 'Savoy 2000' programme has had a positive impact on employee morale as expressed in the results of the employee attitude survey conducted by the Group. Turnover figures at the staff level are difficult to track due to the complexity of contracts and seasonalities of employment. However, tracking of management turnover shows that turnover for this group has levelled off as a result of the quality improvement programme.

'Mystery shopper' scores have steadily increased, as have the number of positive comments on the customer comment cards. Continuous measurement of performance against the Savoy Group's standards has shown consistent improvement.

There is a need for the Savoy Group to continue to measure performance against themselves and the competition. Comparative measures of the Savoy Group's services with that of the competition have shown that the Group surpasses the competition in key areas such as response time to the telephone. The Group can now take comparative analysis one step further and benchmark best practices in other industry sectors.

There is also a need to reinforce the message of 'Putting People First' for all new and existing employees. By continually emphasizing the importance of internal and external customer service, employees will be well groomed to deal with a wide array of 'moments of truth'. Management and employees at the Savoy Group are working toward the common goal of excellence through high levels of customer satisfaction and, as a result of this common goal, the entire culture of the Savoy Group revolves around this central philosophy.

A very tangible and prestigious result of the Savoy's quality improvement programme has been the receipt of 'The Hotel of the Year Award' (The Savoy is world's best hotel . . .', 18 September 1997) voted by readers of *Executive Travel* magazine. This is the first time in fifteen years that the award has been given to a non-Asian hotel. In addition to this award, the Savoy Hotel also received UK awards for best hotel, best rooms and best restaurant.

Expected pre-tax profit levels for 1997 are expected to reach £23 million with estimates of £30 million for 1998 (Ashworth and Walsh, 1997). The Savoy Group has also boosted the level of repeat business up from 49 per cent to 60 per cent. A large sum of money, approximately £425,000 in 1997, has gone into training. The Group has also spent considerable sums (£1.8 million) on a roadshow to thirty-one cities. The Vong restaurant at The Berkeley has seen sales rise 400 per cent in two years.

The Group was founded by a great innovator in his time, Richard D'Oyly Carte. The Company intends to carry on this innovative streak by bringing creativity and value added to its customers, employees and shareholders.

The Savoy Group realizes the importance of maintaining traditions, while at the same time offering the latest technology and the most up-to-date product to the customer. The Group has the greatest respect for the past, a genuine understanding of present needs, and a vision for the future.

Future plans for the Savoy Group include expansion abroad, which in turn will give staff the opportunity to grow with the organization. There are also plans to open up additional sales offices in the United States in order to increase the Group's business in that country.

The Savoy Group hopes to obtain further external recognition for its achievements by entering the National Training Awards for 1998, as well as excelling in achieving other industry and non-industry related awards.

By maintaining well-established traditions at the same time as offering the latest in technology and product features, by the year 2000 the Savoy Group will be able to say that they are the 'Pre-eminent Hotel Group in the World'.

REFERENCES

Ashworth, J. and Walsh, D. (18 September 1997), 'Old guard at The Savoy have reason to be grateful', *The Times*, p. 31.

Pajares, R. (18 September 1997), 'Leaders need to instil a sense of common purpose', *Caterer & Hotelkeeper*, p. 28.

'The Savoy is world's best hotel, say international travellers' (18 September 1997), *Caterer & Hotelkeeper*, p. 18.

Nine

LEGAL & GENERAL ASSURANCE SOCIETY

Breaking the mould of the traditional insurer

Hadyn Ingram
and
Sue Temperton

Nine

LEGAL & GENERAL
ASSURANCE SOCIETY

Breaking the mould of the traditional insurer

INTRODUCTION

The Legal & General Assurance Society was formed in 1836, when King William IV was on the throne of England. The Society's aims were originally to provide life insurance for the legal profession, but it prospered and has expanded into an international group of companies offering a range of financial services products. These include household, life and health insurance as well as mortgages, pensions and an array of investments (Unit Trusts, Personal Equity Plans or PEPs and Investment Bonds). The modern Legal & General Group operates in the UK, USA, Australia, France, The Netherlands and Indonesia (employing 7,500 staff with 2.5 million policyholders). In 1996, the Group was in the top half of the FT-SE 100 with profits of £291.4 million and funds under management of £48.1 billion.

This chapter chronicles the way in which the Group has changed its thinking from a traditional to a customer-centred approach and reports the effects of this change upon performance, profits and people.

BACKGROUND

Financial service companies distribute their products through a number of channels. The Legal & General does this in four major ways:

- Direct sales through people employed by the Group.
- Independent financial advisers who are able to offer any company's products.
- Appointed representatives such as estate agents and solicitors.
- Self-employed financial consultants.

Although this distribution network enables the Group's products to be made available widely, there is limited control over the way that they are sold through non-employed agents, and this is common practice in financial services. It was in this context that the 1988 Financial Services Act (FSA) was set up as the first regulatory framework for consumer protection by controlling providers of financial services products. The FSA formed the Savings and Investments Board (SIB) to oversee strategy, and self-regulating organizations to oversee personal investments (Personal Investment Authority or PIA), investments (Investment Management Regulatory Organization or IMRO) and securities and futures (Securities and Futures Authority or SFA). The SIB is assisted by recognized professional bodies including accountants, insurance brokers and solicitors. One way in which companies must comply with these regulations is to re-draft documents such as brochures and letters so that customers can understand what is being offered and can compare the benefits of competing products. This aid to consumers has caused many financial services to realize the similarity of the product offerings in the market and of the need for greater differentiation. In particular, Legal & General looked to the efforts of consumer-centred companies such as British Airways and Marks & Spencer who were successful in generating demand for consistently high-quality products. These efforts were the catalysts for the current strategy which recognized the need to transform the Group focus from a product- to a customer-centred one. The current Mission Statement reflects these aims:

> By consistently delivering competitive, value for money products and high quality service through the commitment of our people, Legal & General intends to be the customer's preferred choice of financial services.

ORGANIZATION

This re-visioned customer focus is reflected in the current structure of the Group, with its representation by Customer Services and Sales & Marketing as business units at board level, as shown in Figure 9.1.

The direction for policy and strategy of the Group resides within the Quality Council with its representation from all Legal & General business units. Strategy is developed into plans and strategic initiatives by the Total Quality (TQ) Planning Group to ensure consistency and flexibility across the business units.

CUSTOMER SERVICES

The Customer Service Centre of Legal & General offers a service to both agents and existing customers of the Group. The Centre is based at Hove in Sussex, and employs over one thousand people, including 150 in the Call Centre which

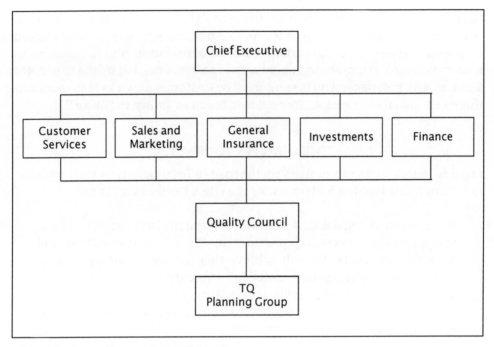

Figure 9.1: Quality structure of the Group

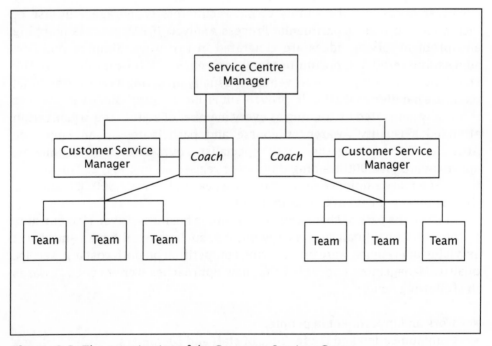

Figure 9.2: The organization of the Customer Services Centre

handles 4,500 telephone calls every day. The Call Centre operates from 8 a.m. to 8 p.m. on weekdays and from 9 a.m. to 5 p.m. on Saturdays. Other staff in Customer Services are concerned with administration and written communications to customers and agents. The facility is headed by the Customer Service Centre Manager who is supported by Customer Services Managers and three self-managed teams supported by a coach as shown in Figure 9.2.

THE QUALITY JOURNEY

Legal & General began its journey on the road to Total Quality in 1991 with the launch of a new Mission Statement for the Life & Pensions division:

> The mission of Legal & General's Life & Pensions Division is to be the best and most successful provider in the UK of Investment and Protection products. We will achieve this aim by providing secure, good value products and excellent standards of service to our customers and our intermediaries on terms that enable us to reward well our employees and our shareholders and to provide a firm base for continuing growth in the future.

'Trust us to deliver' became the slogan, and the focus was on reliability through improved processes. This initiative majored on understanding customer needs and the supply chain. Facilitators encouraged the use of techniques such as Departmental Process Analysis (DPA), process mapping and problem-solving. Ideas are generated in two ways. Simpler, quick-fix suggestions termed Opportunities for Improvement (OFI) are implemented by staff, and more complex improvements, usually involving a cross-functional team, are handled as Quality Improvement Projects (QIPs). Quality awareness is initially generated by training as every member of staff in the organization attended a Quality Awareness course and participated in an Employee Attitudes Survey. Together with specialist courses in TQ techniques, approximately 10,000 training days were registered in 1991/2. The effects were to increase employee suggestions to a peak in 1994 of 2,000 OFIs and 180 QIPs, with 68 per cent of OFIs completed.

In 1994, the pace of change was a continuing business driver. New entrants to the traditional financial services market, such as retail banks and direct servicing operations, were intensifying competition on both cost and service quality. Management concluded that new approaches were needed towards the following factors:

- Work and investment in people.
- Communication and the feelings of staff and customers.
- Benchmarking best practice.

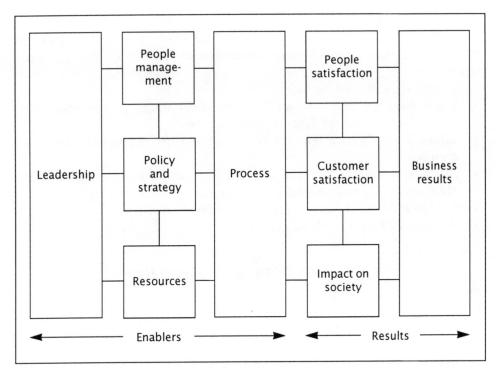

Figure 9.3: The Business Excellence Model

It was felt that the Business Excellence Model (BEM) from the European Foundation for Quality Management (EFQM) could provide a holistic framework for improvement. The model (shown in Figure 9.3) acts as a business planning tool which focuses upon enablers and results.

Enablers include leadership, people management, policy and strategy, resources and processes. Results are measured in terms of people, customer satisfaction, impact on society and business results. The Business Excellence framework highlighted several key areas and these are shown in Table 9.1:

Key area	Focus
Business Excellence Model.	A tool for self-assessment and external benchmarking.
Policy and strategy planning.	Identification of areas for improvement.
	Create the quality infrastructure.
Policy and strategy communication.	Communicate plans and achievements for Customer Services
People management.	Greater involvement through self-managed teams.
	Identification of core competencies.
Communication.	Ease of communication between management and teams.

Table 9.1: Key areas identified by the Business Excellence Model

Teamworking is seen as an activity which assists the effectiveness of planning, communication and people management so that service can be continuously improved. The communication mechanisms used at Legal & General are:

- *Team discussion*: A two-way series of briefings where teams are encouraged to discuss 'What it means for me'.
- *Talkback*: A director-led briefing scheme with facilitated discussion groups.
- *House magazines*: Articles in *Service Lines* (Service house magazine) and *The Gazette* (Legal & General house magazine).
- *Posters and noticeboards*: Both electronic and 'real'.
- *PC displays*: Computer displays.

DEPLOYMENT OF QUALITY IMPROVEMENT

This section records the way in which Legal & General approached quality improvement, including process improvement and resource deployment and quotes the example of successful 'front line' teams at the Customer Service Centre.

In the four years up to 1996, over 5,000 OFIs were raised and over 2,500 completed in addition to 175 successfully-implemented QIPs. In 1996, the suggestion system was broadened to include everyone in Customer Services through a networked PC database. This expanded system has facilitated greater ease of use and availability and continually incorporates new features such as on-line help. It has the capability to include suggestions from customers as well as staff.

Legal & General operate a systematic approach to team-building by providing support through a new team's transition phase to determine its own local business vision and address the concerns of team members. This is achieved by using the experiences of peers who have already been through the transition with their own teams. A new team is launched on Transition Day (or 'T' Day) with a team-building event and, from that point, teams are expected to be involved in every aspect of their business.

Teamworking at the Customer Services Centre

An example of teamworking in action at Legal & General is the Customer Services Centre at Hove. The established teams there are almost entirely self-managed, receiving only broad business guidance. During transition, each team identified their own roles during focus group sessions using Belbin's 'Team Roles'. They agreed the roles they would need to enable better teamworking and who in the team would fill the role to best effect. Some examples of the team roles are Facilitator, Planning Co-ordinator, Training Co-ordinator, Team Communicator, Team Bonus Representative and Specialists (e.g. Statistical Process Control or SPC).

Prior to 1995, there was little evidence of teamworking, but there are now regular team meetings at the Customer Services Centre for 'front-line' staff. There are, for example, weekly operations meetings for Customer Services Managers and the management team as well as monthly communicators' meetings which review staff relationships. Teams raise their own OFIs and QIPs and are expected to resolve the majority of their own issues. Any issues the team cannot resolve directly, through impact on another team or area, may be raised at the operations meeting. There are opportunities to discuss and plan for implementation of policy and strategy in the area, and to contribute to its development. The Group uses the team meeting process to drive their Customer Services Centre mission and values.

Team performance is measured by feedback from a number of sources:

- The team as a whole.
- The team member.
- The Customer Services Manager.
- The coach.
- A sample of 10 per cent of customers.

Since the concept of team bonuses, there has been a 10 per cent improvement in availability of staff to the customer and a recorded 5 per cent improvement in customer satisfaction. There are plans to supplement the reward system to include individual bonuses in the near future.

The success of teamworking with front-line staff the Customer Services Centre has spurred similar transition initiatives with 'back-office' teams who are a critical component in service quality. Their mission is to support the growth in 'one-stop' servicing so as to minimize referrals and handover errors. Conclusion teams have been set up to deal with customer enquiries that require fast or special attention to resolve a problem. Another 'back office' aim is to keep under review the twenty-five or so Service Level agreements with internal suppliers and customers.

Process improvement

In September 1996, the Group introduced Project Deming as a focus for process management. The aim is to demystify Statistical Process Control (SPC) specialist area and to improve process ownership and awareness by training ten SPC specialists who hold regular process improvement workshops with teams across the business. Teams work through data collection, the measurement and action phases of the process, and look after all the measurement documentation as well as the audit trail. The SPC process is outlined in Figure 9.4.

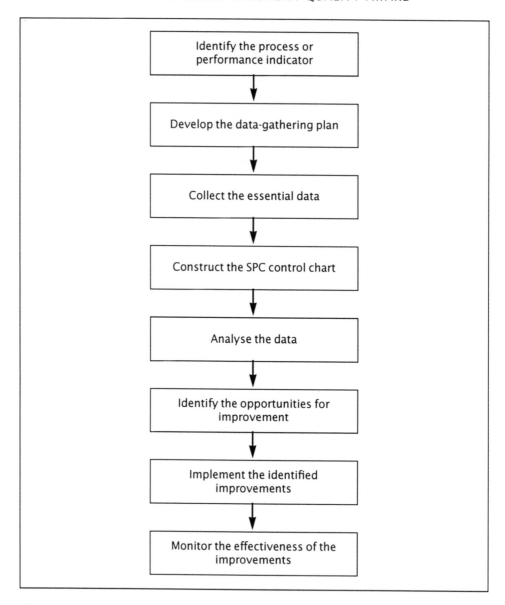

Figure 9.4: The Statistical Process Control Process

To date, there have been fifty-three teams involved measuring eighty-three processes and ninety-five key performance indicators. These projects have directly involved 100 people either on steering teams or as specialists and they have been supported by specialist computer software.

Resource deployment

The introduction of new technology is a major enabling strategy to support the Customer Services vision. There are currently project teams with thirty-two staff involved full-time on projects to improve information systems and product development.

Impact on society

The community relations programme at Hove has the aim of raising the profile of Legal & General as a socially responsible member of the community and the emphasis is on fun and involvement. Current projects include sponsorship of music, youth and schools in conjunction with local media and associations. Management teams are also involved with activities such as work experience, mentoring and skills sharing.

Customer satisfaction

As the programme developed, it was realized that OFIs were a useful form of quality improvement, but that regular communication with customers could provide a rich vein of information. OFIs can now be logged as 'Customer Wants' on the computer database and can originate from a customer or from sales consultants, representatives or independent financial advisers. Priority may be given to suggestions that are made frequently, but none can be ignored. The scheme has been sponsored by the Director of Customer Services who takes it upon himself to give personal thanks to members of staff adding ideas to the scheme. Since many issues involve systems or process changes that cannot be immediately effected, a network of representatives across Customer Services has been set up to take responsibility for the response and implementation of Customer Wants.

QUALITY EDUCATION AND TRAINING

Legal & General believe that the Customer Services mission can only be achieved by investing in people to give them the right tools for the job and the chance to broaden their roles and acquire transferable skills. The first customer care training provided in 1994 concerned the introduction of a central telephone Helpdesk at Hove. This training equipped staff with essential and practical telephone skills which were largely based around scripts and consistent responses to standard customer situations. After initial help from training consultants, Customer Services now have a pool of ten trained facilitators to deliver appropriate training to staff and managers alike.

The next stage for Legal & General in supporting the Business Excellence Model approach is to enable three staff to become British Quality Foundation (BQF) recognized External Assessors.

Standard courses for transition teams include:

- Counselling and the change cycle.
- Undertaking competency assessments.
- Resourcing.
- Leading the new organization.

SYSTEMS OF MEASUREMENT

The measurement strategy at Legal & General is directly linked to the EFQM Business Excellence Model which has been formally adopted as a tool for improvement. Primary measures are based on the results criteria of the model and secondary measures on the enablers, with the focus of improvement being the balance between unit costs and the quality of customer service. The measurement system includes the input of outside firms, such as a MORI survey, and measurement by internal teams. Internal planning is made possible by the self-assessment approach of the BEM model, and the Group encourages the use of the model to report plans and record achievements. There are moves to formalize the use of the model even further by using it as a basis for quarterly activity reviews between the principal BEM facilitators and each of the Customer Services management team.

As part of the communications strategy, there are a range of internally published measures including:

- Communications audit.
- Complaints and customer satisfaction surveys.
- Results of surveys of training evaluation.

In addition, information is communicated through internal magazines and noticeboards.

Legal & General regard customer satisfaction as one of the most important measures of quality and performance. This is conducted for the Group as a whole and, within Customer Services, teams are encouraged to take their own customer satisfaction measurements on levels of service. Teams with internal customers also use feedback mechanisms to measure the quality and type of service offered. An extensive customer satisfaction survey conducted by outside consultants in 1996 revealed a number of critical factors:

- The factors that influence customer satisfaction and their relative importance.
- Variations in these factors across customer groups.
- The Group's overall position in their markets.

As part of the ongoing measurement policy, every front-line member of staff in the Customer Service Centre is required to survey ten customers per month to ascertain levels of satisfaction and to provide opportunities for improvement. Customers are first asked if they would like to participate in the survey, and if agreeable, they are asked questions that mirror Group-wide surveys so that results can be compared.

Complaints volumes fell in 1996 by an average of 16 per cent over 1996. Whilst they are pleased about this improvement, Customer Services would like to develop a greater understanding about how well complaints are handled. Accordingly, they have started work to link reasons for complaints to business process improvement opportunities highlighted by Project Deming. In the last quarter of 1996, Complaints Solutions (part of the Customer Recovery team) conducted a survey of 500 randomly-selected customers and achieved an actual response rate of 25 per cent against an expected return of 10 per cent. The survey generated five recommendations for service improvement:

1   To undertake a personal review with each customer within two weeks of their complaint being fully resolved, and 83 per cent of respondents indicated that they would like to do this.
2   To monitor the impact of telephone responses to establish whether written confirmation is always required.
3   To explain reasons and corrective measures together with reassurance that mistakes will not be repeated.
4   To ensure full resolution so as to reduce follow-up activity and customer uncertainty.
5   To maintain regular contact through acknowledgements and agreement of time-scales.

In the same way, great importance in placed at Legal & General on measuring the satisfaction of employees. There is a formal cycle of attitude surveys conducted by MORI every two years, supported by pre-survey internal publicity, focus groups and internal briefings.

Business measures at Legal & General include unit costs and productivity. Unit costs are currently measured by a system which shows the costs of servicing new business and in-force plans. In future, an enhanced system will enable unit cost for events to be measured, for example the cost of servicing a policy claim. Productivity is not regarded with such great importance in Customer Services because of the variance in processes and because of the focus on quality and compliance. Although there are standard timings, these alter when processes are continually adjusted. The modern telephone technology in the Service Centre enables statutory personal financial reviews for each customer to be processed and stored as well as the automatic logging of volumes and queue adjustment. There is more of an emphasis on the quality of service rather than absolute speed so as to maximize customer satisfaction.

Project Deming was set up in 1996 to measure and manage process improvement; this is very much a team initiative because improvement sessions are run by the teams themselves with the assistance of a facilitator and a SPC specialist. There is a formal cycle and audit trail showing:

- The process and performance indicator under measurement.
- The sampling methodology used.
- Training required and dates completed.
- Progress meetings.
- Results and actions.
- Confirmations of completions.
- Post-improvement monitoring.

Sampling of elapsed time for key processes since 1992 has shown turnaround times have been considerably reduced.

ACHIEVEMENTS

Since the launch of the TQ initiative in 1991, the Group has improved its position in the UK from being a 'Top 100' company to a 'Top 50' company. Profits from Life & Pensions have increased from £220 million in 1995 to £250 million in 1996. Overall funds under management now total £49.1 billion (from £19.3 billion in 1991, when TQ was launched).

There have also been measurable increases in customer and employee satisfaction as well as business results. Independently-commissioned customer satisfaction ratings for life assurance and individual pensions show how Legal & General compare against industry norms. Customer Centre staff have taken their own surveys of customers during 1996, based on samples of telephone callers, and have been able to show improvements in satisfaction with their telephone-based services. Further, monitoring of customer complaints has shown that, although the rate of new plans is expanding, there is a downward trend on complaints.

Externally-benchmarked surveys based on financial soundness, quality of products and services and value as a long-term investment suggest that Legal & General have shown growth against the 260 most admired companies in the UK. Internally, response times for customers have been falling since 1992 and have been reflected in continually improving targets.

MANAGEMENT COMMITMENT AND THE RECOGNITION PROCESS

There is a commitment at all levels of management to continuous improvement and customer service. This is demonstrated in the degree to which management has developed a culture of participation through teamworking and have supported this through positive recognition and rewards. There is new management recognition that there is a limit to which OFIs and QIPs can drive improvement forward. A new quality management strategy at Legal & General is aimed at integrating human resource and technology through the framework of the BEM as the everyday benchmark. Nevertheless, the Quality Council and its supporting infrastructure still has a major role to play and it is supported by training for managers and staff.

Training is now based on the identification of four competences need by staff:

1 Customer focus.
2 Teamworking.
3 Results orientation.
4 Handling change.

Teamworking is the second of these core competencies and Legal & General have demonstrated their commitment to teamworking by the way in which work has been re-structured to facilitate involvement by self-managed teams. The old role of supervisor has been transformed into the new role of Customer Service Manager with specific responsibilities for business planning and enabling front-line teams to give quality service to the customer. In addition, the role of coach has been created to develop team members and enhance team transition.

One example of the way that self-managed teams have led change in working practices in Customer Services is in flexible working. The old system of core hours and flexitime have been replaced by a more adaptable working pattern which allows teams the flexibility to decide how best to serve their customers. The scheme is based on the four principles of the core competencies:

1 *Customer focus:* Flexible working allows the needs of customers to be accommodated. Providing customers with greater access to products and services requires greater flexibility from both managers and staff.
2 *Teamworking:* Teams are responsible for providing agreed levels of service to customers, and have control over the allocation of resources to meet those needs.
3 *Results:* Teams and team members are rewarded for commitment and achievements, rather than the time spent at work.

4   *Handling change:* There is a recognition that people have personal commitments, responsibilities and interests which they have to balance with the demands of work. An ever-changing environment demands that routine is sacrificed for flexibility.

A strategic review in 1994 suggested that communication was one of the significant opportunities for improvement across the Group and in Customer Services. The resulting communication strategy was launched in 1995 under the direction of a small self-managed team. Feedback from a survey in 1996 showed that 85 per cent of teams in Customer Services believe that communication has improved. The commitment to communication includes *ServiceLine*, the house magazine and *The Gazette* as the Group publication. Information is shared through the electronic noticeboard called *Inform* and a timetable of briefings and information-sharing presentations is posted visibly beside the coffee machines on every floor at Hove. The 'Talkback' scheme has enabled staff greater accessibility to feed back their views to Group senior managers. Following the initial presentation, the group breaks out into facilitated focus groups where the implications of the briefing can be considered in a 'safe' environment. Here, people can feel free to ask difficult questions that they may not feel able to ask in open forum. The groups can also agree on the most important issues they feel they want to address. When the groups reconvene, the facilitators can put questions to the senior managers on behalf of each group. This openness of debate also operates in teams, who are encouraged to discuss 'what it means for them'.

Two other ways in which Legal & General are breaking down barriers and improving the quality of information are the 'Ask the Boss' scheme and the 'Pollution' project. Peter Duplock, an Associate Director, has raised his visibility through weekly surgeries for private discussions, focus groups and suggestion boxes. The Pollution project aims at rationalizing electronic mail by filtering what is important information and what is not.

The final way in which commitment at Legal & General is demonstrated is through recognition and award schemes. Every January there is a major awards ceremony for Customer Services and, in 1996, 10 per cent of the service staff attended the function. The process for recognizing achievement is based on nominations from individuals and teams, and winning teams receive a personal letter of recognition signed by the Group Director (Services) together with a scroll. Other examples of recognition include letters of thanks for every 'Customer Want' and schemes for 'OFI of the Month' and 'QIP of the Quarter'.

FUTURE CONTINUOUS IMPROVEMENT PLANS

The plans for future continuous improvement are embodied in the Business Excellence model which is expressed in terms of the BEM:

- *Leadership:*   Maintain and develop the communication strategy. Give encouragement and support to the improvement activity.
- *People management:*   Complete implementation of the HR strategy. Further MORI employee satisfaction surveys.
- *Policy and strategy:*   Develop new products. Rationalize some operations.
- *Resources:*   Optimize use of buildings. Develop central purchasing facility.
- *Processes:*   Develop an integrated servicing operation. Manage customer contact processes more effectively.
- *People satisfaction:*   Improve areas identified by first MORI survey. Build on success of HR strategy.
- *Customer satisfaction:*   Improve reputation among internal customers. Better understand policyholder satisfaction.
- *Impact on society:*   More staff involved in the community.
- *Business results:*   Lower unit costs. Meet sales and profit targets.

The management of Customer Services believe that this plan can be achieved by a combination of enlightened human resource policy and the communications programme. The medium-term targets are to provide excellent service through developing people and effective technology so as to improve performance.

CONCLUSION

Legal & General has always been a successful company in the traditional mould of most financial services companies. A combination of statutory regulation and consumerism has led the Group to re-state its strategy for a more challenging future. A renewed sense of customer awareness was focused through the BEM approach, which highlighted the need for improved human resource management and communication. Early experiments in Customer Services showed that teamworking could facilitate these aims through more effective planning and by continuous improvements generated by self-managed teams. There is now a more open culture at Legal & General which is embodied in the new structure shown in Figure 9.5.

It is now fully recognized that self-managed teams in Customer Services have a special relationship with internal and external customers which can help to improve service quality and customer satisfaction. These 'front line' staff are now supported by their coach as well as departmental and senior management. Greater control over their work has resulted in a happier working atmosphere in which teamworking is firmly embedded by long-term management commitment.

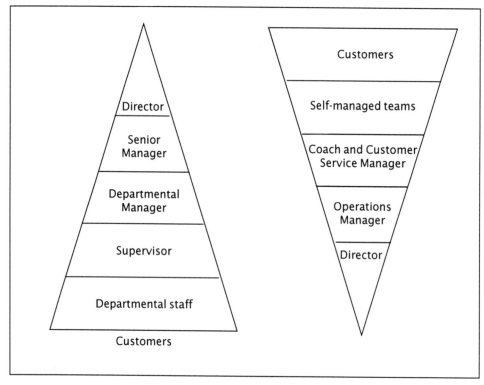

Figure 9.5: The new focus of Legal & General

GLOSSARY

BEM	Business Excellence Model
BQF	British Quality Foundation
CSM	Customer Service Managers
DPA	Departmental Process Analysis
EFQM	European Foundation for Quality Management
FSA	1988 Financial Services Act
IMRO	Investment Management Regulatory Organization
OFI	Opportunities for Improvement
PEP	Personal Equity Plan
PIA	Personal Investment Authority: the regulatory body for UK financial services
QIP	Quality Improvement Projects
SIB	Savings and Investments Board
SFA	Securities and Futures Authority
SIB	Savings and Investments Board: the strategy-making body set up under the 1989 Financial Services Act
SPC	Statistical Process Control
'T' Day	The transition day for new teams
TQ	Total Quality

Ten

LEGAL & GENERAL ASSURANCE SOCIETY

Stimulating opportunities for improving sales and marketing

RICHARD TEARE
AND
MATT JOHNSON

Ten

LEGAL & GENERAL ASSURANCE SOCIETY

Stimulating opportunities for improving sales and marketing

INTRODUCTION

The financial services industry has undergone significant change during the 1990s. Banks, building societies and insurance companies have expanded their product and service range beyond their respective specialist fields and they now compete with one another across a much wider range of business. This means that in today's financial services market-place it is vital to provide the customer with the right products backed by excellent, consistent service, supported by innovative marketing approaches. The chapter seeks to reflect on how teams of employees in Sales & Marketing at Legal & General have been applying proven quality techniques with special reference to the product development process.

Founded in 1836, Legal & General Assurance Society (the Society) is now one of the leading providers of life assurance, pensions and investment products. To mark its 150th year, Legal & General designated 1986 as Customer Care Year but after this, it was business as usual and customer-focused initiatives were less visible. Then in 1992, the Society's Quality Initiative was launched and every member of staff attended a short course designed to explain its importance to the company, its customers, services and employees. Between 1992 and 1994, the application of quality principles in the Sales & Marketing Division had been moderately successful but in hindsight it was hindered by:

- an inconsistent approach to quality across the division;
- a rather limited awareness of the vision of the company as a whole;
- limited recognition of those who were willing to be involved in the Quality Initiative;
- inadequate mechanisms for encouraging feedback, two-way communication and for publicizing success stories and sharing best practice.

A re-structuring of the Sales & Marketing management team in the last quarter of 1994 enabled a number of new initiatives to be undertaken, built around an agreed strategy of commitment, awareness, measurement and recognition. During 1995, all staff attended a one-day Quality Awareness refresher course, and progress tracking systems for two quality schemes – Opportunity for Improvement (OFI) and Quality Improvement Project were refined. Coupled with this, a concerted effort was made to improve internal communications and responsiveness to improvement suggestions made by individual employees. In part, this was to help ensure that staff members were involved and remained interested in the ideas they put forward and to encourage a free flow of further ideas. An improved review system was implemented so that progress from the initial suggestion through to acceptance or rejection of the idea might be monitored at all times.

In 1996, the Society formally adopted the European Quality Model for Business Excellence and every Sales & Marketing Divisional Director and their respective teams have participated in a self-assessment workshop. Today, the Sales & Marketing Division employs some 2,500 staff and encompasses nine spheres of activity. These are depicted in Figure 10.1.

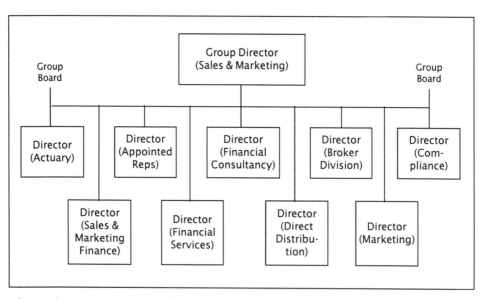

Figure 10.1: Organizational functions of the Sales & Marketing division

EMBEDDING THE QUALITY INITIATIVE

The Society's Mission Statement has been in existence since the launch of the Quality Initiative in 1992:

The Mission of Legal & General's Life & Pensions Division is to be the best and most successful provider in the UK of investment and protection products. We will achieve this aim by providing secure, good value products and excellent standards of service to our customers and our intermediaries on terms that enable us to reward well our employees and our shareholders and to provide a firm base for continuing growth in the future.

In 1995, the Chief Executive decided that added benefit might be derived from developing a short, focused mission statement:

By consistently delivering competitive value for money products and high quality service through the commitment of our people, Legal & General intends to be the customer's preferred choice for financial services.

This statement emphasizes three key elements:

- *Consistency* – lies at the heart of a quality assured service.
- *Commitment* – means convincing employees that quality improvement is a serious business and that everything they do really *does* make a difference.
- *Choice* – means recognizing that customers choose the products and delivery methods that suit their own circumstances and lifestyles.

The Quality Initiative aims to ensure that the Society can say to its customers: 'You decide how you want to purchase this product because we can respond to whatever choice you make.' By implication this meant adopting a wholly different mentality – instead of 'pushing' products out to customers (the traditional way) the new orientation is to attract customers to choose the package of services and benefits that suits them. The organizational imperative therefore is to break down artificial, product-related barriers built up over many years and create integrated processes and teams that are truly customer-focused.

To realize the Sales & Marketing mission it was necessary to develop and implement a quality strategy. The aim was simply to achieve and maintain business excellence. The strategy sought to address five main areas: commitment; awareness; measurement; review, and recognition.

Commitment

In late 1995, with the backing of the Sales & Marketing board, all divisional managers attended a Quality Awareness workshop. As a follow-up, a Quality Communication Day for all staff took place with the aim of introducing the new quality structure, the processes to be adopted and to refresh participant skills in the tools and techniques of quality improvement.

Commitment was to be built around a Legal & General Quality Council made up of the Group Directors (or Managing Directors) of the respective businesses: Sales & Marketing; Customer Services; General Insurance and Investments (see Figure 10.2). The Council meets on a monthly basis and has been responsible for introducing 'best practice' initiatives such as the Business Excellence Model, a Plain English Campaign and a regular MORI staff survey. By establishing the Council, senior level commitment had been secured and the next step was to gain wider commitment by setting up Head Office and Regional Quality Forums so that all Sales & Marketing staff might participate. The Forums bring together Divisional and Regional Quality Co-ordinators to support the implementation of Council initiatives and ensure that upward and downward lines of communication remain open and active. Co-ordinators are responsible for running monthly Quality Improvement Team (QIT) meetings with their divisional management teams, for reviewing and amending divisional goals as part of the 'Plan, Do, Check and Act' quality cycle used by Sales & Marketing, and for ensuring that best practice is disseminated to process owners.

Part of the QIT role is to ensure that managers involve new staff in quality initiatives through induction and training in quality awareness and the use of tools and techniques to explore, test and develop opportunities for improvement. When Sales & Marketing opened its new direct distribution operation in Cardiff during 1996, one of the first tasks was to establish a

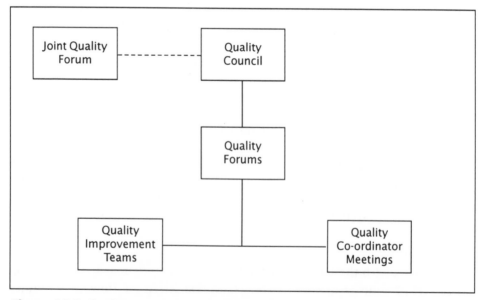

Figure 10.2: Quality structure: Sales & Marketing

Quality Team, who together with experienced coaches, helped to ensure that the many new staff were ready and able to contribute to the quality improvement effort in the shortest possible time. Evidence of early success came less than a year later when Direct won the 'European Callcentre of the Year Telesales Gold Award' in the Telebusiness Awards for Excellence, 1997.

Awareness

A key contributor to the success of Sales & Marketing's Quality Initiative has been the broadening awareness of the Society's vision of the future. In part, this is emphasized in the sharply focused Sales & Marketing Mission Statement that serves to reinforce the consumer-orientated message of consistency, commitment and choice. To build on the vision, the role of facilitator was introduced across the business as a whole. The aim is to ensure that facilitators are accessible – both electronically (by e-mail) and in person. They assist in the promotion of improvement activities, projects and workshops using techniques like brainstorming, mind-mapping, metaplanning and forcefield analysis. Best-practice approaches are now shared widely and many now use these and other techniques on a daily basis in pursuit of personal and departmental objectives. It has also meant that meetings are run to a clearly defined timetable, often guided by a facilitator, and this has produced many benefits. A sense of purpose and of ownership of outcomes arising from professionally run meetings that draw on quality techniques to explore key issues and clarify action lines and outcomes not only ensures that meetings are meaningful, but that time and energy is used productively and positively.

The Quality Initiative uses a number of drivers to identify and deliver improvements. The most recognizable to all staff are the OFI (Opportunity For Improvement) and QIP (Quality Improvement Project) campaigns (see Exhibit 1). Both use 'eye-catching' forms to stimulate creative thinking in the workplace. The form aims to capture the means by which an idea – a suggested improvement to a process or procedure – might be implemented. Ideas range from small, easily-made changes to product literature, to more complex changes involving wide-ranging development work. A variety of media are used within Sales & Marketing to stimulate the flow of ideas from a large and disparate audience. They include: colourful noticeboard posters; e-mail bulletins; quality packs; the *Inform* sales magazine and the Society's internal newspaper *The Gazette*. A recent poster campaign leads with the catchline 'Work improvements lead to stress relief!! . . . Send in that OFI!' In acknowledging receipt of an idea arising from this particular campaign, the Division's central quality team send OFI proposers a stress-ball reliever. This takes the form of a rubberized ball in the shape of a brain and these items have become a fashionable desk accessory as a result of the poster presentation.

EXHIBIT 1
Quality initiative infrastructure

OFIs – Opportunities for Improvement
A standard OFI form is available so that individuals can set out and extrapolate from their own ideas and thereafter ensure that improvements are made to the processes they themselves own. The OFI system also allows individuals to share ideas via the Quality Team structure. Essentially the OFI procedure enables the same individual to propose an improvement idea and to take responsibility for implementing it, with management support where necessary. A process review conducted in 1996 had identified the importance of recognizing the individuals who had proposed any given OFI. To ensure this happens every time, every OFI submitted is personally acknowledged and copied to the Quality Co-ordinator so that it is possible to 'track' OFIs through acceptance (or rejection) and implementation. The same procedure is used to encourage cross-divisional suggestions. If the OFI is rejected, a full explanation is provided as to why the idea cannot be implemented. By ensuring close contact with the OFI originators, it encourages a strong sense of ownership and reinforces the importance of the quality initiative.

QIPs – Quality Improvement Projects
If an OFI requires more than one person to implement it, the OFI is discussed, its implications considered and if it is accepted, it passes from an 'idea' to a project. A central part of the 'ownership' process is to invite the person responsible for the idea to assume the role of project leader, with whatever assistance they need from the quality and management teams respectively and with a management team member acting as the project sponsor. The project leader's responsibilities include selecting the project team, booking a team facilitator to provide team support, arranging meetings and ensuring that the project is monitored and completed to schedule. The project process is underpinned by the quality improvement cycle (Plan, Do, Check and Act) and the relevant quality tools and techniques. Wherever improvement activity has wider application, information and progress reports are shared as appropriate with other areas of the business.

Quality tools
All Sales & Marketing personnel have been trained to use a range of quality tools so that individuals and teams are better equipped to make improvements using a structured, proven approach. The main tools used are: brainstorming; mind mapping; metaplanning; forcefield analysis; quality improvement cycle (PDCA – Plan, Do, Check and Act).

Facilitators
Early in 1995, teams from across the business were encouraged to nominate individuals to train as local facilitators and the original group has since been augmented by a steady flow of individual applicants. The day-to-day role of facilitators remains the same, but whenever an improvement project commences they may be asked to provide assistance and support to the project team.

Co-ordinators
The pool of co-ordinators also draws on a volunteer force of individuals who attend Quality Forum meetings and report back to their sections with current news updates, ideas and information on key activities in and around the sales and marketing function. The co-

ordinators also provide 'first stop' advice on quality and continuous improvement techniques and approaches as well as playing a vital role in ensuring that cross-divisional OFIs are completed and logged for review by members of the management team.

The level of interest and active involvement in the OFI initiative has shown a marked increase during the past few years. For example, the conversion rate of OFIs to projects increased from 40 per cent to nearly 60 per cent during 1995/96.

Measurement

Historically, statistics had been generated on levels of business, but few measurements were taken in relation to quality improvement. In 1995 the Society resolved to tackle this issue and at Group level it was decided that a more advanced measurement and internal benchmarking device was needed. This led to the introduction of the Business Excellence Model which is described in the previous chapter with reference to Customer Services at Legal & General. The model uses self-assessment as a means of identifying areas for improvement. Self-assessment encourages ownership and teamwork by managers and staff alike, related to nine areas:

- Leadership.
- People management.
- Policy and strategy.
- Resources.
- Processes.
- People satisfaction.
- Customer satisfaction.
- Impact on society and business results.

Using this framework, Sales & Marketing is now able to measure its progress both internally and externally with the help of its own divisional assessors. To achieve this, each Divisional Director with his or her senior team, attended a two-hour briefing run by the assessor group. The purpose of the briefing was to explain the model in detail and discuss the scoring method. As a follow-up to the briefing, a one-day workshop session was used to enable senior management to discuss and agree on their achievements using the model's scoring system. After this, each of the Society's core businesses sought to incorporate model criteria and scoring methods for the nine areas into their on-going business plans. New computer-based systems have been implemented by Sales & Marketing's central Quality Team so that qualitative and quantitative data is captured. OFIs and QIPs are 'tracked' and members of staff responsible for the idea are kept informed of progress at regular intervals (see Exhibit 2). Ultimately, a sense of ownership is engendered as individuals at all levels see their ideas being used for the benefit of all.

EXHIBIT 2

Measurement, tracking and research

Legal & General's approach to measurement had to find a way of disaggregating a composite portfolio of services to customers. In Sales & Marketing, this spans three main categories: savings, protection and general protection. While customers receive a policy document, they actually buy a promise: that Legal & General will pay an amount of money on maturity of a policy or, depending on the policy type, on death. The policy is merely proof of the agreement and so the focus of customers' and suppliers' attention is the service it provides in issuing policy documents, answering queries and paying claims. For this reason, surveys are used to monitor and measure levels of customer satisfaction. Sales and marketing has a market research team with two full-time staff. In 1995, £200,000 was spent on market research either conducted by the team or by commissioning an external market research company. This budget was increased to £300,000 in 1996 and to £400,000 in 1997 and serves to underline the importance attached to survey work in the company.

During 1995/96 a series of surveys were conducted and commissioned. A number of these were on-going and have taken place at regular intervals to help gauge trends and to enable Sales & Marketing to benchmark its performance. Projects undertaken during 1996 included:

- Group-wide customer satisfaction survey.
- Appointed representatives' survey.
- Mortgage club survey.
- Independent financial advisers' (IFA) survey.
- Sales and marketing staff research.
- Survey of personal financial journalists (undertaken by Market & Opinion Research International (MORI)).
- Estate agency network research.
- Personal Equity Plan (PEP) mortgage research.
- Internet users research.
- Mystery shopping research.

During 1995 and 1996 each of the four sales divisions – Appointed Representative; Broker Division; Financial Consultancy and Introducer Division – organized roadshows for their team members who work in different locations around the country. It enables the directors and senior managers to talk directly to the sales force and independent intermediaries and to answer their questions. This method of communication has proved very efficient in promoting teamwork/recruitment and in ensuring that the sales force has the most up-to-date information and, at the same time, it enables directors to gather valuable 'hands-on' feedback.

In addition to the annual surveys, more specialized research is conducted periodically. During 1995, projects in this category included:

- An extensive focus group base study of sales representatives to explore satisfaction with the products and services offered by the company.
- A survey of employers to examine the types of occupational pension schemes they offer and how they market them to staff.

- Customer loyalty.
- Attitudes to long term care policies for the elderly/infirm.
- Effects of divorce on pension provision.
- Research by MORI into employee opinions across Sales & Marketing.

Review

As an outcome of measurement, management information is now produced regularly and disseminated to all staff. Of particular topical interest is the number of ideas submitted and the number implemented – both have shown marked increases since the inception of the scheme in 1995. The tracking systems have also helped to ensure greater sensitivity and responsiveness to improvement opportunities and to broaden the search criteria relating to improvement activity and effort. Both OFI/QIP systems allow for the extraction of statistics on any combination(s) of criteria and these are published monthly. They also accommodate rigorous monitoring and review. The concensus view is that the model is a useful tool that helps to focus attention and test the assumptions behind business plans. In this way, incremental improvement and a 'How can we do this better?' culture has become firmly embedded in the organization and the mindset of its members.

The review process encompasses on-going dialogue with employees too and an employee survey conducted by MORI in 1995 sought to uncover attitudes towards: job satisfaction; aspects of working life; working relationships; communications; and Legal & General as a business. Following this, further research was conducted to identify as precisely as possible the improvement activities appropriate to key areas. In 1996, Concensus Research International Ltd were commissioned to conduct a programme of in-depth interviews and focus group discussions among staff employed in the Sales & Marketing Division. The key areas were:

- Company culture and working environment.
- Pay and employment package.
- Job security in a changing environment.
- Job content – interest and extent of teamwork.
- Relationships with management.
- Management's ability to communicate strategy.
- Performance recognition.
- Career development opportunities.
- Company communications.
- Legal & General's attitude to customers.

Taken together, these two surveys provide the foundations of a benchmarking approach which is undergoing further development and refinement.

Recognition

To encourage widescale participation, Sales & Marketing has introduced a comprehensive recognition and reward programme. This begins when an OFI/QIP is generated and if an idea is not feasible the line manager or central Quality Team will report back to the originator with an explanation to a given timescale. Whenever an idea is supported, it is the line manager's responsibility to ensure that the member of his or her team has the necessary resources and support to complete its implementation.

Sales & Marketing's central Quality Team run an OFI of the Month award for all ideas that are registered with them and standard criteria are used to judge the winner who receives a year's free entry to the National Lottery or £50 of retail vouchers. The contributions made by teams' QIPs are also recognized via Quarterly and Team of the Year awards made to head office and sales teams. Publicizing success is also considered to be important and this is achieved by: electronic mail; quality updates; and in-house publications – the *Gazette* and *Inform.* Two project examples are shown in Exhibit 3.

EXHIBIT 3

QIP cases

Case 1: Recruitment assessment centres made easy

A process improvement project in the Broker Division, Scotland

The aim of the project, with Broker consultant recruitment in mind, was to develop the assessment centre concept, launched in 1995, so as to ensure that the centres could be run by two local managers. Prior arrangements had meant that area managers were required to travel from their office locations to act as centre assessors whenever recruitment days were held. The project team consisted of a regional director, an area manager, a personnel manager and a member of the sales support staff. The team re-engineered the procedures used during an assessment centre session. Some exercises were removed, while those seen to be key to the role of a Broker consultant were improved. The single biggest task was to schedule activities so that a smaller team of two assessors could run the entire event. The programme now allows for three candidates to be interviewed on a rolling basis, with four exercises and a psychometric test completing the day. After completing the 'Plan and Do' part of the quality cycle, the team checked the newly designed programme by testing the revised centre concept on three separate occasions in Glasgow. The tests were successful and the new programme is used throughout the Broker Division.

Case 2: A risk-focused approach to compliance reviews

Improving management information in the Sales Division

The project sought to strengthen the basis for making comparisons between Sales Division compliance reviews by improving the quality and accuracy of management information. In particular, the project sought to make cost-effective use of the resources available in scheduling reviews and to improve the quality of information available for forward planning purposes. The project team consisted of eleven compliance review officers and two of their line managers. The importance of the project can be seen in relation to its background:

- A 20 per cent reduction in the number of compliance reviews officers.
- Criticism that the reviews focused on 'petty' issues.
- Different approaches to reviews in different Divisions did not allow for easy comparison.
- The available management information was not being analysed or used effectively.
- Reviews scheduling concentrated on the short term at the expense of the longer term.
- Follow-up of serious issues was inconsistent and largely restricted to the efforts of individual reviewers.

A project plan was drawn up by the team using a brainstorming process. This sought to address the strategic direction and terms of reference, which were:

- Why should reviews be carried out?
- Who should be reviewed?
- What should be reviewed?
- How should the review process by carried out?
- When should the reviews occur?

The project team addressed these criteria and presented their recommendations to the Director (Compliance) for approval and authorization. The newly designed procedures took effect in August 1996, and the measurable improvements derived are:

- Reviews are now planned further in advance.
- More informative and useful monthly reports are produced.
- An internal audit has been completed, guided by the new procedures.
- The procedures have been shown to yield valuable management information.
- Reviews are now completed within the scheduled time plan.

Breaking down barriers and focusing on customers

In order to share best practice, raise business awareness and strengthen morale, Sales & Marketing has actively sought to engender a culture of teamworking, openness and trust. In order that team members might appreciate their role as part of a wider team, attendance of management at quality courses is encouraged. The aim is to achieve a mix of delegates from a variety of business areas and ideally different geographical locations. This helps delegates to forge new contacts, share ideas and best practice and to gain a better understanding of Sales & Marketing as a whole as well as its individual component parts. To assist in fostering a culture of sharing and learning, Quality Forums are also attended by a mix of people from all business areas, and joint Sales & Services Forums meet on a regular basis to discuss issues and seek support and agreement on future plans and improvement activities. Further, visits are arranged to other parts of the business – this is not confined to Sales & Marketing but encompasses Customer Services, General Insurance and the Direct Sales operation – all in different geographical areas.

To maintain momentum, a new post of Development Director has been created and Sales & Marketing has embarked on its most ambitious investment in personal development to date. Some 200 of the Division's managers have attended six half-day workshops over a six-month period. The aim is to equip participants with the skills needed to create a true quality-of-service environment and to sweep away traditional ways of working that impede customer-focused development. The Society supports a range of educational and training programmes as shown in Exhibit 4.

EXHIBIT 4

Education and training

Legal & General's education and training policy:

> By carefully recruiting, training and developing our people, we achieve standards of professionalism that are recognized by competitors and customers alike as the highest in the industry.

Throughout 1996, a range of initiatives were implemented, in addition to standard induction and training programmes.

Quality Awareness Programme
The Society's quality awareness training is an on-going programme which focuses on customer and supplier issues and on continuous improvement initiatives. For example, the programme played a key role during the opening of the new Callcentre in Cardiff where thirteen awareness courses were run for a total of 100 people. In addition to quality awareness for new recruits and updates for existing employees, there are also programmes designed to develop managerial and facilitation/coaching skills.

Facilitation Skills Workshop
The workshop forms the foundation for on-going assessments in key competency areas, and facilitators are developed to play active roles in the regions and at head office. The local facilitator role is now widely embedded in team-based improvement activity.

Professional Qualifications
The Society's professional qualifications training programme supports members of staff who wish to study management and business to degree level. A more specialized form of support relates to the Chartered Insurance Institute (CII) and employees are actively encouraged to enrol for CII qualifications at Associate and Fellowship levels, and where appropriate the Financial Planning Certificate (FPC), to achieve company representative status. Support is provided in the form of study days leave, financial support for examination entry, study material and registration fees to the appropriate professional

body and via computer-based training and distance learning packs. A financial incentive is awarded on completion of the Associateship examinations.

Mentoring
As part of an initiative to encourage and support a wider understanding of business and commerce among schoolchildren, the Legal & General Group invited staff to participate in a mentoring scheme with Highview School, Wallington, Surrey. The scheme was launched in October 1995, with a one-day training course and forty-one employees took part, including eighteen staff from sales and marketing. By volunteering for the scheme, staff took on a mentoring role which involved participating in and organizing after-work activities. The feedback from mentors and mentees indicates that both parties gained from the experience and the scheme is now an on-going one. Commenting on the value of the scheme, the school's headteacher said:

> The majority of students being mentored have improved to a level we would not have expected in the areas of personal organization, confidence and self-esteem: they are developing good, positive adult relationships, which to our students, a lot of whom don't have adult role models at home, is extremely important. In addition, because the journey to the Legal & General site is not an easy one, they have become much more independent, confident travellers.

COMBO: CUSTOMER-FOCUSED PRODUCT DEVELOPMENT

Sales & Marketing see 'Combo' (so called because it combines the mortgage loan and other financial services products) as a revolutionary concept in the mortgage market. The idea arose from a series of focus group discussions held during 1994 with key representatives of Sales & Marketing's distribution channels. A significant slump in the housing market had occurred and this threatened the livelihood of some of the Society's advisers. As key internal customers, Sales & Marketing asked them what it could do to help their businesses and, during the consultative process, a number of quality techniques were used to pinpoint the issues and possible solutions. The group concluded that the best way to create more business would be to deliver a more cohesive service to the end customer, built around the mortgage transaction. It was felt that this would help to generate additional income by enabling the Society's intermediaries to provide a simpler, more complete service.

Integrating systems and processes

To develop and deliver Combo, Sales & Marketing had to draw together products from different divisions – principally Mortgage Services, Life & Pensions, and General Insurance – and package them in a way that would provide 'one-stop' appeal to customers. While most felt that Combo would

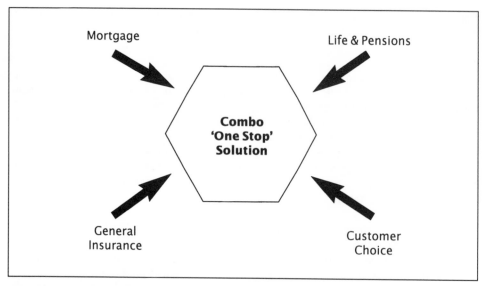

Figure 10.3: The Combo Product

prove to be the ideal way of assisting intermediaries to revive their businesses, an objective view was sought to ensure that the product was in line with customer needs. A research programme confirmed that customers not only wanted value for money but also a much simpler buying process with fewer forms to complete. The key to this was being able to transfer customer details across different organizational divisions – a simple task in theory but not in practice.

It became clear that the essence of the challenge was to develop a product that would work effectively and sell well; but to achieve this, radical changes in processes and systems were needed. The ideal would be to process customer details just once and provide a central, internal point of contact for this information. At its inception, Combo had been treated as a product and marketing project but it had rapidly presented a significant technological challenge too.

Combo had become a large-scale project that demanded unparalleled levels of teamworking and no less than a radical re-think of how systems and processes might be integrated to solve what had seemed a simple, rather obvious set of customer needs. Quality tools and techniques were used throughout the project and advisory groups of intermediaries met on a regular basis to check and validate requirements and to test proposed solutions to problems as they emerged. Further, a programme of focus group discussions with customers sought to probe key issues to ensure that 'ideals' had been interpreted accurately and that customer concerns, needs and expectations could be met by the emerging features of the Combo product package. At the point when most of the package had been framed, Combo was piloted so that feedback from customers and intermediaries could be used to fine-tune the package. Combo was launched in late 1996 and began to penetrate the market in the early months of 1997. Since then, a phenomenal increase in take-up has occurred; especially in what were traditionally more peripheral product areas such as buildings and contents insurance, accident, sickness and unemployment cover. These product areas experienced 100 per cent increases in sales revenue during the launch period and the Combo product is now applicable to some 25 per cent of the Society's mortgage business. In addition, Combo has been universally well received by intermediaries, many of whom have been able to strengthen their business as a result of being able to offer a product that is genuinely crafted to address customer needs and concerns.

Learning from the Combo project

The Combo product development experience taught Sales & Marketing a number of important lessons. First, that to develop a valued, quality product it is essential to begin by listening to the needs and concerns of customers. This means much more than asking them once and hoping for the best – it requires a continual process with in-built customer feedback throughout the project. If this is in place, it is possible to check frequently so as to address the inevitable problems that arise in translating customer requirements into actual product benefits. If the product is to work, it must be mapped as closely and accurately as possible against the customer specification at all stages in its design and implementation. The second lesson arose from reflecting on the integral role that employees and others play in the product development process. The project involved the IT department, customer services, sales, marketing and intermediaries. At its inception, they all had different priorities, but by team-building it was possible to secure a shared vision and the realization that all those involved had something valuable to contribute to the successful conclusion of the project. The third key success factor relates to the need to ensure that systems are kept in step with the thinking and actions of teams and the processes that they need to re-invent to deliver improvements. The Combo project required an integrated IT solution and in this case, it meant bringing three different systems together and thereafter, customizing inputs so that all transactions could be handled from one central point.

The Combo team found that responding to customer needs can and does precipitate a fundamental re-think of the way in which products are conceived, constructed and delivered. Providing customer-driven products is demonstrably the way in which 'choice' has to be presented in a ever more crowded financial services market-place. The lessons from developing Combo have already been applied to all new product planning priorities and the key driver is a desire to improve and re-focus on dynamic customer needs rather than a static product portfolio.

KEEPING PACE: QUALITY-DRIVEN CHANGE

The success of Combo and improvements to a wide range of processes across the organization have helped to signal the way ahead. But the challenge of keeping pace with the market would be difficult to meet without first creating and embedding a total quality approach. This is characterized by a practical infrastructure for discussing and actioning quality improvement ideas and maintaining momentum through an open communications network:

- The Quality Council and related forums had been established to formulate plans for quality improvement and to provide direction and guidance on a wide range of issues and initiatives.
- A Quality Pack is distributed on a monthly basis, consisting of minutes of the Council and Forum meetings, OFI and QIP statistics and other topical news and information.
- The Sales & Marketing training department sends out bulletins on any new compliance issues and provides training courses with the aim of keeping managers and sales personnel up-to-date on new developments.
- Sales personnel receive a topical newsletter called *Inform*, established in April 1995. The newsletter came about as a result of a quality process improvement project and is an amalgamation of different newsletters.
- *IFA News* is sent on a monthly basis to the Society's independent financial advisers to maintain open communication channels, keep advisers up-to-date with new developments and encourage them to feel part of the Legal & General team.
- All work areas now have notice boards on which to post news, OFI statistics and details of competitions. Further, posters are regularly distributed by the central Quality Team responsible for promoting the OFI culture.
- Each of Sales & Marketing's three sales divisions – Appointed Representatives; Broker Division; and Financial Consultancy, organize their own 'roadshows'. These are essentially conferences where each sales division's customers are invited to attend and to hear latest news on the Society's plans for the coming year and how the various stakeholders might work together as a team to improve on past performance.

As the insurance industry moves towards a new millennium, Legal & General is responding to the pressures from tightening margins and intense competition among pensions and life products providers. For example, the Society is developing a 'Future Product Framework' (FPF) to help minimize the time it takes to develop new products and reduce costs. At the same time, a wide range of quality improvement plans have been initiated. An indicative list of projects is shown in Exhibit 5.

EXHIBIT 5

Future improvement plans

Quality awareness programmes for managers and staff have helped to re-focus the Society's efforts and provided a basis on which to build. Key activities like OFIs, QIPs and the concepts of ownership and responsibility will assume even greater importance in the future. On-going changes to the corporate quality system reflect this. In 1996 the system was rated 'below average' (rating of 4 out of 10) by company staff and, arising from this, a value added approach was adopted to re-engineer quality processes. To assess progress so far, the original survey group were re-visited in September 1996, and on the same scoring basis, the average rating has improved to 6.4 from 10, denoting 'above average' performance. Clearly internal perceptions are an important measure of confidence in the quality process and improvements so far are having a positive effect on confidence and morale.

Development team

A development process has been introduced and built around two-day assessment centre sessions. These are designed to assist employees to appraise their relative strengths and identify opportunities for personal development. Individual feedback derived from three or four trained observers is given to each attendee, based on contributions made over the two-day period. A total of forty development centres ran during 1996 with a further fifty-five scheduled for 1997.

Self-managed teams

The introduction of self-managed teams in the various sales environments is viewed as a logical and desirable development. The perceived benefits are:

- Increased employee motivation and satisfaction;
- improved customer/supplier satisfaction;
- the prospect of enhanced work outputs from teams motivated to achieve goals that they themselves set and own, relating to customer and supplier relationships.

Introduction of flexible working

Prior company flextime arrangements had proved difficult to reconcile with the needs of customers at any given point in the working day and of staff who in practice were not able to arrive later than 10 a.m. or leave before 4 p.m. A fresh approach was needed and teams are now encouraged to exercise greater freedom by organizing themselves so that customer needs are met without having to conform to a formal system of recording hours worked. The fresh approach is very popular – typical reactions include:

'I have more freedom to plan my time and work as best fits me and my team.'
'I would recommend flexible working to anybody. Everyone should give it a go.'

Commitment to the environment

Legal & General is committed to caring for the environment, and a recycling procedure for plastic cups, paper and cardboard has been operating for two years. In November 1996, a further enhancement known as the 'recycling at your desk' scheme was launched. Each member of staff was issued with a twin compartment desk bin. The blue section is used for recyclable mixed paper and cardboard; the grey section for non-recyclable general waste. There is a 100 per cent participation rate in the scheme as there is a minimum effort and disruption to work patterns and flows. The cumulative annual tonnage of recycled plastic cups is around five tonnes, and for recycled paper and cardboard, the figure is in excess of 100 tonnes. Detailed updates on recycled materials are prominently displayed throughout the building.

Reviews

Reviews are a fundamental part of the process of continuous improvement, so teams are encouraged during the quality awareness programme to re-visit their processes and see whether any improvements might be made. The first step is to 'process map' the activities used in a given area and 'challenge' current practice. Teams use the quality improvement cycle which takes the improvement activity through four stages: plan; do; check; act. In following this cycle, teams have the opportunity to make improvements in a structured way.

A QUALITY FUTURE

In summary, the Quality Initiative has had a significant impact on corporate thinking and action in a comparatively short space of time and is yielding significant benefits for Sales & Marketing and the Society as a whole. The current structure means that with the support of a small central team, everyone is encouraged to look for and implement opportunities for improvement and this includes questioning and testing existing systems, processes and procedures.

Achievements so far provide a good foundation on which to build the company-wide future product framework (FPF) initiative. The FPF aims to provide consistent quality service and to deliver a continual stream of innovative products to the market-place. The project was launched in October 1996 and, following twelve months preparatory work, has become the biggest project of its kind undertaken by Legal & General. At the heart of FPF is a new administrative system, designed to deliver well-integrated responses to customer needs and market-place opportunities.

In summary, this high-tech project offers a glimpse of the future of financial services. In this, continual improvement is a key driving force which has already helped to change the way people work, think and act. A pattern for the future has already been set by stimulating opportunities for improvement.

Eleven

MAGNOX ELECTRIC PLC

'Brains off the peg' – quality improvement initiatives

NICK JOHNS

*The author wishes to thank
Mike Shannon, Head of Maintenance,
Dungeness 'A' Power Station,
for his assistance in compiling this chapter.*

Eleven

MAGNOX ELECTRIC PLC

'Brains off the peg' –
quality improvement initiatives

BACKGROUND

Nuclear energy is generated by producing a controlled chain reaction in the element uranium, which spontaneously breaks down, emitting neutrons. In a small mass of uranium this reaction is slow and the heat it generates is very small. In larger masses of uranium, there is a higher probability that each neutron emitted will collide with the nucleus of another atom. Each time a collision occurs, more neutrons are produced. When the amount of uranium reaches a certain 'critical mass' the number of such collisions accelerates rapidly, releasing energy. In order to produce a controlled flow of energy, the neutron flow must be slowed, and excess neutrons absorbed. In nuclear power stations this is achieved by bringing rods of uranium metal close to one another. In order to slow and control the flow of neutrons the rods are inserted into an inert substance called the moderator. Rods of a different chemical element (usually boron) which absorbs neutrons, can be inserted into the moderator block among the uranium rods, if any further control is required. Some kind of fluid medium (a liquid or gas) is also needed to carry away the heat that is produced to heat exchangers, where it can be transferred to superheated steam and then converted into electric power.

'Magnox' is an oxidation-resistant alloy of magnesium and aluminium which is used to encase the uranium rods in a 'Magnox' nuclear reactor. The uranium rods, in their Magnox 'cans', are inserted into a block of graphite which acts as the moderator. Boron rods can be inserted in between them to calm or stop the reaction, and the heat is carried away from the reactor by carbon dioxide gas. The Magnox reactor system was developed in Britain in the years immediately after the Second World War, and the first working power station of this type was opened by Queen Elizabeth II at Calder Hall, Cumbria in 1956 (British Nuclear Fuels plc, 1997). The Magnox system has proven itself extremely robust, with an excellent safety record. Calder Hall, and its sister station at Chapelcross in Scotland, have recently been given the go-ahead to operate for a further ten years: a total of fifty, well in excess of the thirty-year lifespan cautiously forecast when they were built (Nucnet News Briefing, 1997). However, the system is not highly efficient in today's terms, carbon dioxide being a comparatively poor transmitter of heat. The modern pressurized water reactors are significantly more reactive.

Nuclear power stations were built in a climate of technological optimism. Nuclear power consumes only small amounts of fuel, and at the outset it was hoped that electricity would become much cheaper as a result. However, in subsequent years it became clear that the cost of decommissioning nuclear stations and dealing with nuclear waste was substantial. Reactors leave long-lived isotopic contaminants behind, from which the public and the environment have to be protected. A considerable cost is associated with closing down the operation and making the sites secure while the radioactivity (usually sealed inside a massive concrete capping structure) dies down to a safe level.

Until 1990 all power stations in the UK were owned and operated by a public corporation, the Central Electricity Generating Board (CEGB). As part of a general government agenda of privatization, the conventional power stations were taken over by private operators during 1990, but the nuclear stations remained under the control of the government-owned company, Nuclear Electric plc. During the period immediately following this there was an emphasis upon efficiency and profitability, as the nuclear power industry made itself ready for full privatization in 1996. For mostly historical reasons, the power stations at Calder Hall and Chapelcross came under the aegis of British Nuclear Fuels plc. The other Magnox stations became part of Magnox Electric plc, under the shareholdership of the British government.

As can be seen from Table 11.1, Magnox Electric plc, which is based at Berkeley in Gloucestershire, owns nine Magnox stations. Six of these are still

Station name	Type	Operating status	Location
Bradwell	Magnox/nuclear	Operating	Essex
Dungeness A	Magnox/nuclear	Operating	Kent
Hinkley Point A	Magnox/nuclear	Operating	Somerset
Oldbury	Magnox/nuclear	Operating	South Gloucestershire
Sizewell A	Magnox/nuclear	Operating	Suffolk
Wylfa	Magnox/nuclear	Operating	Anglesey
Maentwrog	Hydroelectric	Operating	North Wales
Berkeley	Magnox/nuclear	Decommissioning	Gloucestershire
Hunterston A	Magnox/nuclear	Decommissioning	Scotland
Trawsfynydd	Magnox/nuclear	Decommissioning	North Wales

Table 11.1: Power stations owned by Magnox Electric (summer 1997)

operating and three are in the process of being decommissioned. The company also owns one hydroelectric station, at Maentwrog in Wales.

There are currently no plans to close any of the operating stations, but they are certain to be phased out in the long run. Magnox stations were augmented during the 1970s by a new technology: the Advanced Gas-Cooled system. The intention was to phase in pressurized water reactors (the type of nuclear power stations operating in France and the USA during the 1980s). However, only one of these (Sizewell B) was in fact built, with British Energy announcing the abandonment of two further stations of this type in 1995 (UI News Briefing, 1995). However, the existing stations, and particularly those operating the Magnox system, have demonstrated themselves to be both safe and reliable, and as a result their life-span has steadily increased (UI News Briefing, 1995).

The present chapter is concerned with Dungeness A, commissioned in 1966 in the heyday of Magnox nuclear technology. In 1997 this station employed just under 10 per cent of the total workforce of Magnox Electric. Managing a nuclear power station hinges upon safe, effective maintenance. Therefore this chapter is mainly concerned with the maintenance department at Dungeness A, which demonstrates clearly how the quality process unfolded at Magnox Electric, both at management level and among the workforce.

THE QUALITY JOURNEY AT MAGNOX ELECTRIC

Although the nuclear power stations remained under government ownership when the electricity supply industry was broken up in 1990, they became subject to more intense commercial pressures than they had ever experienced. Dungeness A had particularly high operating costs, and the deregulation and privatization of electricity generation had reduced the market price of electricity considerably. Faced with rising costs and diminishing revenue, senior management realized that rapid action had to be taken to avoid closure. The station's high running costs were partly due to over-staffing. In 1990 there were more than 560 staff in post, compared with 360 in 1997.

However, there were also a number of other factors contributing to Dungeness' inefficiency. Chief among these were outdated working practices, which had been set up during the 1960s and 1970s and reflected a very different working environment and ethos. There was clear demarcation between trades, for example. Workers from one department were not allowed to perform tasks designated as belonging to another, even if these were low in skill content. Thus a mechanical craftsman was not allowed to do a simple job like disconnecting a motor, even if he had the appropriate qualification and could undertake complex jobs like rewiring a house outside working hours. Demarcation of this kind made labour scheduling unduly complicated and

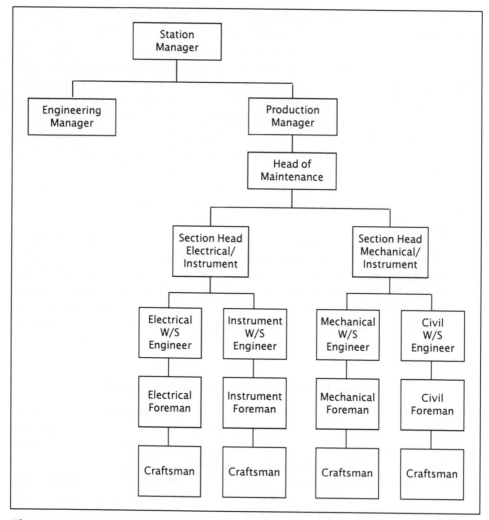

Figure 11.1: Original maintenance team structure

meant that far more people needed to be assigned to a job than were actually needed to get it done. Jobs also took longer; the annual maintenance shutdown took ninety days at this time, one quarter of the working year.

Another problem was the management structure, which was very hierarchical, as can be seen in Figure 11.1. Throughout the company, and specifically in the maintenance department, there were seven layers of management, all with designated grades of pay. This tended to inflate wage costs and the jobs frequently had such fine gradations of status that the boundaries of each job were unclear and the opportunities for overlap, or for avoiding responsibility, were correspondingly great.

In 1992 the Management Team at Dungeness A conducted a staff attitude survey. This confirmed the conditions and structures of working within the station, and also provided further insight into them. The survey showed that communications were poor. There was no communication between different teams or sections, and the senior management team was unable to communicate effectively with shop-floor employees. Informal communication through 'the grape vine' seemed to be the main means by which information was disseminated. Staff also felt that accountability was poor. Responsibilities and decisions tended to get lost or obscured among the levels of management and supervisory hierarchy. Middle managers could hide from the consequences of their actions, or pass the buck. Foremen and lower management were not perceived as accountable for anything.

The work of the station was subject to delays and there were long shutdown times for maintenance work. This was partly due to poor communication and to the bureaucratic intricacy of the management hierarchy. Impermeable boundaries had also grown up between departments and sections and this further complicated the problem. Strict demarcation between trades increased the pressure on manpower and added to the delays. Staff had constantly to refer up the line to get simple jobs done. For example, in order just to disconnect an electric motor they had to ask the foreman, who had to ask the Work Schedule Engineer, who had to ask his colleague in the Electrical Section, who asked his foreman if he could do it. If it was a priority it might be done almost at once, but if not it would wait for hours, days, or sometimes even weeks. At the time, this had become 'the system' and was accepted by everyone without question, even though it caused a general feeling of constraint and frustration.

Demarcation was another major frustration. Many workers had augmented their original skills in their spare time, for example electrical engineers went home to build complex model steam engines. Demarcation prevented them from using their full range of skills at work. Besides causing delays and frustration, it made workers feel undervalued. Respondents in the attitude survey felt that management asked them to leave their brains on the peg with their coats, when they came into work. They asked why certain tasks were forbidden to them, and said that when they came to work they wanted to get on with their job, rather than waste time in hanging around.

On the basis of the evidence they had gathered, in 1993 the management team put forward a business plan designed to improve performance at Dungeness A. The target was to produce a step-wise improvement in the cost of generating electricity, accompanied by an increase in personal productivity of 50 per cent and the modernization of working practices and procedures. At the same time, management aimed to improve the station's safety record and boost employee morale and job satisfaction. In order to do this they asked staff to work on Change Teams, which were charged with reviewing existing working practices, recommended improvements and carried them through to implementation.

The company had always had a good relationship with its trade unions, and naturally discussed the proposed changes with union officials, both full-time officers and shop stewards. The full-time officers were receptive to change of this kind, which was by then the norm in most areas of industry. However, the shop stewards were more suspicious, and reluctant to come forward with their own ideas. They would have preferred simply to be presented with management's plan, which they could then criticize. The answer to this was to involve shop stewards in the Change Teams, where they could be involved in decisions along with their colleagues. In this way a mood of common purpose developed, where shop stewards could see their role in the context of their colleagues' and management's views.

The quality structure

The Maintenance Change Team was one of those set up set up in 1993 during this initiative. It consisted of seven maintenance staff, management, supervisory and workers, and included an AEEU shop steward. It began its work by identifying the areas of existing maintenance work which went well, and those that did not. The second list was somewhat longer than the first. They investigated this list of problems and difficulties in detail by discussing it on a one-to-one basis with all their colleagues. They also contacted their 'internal customers', Production and Engineering, to ask their views. From this exploratory work they confirmed that skill demarcations and the organizational structure were adding to the delays. However, they also identified the following other factors which needed to be addressed.

- Different categories of staff had different working hours, with different start and finish times, which unnecessarily complicated the scheduling of work and helped to produce delays.
- Tea breaks were taken at prescribed times, putting the whole workforce out of action at once and disrupting jobs.
- Radiation monitoring had to be carried out by a member of the Health Physics Department, which meant that an extra specialist had to be scheduled for many of the jobs, as well as the various, strictly demarcated, tradesmen.
- Planning of work was carried out in another department, which meant extra communication lines, and removed the planning process from the expertise that was needed to actually accomplish the work.
- Authorization was a problem, because many signatures were often needed to initiate a job or to issue material from Stores.

The Maintenance Change Team also reviewed numerous published articles on change management and visited various modern process industries in the UK to find out how they had tackled similar problems. After this, they reported, with other Change Teams, to the management team. As far as the Maintenance Department was concerned, key recommendations of the Change Teams were:

- Replacement of existing trade-based sections (mechanical, electrical etc.) with multidisciplinary teams. This would result in more flexible units, which would be better able to tackle maintenance jobs as they came up.
- Flattening of the management hierarchy into the four-tier structure shown in Figure 11.2. Each multidisciplinary maintenance team (designated by colours, to avoid connotations of trade, function or hierarchy) would thus report to a team leader, who would report directly to the Head of Maintenance. The result would be a clearer line of communication, authorization and accountability.
- Skill broadening, in which craftsmen would receive additional modules of training. This would enable them to understand each other's jobs, remove many of the delays and constraints formerly encountered under demarcation, and allow them to become more productive.
- Self-monitoring: maintenance personnel were trained to check their own radiation levels, promoting personal responsibility, increasing safety and removing the need to deploy Health Physics personnel on routine maintenance tasks.
- Introduction of the planning function into the Maintenance Department. This recommendation aimed for a more flexible planning process, geared to the needs of the people who would actually be doing the work.

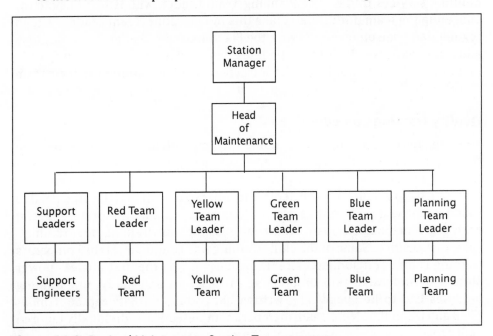

Figure 11.2: Revised Maintenance Section Team structure

Team structure in action

The 'Red Team' provides an example of a typical Maintenance Section substructure. Its team leader has a background in electrical maintenance, but this is not specific to this team. Other team membership is as shown in Table 11.2.

Trade/Discipline	No.
Mechanical maintenance craftsmen	4
Electrical maintenance craftsmen	4
Instrument maintenance craftsmen	4
Mates (various disciplines)	5
Welder	1
Riggers	2

Table 11.2: Composition of 'Red Team'

One of the mechanical craftsmen is designated as Red Team's working deputy, and stands in for the team leader during holidays. At other times he performs the same duties as the other craftsmen. All of the team's members have been trained to self-monitor, so there is no need for a health physicist to be attached to the team.

The colour teams vary somewhat in their skill base; for example, Green Team has a higher skill base in electronic expertise and Blue Team has more building services trades. The Planning Team Leader, who is responsible for allocating the team duties, must take this into account. Team Leaders attend regular daily liaison meetings with the Planning Team Leader. They may also add some extra work to the schedules, which does not pass through the planning system. In addition, Team Leaders arrange training for their team members and authorize minor paperwork, such as holiday applications.

Quality training and education

When the new organizational structure was implemented in 1993, it became the responsibility of the 'colour' Team Leaders to assess the training needs of each of their members. The device for this was a 'skills grid', which ensured that each team would have the depth and breadth of skill that it would need to function correctly. There was a conscious effort to take the preferences of each team member on board wherever possible, but training 'for training's sake' was avoided. Some of the skills training was conducted at the company's training centre and some on site. Dungeness A was the first nuclear power station to undertake skill broadening in this way, and many new training modules had to be specifically written and validated. Between September 1993 and December 1994, team members completed 116 individually tailored skill broadening packages. Typical examples were:

- Electrical skills for fitters and instrument technicians.
- Mechanical skills for electricians and instrument technicians.
- Instrumentation skills for fitters and technicians.
- Health physics self-monitoring for staff working in the reactor areas.

In order to ensure that team members had reached the required level of competence, each individual underwent an assessment interview and a test on completion of each package.

Leaders of the 'colour' teams received training in leadership, coaching, planning and budgeting. They also underwent programmes of communication skills training, to equip them for their new role. Some of them had been foremen within the previous system and others workshop managers. However, the new role in general exercised greater responsibility and demanded much greater people-management skills than their previous job. The Team Leaders were encouraged to discuss the day-to-day organization of work with their team members. Their roles also included making recommendations to the Head of Maintenance, and implementing their preferred solutions.

Measurement and achievements

Team accountability was introduced at Dungeness A, to encourage teams to monitor three main target areas: safety, human resources and finance. These targets are geared to the station's business plan and are monitored on a monthly basis at the organizational level. Teams review them weekly. At the local level, typical measures relate to the numbers of personnel employed on a job, the duration of jobs, the down-time of machines and the estimated cost.

For example, one of the maintenance teams analysed the overhaul of a charge machine bottom machine valve. Under the previous system, this job had previously taken ten days and had involved six maintenance personnel. Using the benefits of skill broadening, the team reorganized the job so that it can now be completed in 4.5 days, by just three people. Other areas studied, measured and reorganized by the teams in this way include:

- The issue of materials from stores.
- The timing and frequency of meal breaks.
- The planning and allocation of maintenance jobs.
- The introduction of regular two-way communications.

Each Maintenance Team holds regular workshops with their internal customers. These meetings discuss the progress and completion of specific maintenance jobs. They assess positive and negative aspects of performance and look at ways in which further improvements can be made and work practices rendered more efficient.

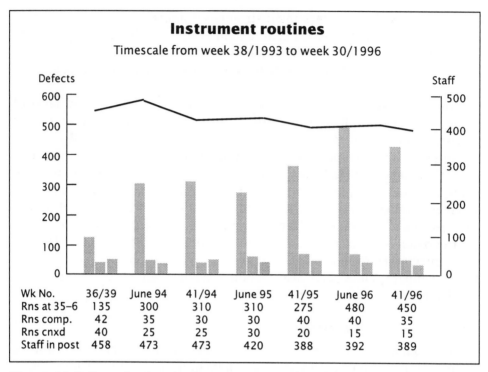

Figure 11.3: Example of output from computerized work control system

Dungeness A is keen to benchmark its progress, but being the first nuclear station to embark upon a quality journey of this kind, there have been no comparable operations against which to compare metrics. For this reason the station has concentrated its benchmarking process on historical data. This gives a clear base from which to work, but of course does not assure competitiveness, a major goal of the quality process at Magnox Electric. The company is seeking other operations with similar process measures, against which it can compare itself.

The effectiveness of teamworking can also be monitored on the station's computerized work control system. Data fed regularly into this system are presented in the form of easy-to-read graphs (see Figure 11.3). Typical measures employed include mechanical, electrical and instrument defects, numbers of staff in post, and the number of routine jobs undertaken and completed in each area.

Management commitment and recognition

Probably the most important mechanism for demonstrating management commitment, and for integrating the ethos and teamwork of the station, is the team briefing system. This begins with a weekly briefing meeting held by the station Management Team, the outcomes from which are cascaded down the organization structure. This allows all sections to be briefed on the issues that affect the company, its sections and teams. Monthly Link-Line briefing sessions provide an opportunity for a more formal briefing process of both delivery and feedback, between the various management levels and the Station Manager.

The efforts of sections are formally recognized through schemes such as the Magnox Magnum Award. This is presented every year to a unit within the company which has demonstrated its teamwork. In 1996 it was won by the Maintenance Section. The efforts of staff are also formally rewarded through an incentive scheme. For example, craftsmen receive a financial bonus (£200 in 1997) for successfully completing each training programme. They receive one pay increment for each extra skill they can use in their work. In addition, financial incentives are paid to staff involved in structural change.

Future continuous improvement plans

Dungeness A has continually refreshed and updated its quality improvement process since it commenced in 1993. The training system is evolving as the organization gains more experience. New initiatives have been undertaken; for example the station received the Investors in People (IIP) award in 1995. A new development being explored at the time of writing is the concept of self-managed teams. At present, craftsmen are taking responsibility for planning large maintenance projects and are also responsible for deploying skills and materials to meet project deadlines. This development is to be evaluated in the near future, and the lessons learned applied to team management and team structures. It is hoped in this way to further flatten the organizational structure, with consequent improvements in communication, motivation and accountability.

The benchmarking process also continues to develop. Dungeness A has extended this initiative to include comparison with other large process industries in the UK. The quality improvement drive has now also spread to other stations within Magnox Electric, providing opportunities for like-with-like comparisons. Future benchmarking will also consider Dungeness A's performance in the light of that of other nuclear power stations in other UK companies. It is hoped that the benchmarking net can be spread worldwide, to produce the most helpful comparisons and render the operation still more competitive.

IMPLICATIONS ARISING FROM THE QUALITY PROCESS AT MAGNOX ELECTRIC

Unlike manufacturing processes, which tend to focus on product quality, a public utility operation such as a power station has to define quality in terms of *process quality*. For a nuclear station such as Dungeness this focuses on two things: the ever-present issue of safety, and the efficiency of operation. Thus, quality improvement in such an operation is bound to go hand-in-hand with the management of productivity. This is clear from the experience of Magnox Electric, which faced the problem not merely of achieving higher productivity, but of maximizing operational safety (always a major consideration in the nuclear power industry) at the same time.

Up to 1990 the nuclear power industry was largely sheltered from international developments in the commercial world. It could virtually conceal itself from public and commercial scrutiny within a vast nationalized corporation, and, at least during the early years of the Cold War, it enjoyed a status of national priority as a vital national energy resource. The manpower and management structures of Dungeness A were established during the first flowering of a Labour government and the height of trade union power. This contributed considerably to the restrictive practices discussed above and provided the station with plenty of scope for improving its productivity. It must also have left a considerable cultural legacy within the organization, and Magnox Electric's management and staff are to be congratulated on their achievement in overcoming this.

It is clear that the culture has now changed for the better. All staff understand the need for change and there is a general feeling of progress and benefit. An instrument craftsman from 'Blue Team' explained this as follows:

> I have had five weeks off site, on a skill-broadening course, which now means I can monitor [the safety of] my own work and also use the mechanical and electrical skills I have learned. Because I was successful in passing, I received a £200 lump sum and got an extra increment on my salary, so there is an incentive to do the course and pass it. The benefits to me are a greater scope for my career, less time for the station and a reduction in cost for the company.
>
> One of my most important jobs is a two-yearly overhaul of a precipitator, which is a critical piece of equipment for the safe running of the station. I used to need the help of a skilled monitor [health physicist] for three days to complete this job, but now, because of skill broadening, I can do the work myself, which saves the station 33 per cent manpower. I can now see the job through, which gives me job satisfaction.

Quality and productivity improvement remain in sharp focus at Magnox Electric. The company and its workforce are aware of the need to continuously develop and change. Competition within the electricity industry continues to intensify, and it is particularly easy to settle down to a period of inactivity following major changes of the type experienced in the company's recent past. Nevertheless Magnox Electric is committed to reducing costs still further. One way to do this will be to develop the present team structure, and there are plans afoot to further reduce levels of hierarchy and to maximize multiskilling within the labour force. The result will be the High Performance Teams, which Magnox hope will carry the company into the twenty-first century.

From a culture in which workers were encouraged to leave their 'brains on the peg' has developed a new approach to nuclear power generation. Everywhere in the company there is a new air of empowerment and accountability. As the instrument craftsman from 'Blue Team' puts it:

> If we were back in the old days now, I would not be here talking to you, because my brain would still be on that peg.

REFERENCES

Collins Concise Dictionary (1989) Collins Ltd., Glasgow.

UI News Briefing (1995) *Plans to build two new power stations in the UK have been dropped*, NB95.50-4, www.uilondo.org/nb/nb95/nb9550.html.

Nucnet News Briefing (1997) 'World's First Major N-Plant Celebrates 40th Birthday' http://www.aey.ch/nucnet/News/960904a.html.

British Nuclear Fuels PLC (1997) 'Where science never sleeps. Calder Hall' http://www.bnfl.com/calder.htm.

Twelve

LAND ROVER VEHICLES

The quality journey

ANTHONY INGOLD
AND
NICK HADLEY

Twelve

LAND ROVER VEHICLES

The quality journey

THE COMPANY

Introduction

Land Rover Vehicles (LRV) is a 4×4 vehicle manufacturer and is a business unit within Rover Group which has been owned by BMW Group since 1994. Each business unit within Rover Group has its own business objectives and distinct cultures, but each individual unit is closely aligned to the rest of the Group and aims to work towards achieving the overall goals of the organization.

Land Rover is in fact the only vehicle manufacturer that concentrates solely on 4×4 vehicles. The product range includes New Range Rover, the luxury flagship model, and is a development of the Range Rover Classic launched originally in 1970. The Defender was launched in 1991 and is based on the Land Rover 90 and 100 range; the vehicle is known as a tough workhorse able to venture into areas impassable to other vehicles. The final model is Discovery. This is an award-winning vehicle, sold in more than fifty countries. Soon to be launched is the new small model, Freelander.

The business unit is headed by a Managing Director (Ian Robertson) who in turn has seven Functional Directors reporting to him. The functions include Personnel, Logistics, Finance, Manufacturing Engineering, Quality Assurance and Manufacturing.

Personnel

The Personnel function at Land Rover has moved away from the traditional role of pay and employee relations towards a broader and more proactive developmental role. Personnel has a strategic role in shaping the people policies of the future, alongside a day-to-day role of supporting line managers on people issues. This entails working with managers to place a greater emphasis on learning and development, thus the existence of a Learning &

Development team at Solihull. The overall emphasis for all associates (employees) includes introducing new levels of flexibility and contribution, improving communications and working towards a new approach to relationships within the company.

Logistics

Logistics is perhaps one of the fastest-growing areas in the manufacturing sector. Ever-increasing emphasis is being placed on the importance of developing systems which can deliver customer satisfaction in this field. It can be delivered into two areas – Inbound Logistics, which involves ensuring that materials from suppliers are available in the right quantity, in the right place and at the right time twenty-four hours a day. The other area, Outbound Logistics, is concerned with the effective transfer of finished products from the manufacturing site to customers worldwide.

Finance

Finance within LRV seeks to provide a comprehensive service which optimizes the use of resources and influences the planning and decision-making processes.

Manufacturing Engineering

This is the technical side of the manufacturing process. It includes specifying, developing and installing of all the processes, machines, buildings, tools and computer and control systems used directly or in support of manufacturing. They have an important part to play in site strategy.

Manufacturing

This function is concerned with the manufacture of the actual product. In the case of Land Rover this is 4 × 4 vehicles. The range includes Discovery, New Range Rover Defender and Freelander vehicle manufacture. This involves three basic processes and thus the manufacturing function splits into the following areas – Body-In-White, Paintshop, and Trim and Assembly. As suggested from the names, Body-In-White is where the body shell is welded together, it is then 'painted' and finally it goes into Trim and Assembly where final fixtures and fittings are added, including seats, engines and gearboxes.

Quality Assurance

This team is dedicated not only to the measurement of product quality performance, but to devising and implementing strategies for the continuous improvement of processes and quality.

THE CULTURE

In the 1960s and 1970s Rover Group was a conglomerate with many products and little focus. By 1986 the corporate structure was very complex. The decision was made to reposition from an unsuccessful volume producer into a successful, specialist producer. The result was the formation of Rover Group, with a core business of designing, manufacturing and selling motor cars.

Around the same time Rover Group put plans in place to train all their workforce (over 35,000 people) in the philosophies and tools of Total Quality Improvement (TQI). This was essential if there was to be a step change that would lead to improved quality and provide a competitive edge in customer satisfaction. TQI is a continuing activity focusing on:

- *Philosophy:*   Prevention not detection.
- *Approach:*   Management-led.
- *Scale:*   Everyone responsible for quality.
- *Measure:*   The costs of quality.
- *Standard:*   'Right First Time'.
- *Scope:*   Company-wide.
- *Theme:*   Continuous improvement.

A strong thread of TQI is teamwork and working to common goals.

The next stage was to create an environment of empowerment, where everyone could play a part. In a programme called 'Rover Tomorrow' was developed, the strategic vision of the company was communicated to all employees. Radical changes in products and the way in which they would be made were shared, as were details of the competitive threats. Agreement was sought on:

- *Total flexibility in working practices* – which was backed by the statement that no employee would be laid off; where problems disrupt production or the job is no longer in existence, all employees will be engaged in worthwhile activities.
- *Single status for all employees* – thus the development of the term 'associate' for all employees of the company whether manager or shop-floor worker.
- *Forward-looking relationships* with the trade unions and single table negotiating procedures.

The new philosophies are based around the term 'Class Act'. Land Rover want to ensure that at all times they are meeting the prime business objective – delivering 'extraordinary customer satisfaction'. The way ahead requires there to be strong leadership, a high importance based on quality of the product and planning and implementing the business strategy. A recent management conference held at Land Rover Vehicles expressed the changes that were needed in the coming year. The Investors in People (IIP) standard is an important step towards the goal.

THE QUALITY JOURNEY

Development of a clear strategy and plans

Quality Strategy
The Rover Group vision is that:

'Rover is internationally renowned for extraordinary customer satisfaction.'

To ensure that the business realizes this vision, the Quality Strategy was developed by the Rover Group Board.

The strategy, called QS2000, details key processes and critical success factors leading to a process vision. Along the way to achieving the process vision are yearly milestones for the years 1996 to 2000. These milestones are reviewed annually and the process will continue throughout the lifetime of the strategy.

OS2000 is the second Quality Strategy developed by the Rover Group Board. The first covered years 1991 to 1995 and was developed and deployed on a similar basis to QS2000. This conforms to a five-year business planning cycle. The importance of the strategy, and how successful delivery of its goals is critical to the business, is underlined in Dr W. Hasselkus's Communication to all Rover Group managers. This summarizes QS and is part of the overall communication/deployment cascade.

Business Plans
Each Business Unit develops their own Quality Strategy and Business Plan covering the same period (i.e. 1996–2000) as the overall Group Quality Strategy. Land Rover Vehicles is a Business Unit within Rover Group and has developed its own Strategy and Business Plan. This Strategy/Plan has its own vision and mission, processes, process visions and Critical Success Factors that relate specifically to the nature of its business; in our case the manufacture of 4 × 4 vehicles. All processes have owners and yearly milestones. The owners are Directors at Land Rover Vehicles.

As a communication aid, the 1997 Business Strategy 'tree' has been developed which shows how the various functions within the Business Unit provide the 'roots' for the delivery of Key Business Plan objectives.

Functional Plans

Obviously QS2000 and the Land Rover Vehicles Quality Strategy and Business Plan are the company plans at the highest level. In addition to this each function within Land Rover will devise its own functional plan. Each functional plan will support the delivery of the overall Business Unit Plan. In turn the Business Unit Plan supports QS2000.

These functional plans tend to be one-year plans so they are reviewed on at least an annual basis in line with QS2000 and Business Unit Plan. These plans are then translated into detailed Action Plans and linked to Associate Development Process (ADP) objectives.

Communication and Deployment of Plans

As already explained, communication of the vision of the organization takes place through QS2000 and the Business Unit Plan, but the individual contribution of associates is determined and communicated through individual development discussions between associates and their manager. In the past this has usually taken the form of the Performance and Development Review (PDR) for management and staff associates. In 1997, Rover Group is launching the Associate Development Process. This will enable every associate in the business to become involved in the deployment of the business key plans and objectives – either individually and/or in their teams.

'Team Talk' is a vehicle for communicating Key Business Goals and Performance. It is a written brief that contains business information which should be communicated verbally. Each area has the option to add local information as appropriate.

Other communication processes used to communicate visions, strategies and the plans are:

- Associate roadshows.
- Management conferences.
- Newsletter – Weekly News.

Self-Assessment

Another important process that evaluates achievement of the business goals is the self-assessment process. The model used is based on one devised by the European Foundation for Quality Management (EFQM). The purpose of the activity is to review the organization's activities and determine its strengths and weaknesses. The key is to maintain the strong areas and improve the weak. An organization must ensure the foundations are there for enablers, deploy those enablers and then systematically improve them. The enablers within Land Rover Vehicles include: Quality Strategy, Information and Resources, Leadership, Process Management, and People Management. The results that we measure and report back on are: customer satisfaction, people satisfaction, impact on society and business results.

Deployment of quality improvement throughout the organization

The introduction, or developmental of people involvement activities

Land Rover Vehicles has a mature and vibrant Involvement Strategy that goes back to the transformation of the business in the 1980s when Total Quality Management was established and working practices were radically revised. This enabled a variety of involvement processes to be put in place and although there were some initial reservations from trade unions, these were addressed through full consultation and their stance has changed from tacit acceptance in many cases, to positive support and participation. The fundamental changes to the organization of the business in the late 1980s, particularly the introduction of Cell Management and the roles of production manager and team leader, has greatly enhanced the effectiveness of associate involvement and contribution. An overview of involvement at Land Rover is given in Figure 12.1, the Involvement Jigsaw. The Involvement Strategy is made up of the following components.

Team Talk

This is a process of, at least monthly, two-way communication sessions involving the Team Leader/Section Manager and all team members. They

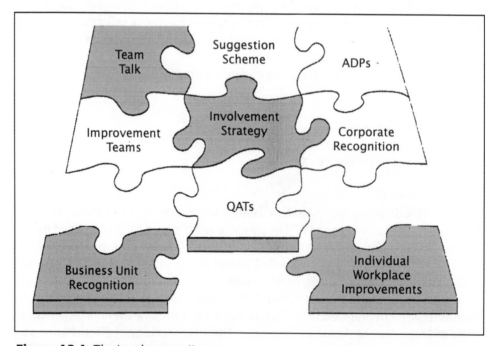

Figure 12.1: The Involvement Jigsaw

brief, and discuss with each other, business unit-wide and local issues relating to Product, Process, People and Pounds (the four Ps).

Suggestion Scheme
The scheme has been continuously improved since the 1980s and its effectiveness in terms of participation and savings accrued have grown significantly during this time. One of the key changes that led to improvement was the introduction of local ownership in 1991. This gave accountability to the Cell Manager to provide the initial assessment of the suggestion giving a very quick response to its viability as an acceptable idea. In March 1996 the scheme was changed further. It was felt that while participation levels had grown from 1991 to 1995, there had been some decline in the overall quality of suggestions submitted and the new, relaunched puts the emphasis on cost-saving ideas of some significance. This will inevitably lead to fewer suggestions, but has improved the adoption rates and value-added quality of the ideas submitted. As an illustration of this the first sixty-nine suggestions submitted post-March 1996 when the new scheme was launched have potential savings in excess of £2.1 million.

Associate Development Process
The ADP process, launched Quarter 1, 1997, involved all associates in the deployment of the Quality Strategies and the Business/Functional Plans. The ADP Planning Process is shown in Figure 12.2.

Improvement Teams/Discussion Groups /Quality Action Teams
In 1996 following a period of decline in the number of functional/effective Discussion Groups, due to a combination of natural 'wastage', volume uplifts and shift changes, a new strategy for Improvement Teams was launched. This has now been piloted in Defender Assembly and the company agreed plans to 'roll out' to all parts of the business by Quarter 3, 1997.

Discussion Groups, of the original sort, will continue to function where they are robust but are likely to 'metamorphose' into the new type Improvement Teams. Indeed Land Rover are already finding that Discussion Groups recently disbanded are forming the basis of the newly created Improvement Teams. This is beneficial in terms of sharing and passing on skills and past learning.

Quality Action Teams are multi-functional teams of relevant fact-holders who come together voluntarily for the purpose of resolving a product quality related problem. As such, they have clear objectives and have a sponsor from the product area involved who, if necessary, will provide any necessary coaching to other areas to support the work of the QAT and to whom the result will be presented.

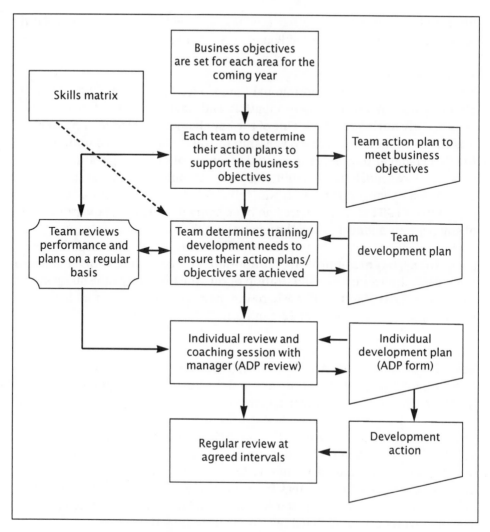

Figure 12.2: ADP Planning process: 'The big picture'

Associate Recognition

Since 1995, Rover Group has held Recognition Events for associates who have made outstanding contributions to the business. Each Business Unit in the Group submits nominations (approximately twenty-five to thirty per Unit) following a selection process with their respective units. The associates, and their partners, attend an evening and overnight event at a local hotel, hosted by the Senior Management Team of the Rover Group managers and associates. Local Business Units also recognize their nominees by giving widespread publicity in their newsletter.

Business Unit Recognition

Land Rover Vehicles has its own associate Recognition Scheme – the Quality Excellence Awards. These awards are designed for peers to nominate fellow associates in recognition of their contribution to quality excellence. These nominations are then considered by various levels of management and awarded either Gold, Silver or Bronze awards.

The scheme allows recipients to be registered on a plaque/roll of honour in the main reception and all Gold and Silver recipients are invited to a celebration annual dinner hosted by Land Rover Vehicles Senior Management.

Individual Workplace Achievements

Since the ending of RISE in 1995, Land Rover Vehicles have been piloting a scheme designed to capture and recognize individual associates or teams, who make improvement contributions that are not captured by the Suggestion Scheme. This is an attempt to stimulate, and reward in an essentially non-monetary way, the small step improvements and contributions that are made daily and do not require in-depth assessment prior to implementation. One thousand small steps have more impact than a giant step.

Increase in the willingness and extent of participation in improvement activities

The years 1990 to 1995 saw a significant growth in the participation in involvement processes such as the Suggestion Scheme, Discussion Groups, and QATs. 1996 saw fundamental reviews of the effectiveness of these processes and has led to a shift in the emphasis from the pure numbers involved in these activities to the quality of contribution. That shift has underpinned the changes to the Suggestion Scheme and Discussion Groups that took place in 1996. The introduction of the Associate Development Process and the roll out of Improvement Teams during 1997 gives Land Rover real opportunities to involve all associates in a value-added way.

The extent of teamworking and people involvement activity and the innovation employed to overcome barriers and difficulties

The changes to the Suggestion Scheme and Discussion Groups described above show examples of where the business has been innovative and creative in order to overcome barriers and difficulties. Teamworking has been deeply ingrained in the business since the introduction of Total Quality Management, and the Cell Manager/Team Leader structures have greatly assisted the effectiveness of work teams throughout the business.

The effectiveness of the management system that supports the teamworking activities, personal improvement, problem-elimination and system improvements

In 1996, Land Rover Vehicles established Involvement Committees for manufacturing and non-manufacturing areas, chaired by senior managers and supported by managers from each main function and department. Their terms of reference cover all existing and developing involvement processes in the Business Unit, as well as spending time developing longer-term strategic issues.

In 1993, Land Rover Vehicles gained investors in People status and was re-accredited in 1996. This status is given by the local Training and Enterprise Council (CENTEC) and follows a very detailed audit of the People Management Processes.

Quality education and training

Land Rover training – internal
The Rover Group firmly believes that its people are the key to its continued success as a company. To this end, training is seen as a crucial aspect of its people's working life. Each site has a dedicated Training Department which can offer people at all levels within the location appropriate training and advice to satisfy their needs and those of the business. Uniquely within the British industry, a separate company, the Rover Learning Business (RLB) has been created to ensure concentrated focus on training for all people within Rover. More numerous and more easily accessible training opportunities have been developed including the REAL scheme which pays for non-job-related training for all associates. The RLB complements site Training Departments – the relationship is one of close partnership.

Associate Development Centre (ADC)
There is an Associate Development Centre at Land Rover Vehicles which aims to provide a facility for individual learning and development of any associate. The majority of the 170 courses provided at the ADC are computer-based, although there are also audio and video learning packages. The Learning and Development team produces an ADC course brochure for individuals to choose the course they wish to study.

The principle of the Centre is that every individual is responsible for his/her own learning and all courses are designed to meet this aim. However, there is a full-time member of the Learning and Development Department on hand to offer help if it is required.

Associates can undertake courses which are either job-related or purely of personal interest. Generally, when a course is job-related, people can study in the ADC during working hours. If a course is non-vocational, bookings can be made outside working hours.

The ADC is open during normal working hours from Monday to Friday and in addition is open until 7:30 p.m. from Monday to Thursday. No charge is made for any courses undertaken in the ADC.

Off-job training

The Land Rover Vehicles Learning and Development team offers a wide range of in-house courses which are run 'off-job' in our own facilities. Supplementing these are courses run by external bodies on behalf of the company. The 'Purposeful Management' programme is an example of such a course which has proved a very successful programme for newly appointed first-line managers. The recently launched Effective Manufacturing Management (EMM) programme runs off-site but its various modules are delivered by line managers and/or subject specialists from within Land Rover Vehicles. The programme is designed for production managers within manufacturing.

External customers and suppliers

The training of dealers and suppliers does not directly come under the Business Unit but has been undertaken by our Rover Learning Business (RLB) with respect to the dealers and the Group Purchasing Unit regarding the suppliers.

Quality management and measurement (QMM)

During the first six months of 1997 Land Rover introduced QMM. Prior to that there was a systematic programme of management education within the Business Unit. QMM is a management tool for driving the systematic and timely resolution of customer-relevant product problems.

The education and training implemented and the perceived and measured effectiveness

The biannual Attitude Survey – Viewpoint – has a section dedicated to associate opinion of the effectiveness and availability of learning and development opportunities. The trend since attitude surveys began in 1988 has been a positive one, with levels of satisfaction improving significantly.

The system of measurement applied
Product quality measurement and improvement

Internal

Product quality is measured and audited, and via the 'Blue Card Process' in particular, picks up quality issues and identifies areas of the manufacturing process that have caused problems.

The local management team then put in solutions to not only fix the problem short-term, but to eradicate the cause for good. The 'Blue Card Process' is visibly displayed on local team noticeboards so that every associate in the team is aware of the key quality issues in their zone or cell. It is also known as the 'Level O' process.

Customer driven
The key internal audit process is the 'QZI audit' (Qualitäts Zahl, or Quality Figure). This takes in sample vehicles from the sales areas and audits the basic features of each vehicle. The audit includes a static audit and road test. Any faults are scored as points depending on the degree of severity. The numbers of vehicles in each sample are individually scored and a sample average is calculated. This produces a mean score for the month and results are published. A range (i.e. difference between best and worst vehicle in the sample) is also calculated. Faults detected in the QZI audit then form part of the programme for quality improvement actions. They also act as an on-going measure of quality performance and quality/year end improvement targets are set. These are widely publicized within the business via Team Talk, weekly newsletters and on team noticeboards.

Customer-driven/external measures
Customer Quality Tracking Surveys
(CQTS) are carried out at least once every year for each Land Rover product. An independent market research company conducts telephone interviews with a randomly selected sample of owners after approximately thirty days of ownership. They then calculate Faults Per Vehicle (FPV) and Freedom From Faults (FFF) satisfaction rating (0–10). These survey results are closely analyzed and a set of improvement activities put in place to solve quality issues/vehicle faults identified by CQTS.

There is also in North America the J. D. Powers survey which samples owners of vehicles bought in a specific vehicle build period. Figure 12.3 shows the rigorous nature of the process that Land Rover have in place to ensure good performance in the J. D. Powers survey. This survey is probably the most important indicator to motor manufacturers worldwide on customer recognition of quality. A sample of owners are sent a questionnaire by post ninety days after they have purchased a new car, and a Faults Per Vehicle rating is calculated. Powers conducts the survey for every vehicle manufactured in certain market sectors so competitor comparisons can be made. Again these results are closely analysed and improvement actions put in place.

The third key external customer measure is warranty. This data comes directly from the dealers in the UK, Europe and rest of the world. Faults detected in warranty claims are driven down to root courses and remedial actions are put into place.

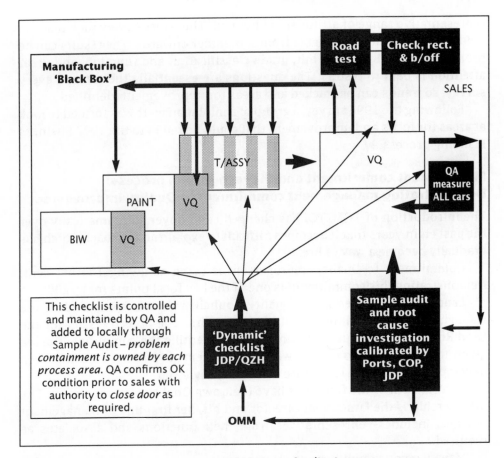

Figure 12.3: JDP Power Programme 1997: Basic Quality Improvement process

Improvement actions

The process QMM (Quality Management and Measurement) has already been described above. All of the quality issues raised by internal measures such as QZ or external such as CQTS, warranty and powers are associated with solution providers and owners and timed action plans for problem resolution.

Land Rover Quality Council meeting

At the Land Rover Quality Council, which is made up of the Land Rover Vehicles directors, and supported by quality assurance specialists, a whole range of quality indicators and measures are shared and new significant product quality issues debated. The input and output measures drive quality improvement indicators at the very senior level of the organization.

Associate/employee measures

Every two years, a random sample of associates in Rover Group participate in an attitude survey called Viewpoint. Every grade of associate is sampled, so a representative range of attitudes is obtained. The latest survey took place in 1996 and results were available from September onwards. The results can be broken down by Business Unit, grade classification and function, and great attention is paid to results. The questions are essentially the same in every survey, so trends can be tracked and areas for improvement identified.

Following the 1996 survey, a group of senior managers was formed to look at areas for focus and improvement that could be fed in to the 1997 Business Planning process.

Management commitment and the recognition process: Demonstrating management commitment to Quality Improvement

The introduction of TQM/TQI has changed Land Rover so dramatically over the past eight years that it becomes difficult to explain an approach which has gradually become a way of life.

Commitment to Quality Improvement is taken as giving 100 per cent. Demonstrating this commitment is one of the key focal points for QS2000.

Land Rover Vehicles has a Quality Council, which is composed of the Managing Director and his first line of directors. The objectives set for the Land Rover Vehicles Quality Council clearly identifie the commitment being given to Quality Improvement with a measurement structure having been developed to ensure that they are constantly reviewed.

In turn, each of the functions have their own Quality Strategy Group. The membership is the Functional Director and his/her first line of management but also includes representatives from their functions and associates as required.

Management commitment is also demonstrated by:

- Support given to the associates in their release from their normal occupation in order to participate in Improvement Teams.
- Attending/mentoring Improvement Teams.
- Sponsoring QATs which not only requires the release of their own associates to resolve their concerns but also to assist other managers in resolving their problems. This applies equally to Improvement Teams.
- Team Talk occurs across the Business Unit with production stopping for around twenty minutes weekly to enable production managers and team leaders to carry out the briefings. Where there is a two- or three-shift pattern operating there is also a daily shift briefing to communicate problems and actions taken during the previous shift.
- The emphasis on team recognition and publicity through:
  - Coverage of Improvement Team/Discussion group successes through the weekly newsletter.
  - Submission of nominations for the Rover Group Wide Recognition Event.
  - Running of the Quality Excellence Awards for Land Rover Vehicles

associates and the presentation of the Gold/Silver awards by the Rover Group Chairman/Chief Executive Dr Walter Hasselkus at Business Reviews.

- The running of the Education Partnership Centre for the purpose of opening up our facilities for the development and education of schoolchildren and students of all ages.
- Through the belief that Total Quality is not just for our industry but for everybody. Land Rover welcome and encourage other companies to visit and share Land Rover's experiences in implementing a Total Quality Improvement Programme.
- Stopping the track is a problem which was in the past considered a cardinal sin. It is now encouraged in order to ensure 'Right First Time' is achieved, and crucially, that the customer is protected. The restart is only made after either an Engineering Concession is provided to give assurance that the concern will not affect either the quality or vehicle reliability.

Management commitment does not just extend to activity relating to improving the product but also the quality of our associates' working life. There is an Associate Care Programme which, via an Occupational Health Centre, provides a range of services including physiotherapy, chiropody, audiometry and optician service as well as the ability to treat accidents. It is managed by a qualified doctor and is moving much more towards preventative medicine and advice as opposed to the treatment of accidents and illness. It is hoped that this will have a very positive effect on long-term and short-term absence. They already provide advice on ergonomics, workplace layout and process/method design so that potential health and safety risks are minimized.

There is also a comprehensive range of health and safety training programmes available for managers within Land Rover Vehicles.

Other evidence of the company's commitment to quality in all aspects of the business is the National Energy Awards won by Land Rover in 1997.

FUTURE CONTINUOUS IMPROVEMENT PLANS

QS 2000/Land Rover Vehicles Business Plan

To a very great extent, the Quality Strategy and Business Unit Plan, already fully described, provides the basis of the company's continuous improvement plan. However, each year sets ever more demanding milestones along the path towards the company's process vision.

	Process	Vision
1	Develop people's contribution.	Best people. Best contribution. Best results.
2	Product development and delivery.	4 × 4 engineering leadership for the twenty-first century.
3	Fulfil demand-supply chain optimization.	Planned, predictable seamless supply.
4	Manufacturing conformity.	On-time delivery of predictable product built to process and validated.
5	Infrastructure provision.	Excellence through people and technology.
6	Business strategy and leadership.	Everyone understanding their part.

Table 12.1: Land Rover's process vision

This vision and vitality of the company is perhaps well expressed in the development of the new model, the Freelander. This is a smaller three-door vehicle, available in soft or hard top configuration. Innovative for Land Rover, the vehicle is of monocoque design, rather than chassis based, with independent suspension and having a transverse engine. With prices starting at £15,000 the vehicle spans the range from utility vehicle to luxury vehicle. Due to high levels of demand, the launch was brought forward to December 1997 and pre-sales greatly exceeded all the company's expectations.

The Group Quality Strategy, Business Unit Plans, Functional Plans and Associate Development Team Plans come together to provide the coherent and cohesive structure that drives the high-level company goals down to the individual associate actions. The quality improvement programme is now firmly embedded in the business culture, and the robust measurement and monitoring process is intended to ensure long-term adherence with continual review. The company have derived vision, clarity and strength from the continuous quality improvement programme. Land Rover aim to achieve their QS2000 goals and to attain the status of a world class company, with a range of products to match by the year 2000.

Part 3

THE WEDGWOOD NHS
TEAM OF THE YEAR AWARD

Thirteen

YORKHILL NHS TRUST

'What's up Doc?' –
the Bugs Bunny Project

RICHARD HALE
AND
LINDA FLEMING

Thirteen

YORKHILL NHS TRUST

'What's up Doc?' –
the Bugs Bunny Project

PART 1: INTRODUCTION

Yorkhill is one of Scotland's principal centres of maternal and child health. It comprises Scotland's largest children's hospital, one of the area's foremost maternity hospitals, several community services, and houses seven academic departments of the University of Glasgow. Uniting this multidisciplinary body of skills, expertise and resources is the common cause of caring for the health of mothers and children in the area.

Yorkhill cares for over 25,000 in-patients, 26,000 new out-patients and around 9,000 day-patients each year. In addition, in excess of 33,000 children attend the Accident and Emergency department and the Queen Mother's Hospital accommodates the birth of around 3,600 babies every year. As can be seen from these figures alone, whilst this is essentially a caring service, the effort required to maintain and improve the service presents a logistics and organizational challenge equal to any commercial venture in the private sector. Indeed it might be argued that the situation is even more complex given the diversity of disciplines represented and the fact that the 'customers' are by definition real people facing personal trauma.

This chapter focuses on the achievements of one team that was set up within the Trust in order to address a specific organizational problem. The problem was essentially that of increased demand for their services at a particular time of year, in other words seasonal peaks. We will show how a truly multidisciplinary team set about exploring this problem and ultimately was charged with implementing real organizational change. Various terms may be used to categorize this project – organizational development, quality improvement, business process re-engineering, continuous improvement – but the fact is that this is about how a service organization re-focused itself around the needs of its customers. There are lessons to be learnt here for anyone interested in how an imminent business problem was seen as a great opportunity for change.

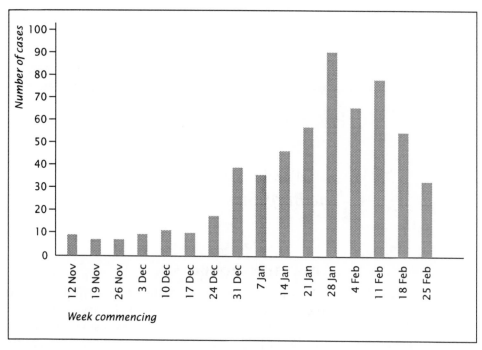

Figure 13.1: Incidences of Respiratory Syncytial Virus (RSV), winter 1996–97

Birth of the project

During the autumn of each year emergency admissions of children suffering from respiratory illness, especially Respiratory Syncytial Virus (RSV) begins to rise and this peaks in December to January and then eases off by early spring. The extent of the problem can be clearly seen from the graph shown as Figure 13.1. The implications of this seasonal epidemic are dramatic, leading to a significantly increased demand for clinical and non-clinical resources. Paediatric medical bed occupancy within wards runs at around 85 per cent and on a daily basis occasionally exceeds 100 per cent. In addition, there is a similar scale of increased patient activity during the summer period in orthopaedic surgery as a result of children becoming involved in accidents during play.

In a sense the project team was born out of the adversity which the Trust had experienced following the winter of 1995/6. The Chief Executive of the Trust, Gerry Marr assured nursing and medical staff that in organizational terms: '. . . they would not experience another winter similar to the last one'. Although there was nothing they could to reduce the seasonal variations, they could develop a better way of managing their response to it.

Whilst a formal team vision was subsequently articulated in the terms of reference, it might be considered that this was the implied vision which the project team worked towards. Specifically the terms of reference for this team, as approved by the management group were:

> To consider the flexible use of resources to cope with summer and winter in-patient demand. Essentially the group should examine seasonal bed utilisation and link this to the impact on resources, i.e. clinical staffing and other ward-based support services. The recommendations must also be financially sound and take account of intra-directorate issues.

So a multidisciplinary team was to be established to address the needs of clinical staff to enable them to provide an improved quality of care provision during the period of peak demand. The leader of the group was appointed and an overall goal was set: to produce a Business Plan with clearly defined solutions by the end of May 1996. The Chief Executive attached a great deal of importance to the outcome of the group and raised the profile of the team internally. As has been recognized for some time in the field of team development, a critical relationship is that between the team and its 'sponsor' or 'sponsors', as well as its stakeholders. It can be seen here that a key issue was the seniority of the sponsor and how he ensured the staff and managers internally, who might be considered stakeholders, were made aware of the importance of the project. Arguably he also created the potential for a 'self-fulfilling prophecy': while team members described feeling apprehensive at the start, they were well aware they had certain expectations to live up to. The team members were under no illusions as to how serious the task ahead of them was.

Formally the team was known as the Flexible Use of Resources Working Group; however, like many successful teams, they self-selected a more imaginative project team name: 'The Bugs Bunny Project'. Why? Because they were basically tackling the management of children as patients who had caught a bug. Furthermore, the catch-phrase which the famous cartoon rabbit uses – 'What's up Doc?' – was essentially the same question the team found themselves asking as they set about trying to define the problem they were tasked with addressing. And so the project was born.

PART 2: THE PROJECT

The team structure

Certain members of the team had worked with each other previously, but they had not worked together as a team before. The team brought together staff from many functions including service managers, business managers, a general manager, an assistant director of finance and a contracts and planning manager. The director of contracts headed up the team and had a key role in selecting team members. In total there were nine core team members. Some of the team members had in the past been involved in successful quality improvement projects within ward areas. This previous experience of teamworking meant that these members were sensitive to the requirements for looking across activities and processes to achieve improved results in support of the seamless delivery of patient care.

In many ways the establishment of this team supports the findings of Katzenbach and Smith (1993:12) who through the study of a number of business teams identified that 'Significant performance challenges energise teams regardless of where they are in the organisation' and '. . . a common set of demanding performance goals that a group considers important will lead, most of the time, to both performance and a team.' It was also found that when these conditions prevail, the environment creates a climate for learning and personal development. This is precisely what the team members at Yorkhill Trust describe in their own words when comparing how they felt upon being asked to join the team as compared with their personal lasting impressions after the team project had concluded.

Comments before included:

> I felt quite happy to be part of the group although I was unsure exactly what I would be able to contribute . . .

> As team leader, I welcomed the opportunity to deliver the task by teamwork but I . . . questioned to myself how the piece of work would develop.

and afterwards:

> I learned that sometimes solutions stem from co-operation and empathy with others rather than through increased funding.

> One of the most important things that I have learned from working in the group was the power of multi-disciplinary and cross-functional project groups.

Defining the problem

Initial efforts were spent trying to understand the nature of the problem; in what areas might the Trust be able to improve its response. This was evidently time well spent given that a common barrier in problem-solving is that teams are often overly solution-oriented and rush prematurely into the decision-making stage. The key problem areas that had to be tackled were identified as falling into two categories: those relating to non-clinical support service and those relating to clinical support services. The non-clinical issues were:

- Availability of discharge transport.
- Case notes not always immediately available for all emergency admissions.
- Newly admitted patients often having to wait before a vacant cubicle is cleaned or a clean bed to become available.
- Considerable delays in keeping up with routine admission/discharge documentation, particularly at weekends and evening peak periods.
- Routine patient-related paperwork being conducted by medical personnel.
- Test results not always automatically following ward transfers.
- Delays in accessing updated admission forms resulting in inconvenience and delays in discharge decision-making.
- Nursing time used to 'fetch and carry', for instance, meals, test results and case notes.
- Uncomfortable facilities for parental overnight accommodation.

The clinical issues were:

- The amount of nursing time spent on preparing intravenous drugs at ward level.
- Once the clinical decision had been taken to admit a patient, the RSV status was unknown until test results became available.
- Delays in the issue of drugs for discharged patients.
- Poor management of the wheelchair provision.

In summary, the project was concerned with introducing a series of practical solutions, designed through teamwork, to relieve the pressure on ward staff and enable them to spend more time with patients and their families during the peak periods, which in turn would greatly improve the overall quality of care provision as well as reducing employee pressure and stress.

The team process and business solutions

The team made a clear commitment to take personal action in the interest of the common goal. Initially, however, team members met and agreed individually to work up, examine and clarify specific action points and report their findings to the following meeting. It was agreed that co-opted members should join the group to provide expert opinion. Interestingly this reflects one of the more recent developments in the Belbin model of team roles, which now incorporates the role of the 'specialist'. Belbin (1993: p. 23) suggests that the significance of the specialist role in contributing to teams is often underestimated: 'in much project work a given form of professional expertise counted for a lot and could be ignored only at peril'. Here the specialist included medical professionals and technicians from a number of areas such as microbiology, laboratory members and clinicians.

In the early days of the project the team would have described themselves more as a group of individuals than a cohesive team. By the third or fourth meeting, though, people were starting to meet outside the formal meetings in order to progress project objectives. A pattern of teamwork began to evolve over time. It was quickly realized by individuals that they could not progress action points on their own and that there was a need to meet informally with both team members and with those outside the team structure.

As group members became familiar with each other, so the reporting back process to the team tended to become a joint effort with two or three members working as a team. So the benefits of teamwork within and outside the formal structure of the group of nine, coupled with shared responsibility, created an environment where trust and support grew and ultimately thrived. Discussions became more open and frank and, as team members began to feel less inhibited, creative ideas and practical solutions emerged.

A good example of this was the introduction of the near patient testing for RSV infection. This is a test which can detect whether a patient is RSV positive within twenty minutes of the test being carried out. This compares with twenty-four hours using the traditional process where the test is carried out in the hospital laboratory. This allowed patients to be tested and categorized and segregated for cohort nursing immediately. The benefits of this change were evident. Nursing staff were able to plan and manage in-patient accommodation, and the level of cross-infection and hospital-acquired infection has reduced to the lowest for many years. This specific idea was developed by core team members and co-opted members such as medical professionals and technicians.

It was recognized that the team needed to continue to develop awareness of its existence and role at the grass-roots level and each core team member undertook to communicate extensively within their respective Directorates. As with any successful team, they broke down rather than erected barriers between the team and the outside world and they built an extended network to gather ideas and suggestions and evaluate proposals for change.

The team was also careful to identify and communicate with other working groups which had been tasked with addressing service improvements. Apart from ensuring compatibility of recommendations this proved to be a politically astute approach and no doubt helped gather support at an early stage for the ultimate proposals.

A summary of the solutions that were proposed by the team is shown in Table 13.1.

Following approval of the Winter Business Plan the Chief Executive invited the team to extend the role of the group to co-ordinate the implementation of the proposals. So the role of the group turned from problem-solving, its

NON-CLINICAL SUPPORT AREAS

Business Problem	Proposed Solution
Availability of discharge transport.	Establish taxi service.
Case notes not always immediately available for all emergency admissions.	Extend existing accident and emergency-based shift pattern to ensure sufficient cover.
Considerable delays in keeping up with routine admission/discharge documentation particularly at weekends and evening peak periods .	
Test results not always automatically following ward transfers.	
Newly admitted patients often have to wait before a vacant cubicle is cleaned or a clean bed to become available.	Increase availability of evening cleaning services to match peak demand and increase cover for evening bed store service.
Routine patient related paperwork being conducted by medical personnel.	Extend use of bank funding to allow increased overtime working from clerical bank.
Delays in accessing updated admission forms resulting in inconvenience and delays in discharge decision making.	Introduce a bank of funds to allow overtime working during evenings and weekends to cover extra admissions, discharges and transfers.
	Surgical to introduce a nursing auxiliary and clerical bank.
Nursing time used to 'fetch and carry', for instance meals, test results and case notes.	Extend shift pattern to provide a 'fetch and carry' service.
Uncomfortable facilities for parental overnight accommodation.	Investigate wider introduction of more comfortable facilities.

CLINICAL SUPPORT AREAS

Business Problem	Proposed Solution
The amount of nursing time spent on preparing intravenous drugs at ward level.	Provide a seven-day-per-week dedicated intravenous service.
Once the clinical decision had been taken to admit a patient, the RSV status was unknown until test results became available.	Introduction of near patient testing with twenty-minute result.
Delays in the issue of drugs for discharged patients.	Messenger service to be available on pager.
Poor management of wheelchairs.	Appoint maintenance assistant.

Table 13.1: Summary of team proposals

original remit in June 1996, to practical implementation of the recommendations. Until October 1996 the group met on a regular basis to monitor implementation in advance of the winter season.

Funding was largely covered through the 'ring-fencing' of existing budgets, though the group did identify where additional investment funding was required. For non-clinical support services £33,900 came from ring-fenced sources and £5,200 new investment was provided for taxi service and clerical support. For clinical support services £11,000 came from ring-fenced sources and £10,000 was invested in RSV testing and the employment of a maintenance assistant.

Formal channels of communication were set up to monitor implementation and this included the following groups:

- Ward-based nursing/administration/clerical.
- Medical records.
- Sisters group.
- Heads of Department.
- Directorate teams.
- The Trust Board.
- Purchasers.
- Clinical Strategy Group.
- External audit.

Impact on the business

The impact of the team's work has been significant and improvements were sustained throughout the winter in both the non-clinical support and clinical organization. The main benefits related to improved staff morale and organizational processes. The impact on clinical activity may be less directly related to the work of the team but it is of interest to note that despite a continued increase (by 10 per cent) in the winter epidemic caseload there was a fall of 12 per cent in admissions, resulting in 1,930 fewer bed days (or 16 per cent). This was evidently related to the increasing emphasis on assessment and treatment prior to a decision to admit.

The number of emergency admissions fell by 10 per cent reflecting the true impact of the revision of the initial management of acutely ill medical patients arriving at the Accident and Emergency department.

These examples and statistics represent only part of overall benefits that were seen, but some qualitative comment from the medical staff and nursing staff is also worth noting. Medical staff have said:

New patients admitted, especially during the night, are better prepared than ever before.

Fully documented patients who transfer from Short Stay can begin treatment on the main ward immediately and this often leads to speedier discharge.

Nursing staff have said:

A great deal of pressure has been lifted from ward nursing staff due to the results of acute work-up in short stay being available to us; this also allows a smooth settle-in for new patients and parents have expressed their confidence in these arrangements.

They have certainly lightened the load on nursing staff with regards to paperwork, messages and telephone answering – any extra time nurses have is now spent on caring for patients and supporting parents.

Overall it was recommended that the multidisciplinary approach for the future development of paediatric medical services be continued.

PART 3: SUMMARY OF TRANSFERABLE LEARNING POINTS

Hale and Whitlam (1997:166–72) identify the importance of teamworking in the future organization, but warn of the difficulties in making it work. They show how dysfunctional teams display certain characteristics such as being introspective, intimidated by their leader, failing to challenge, creating a blame culture, engaging in escapist behaviour and being functionally focused. Many researchers and authors have stressed the importance of teamwork but these negative characteristics are a real threat when team structures are overlaid on an established functional structure. At Yorkhill Trust the team openly admit that partisan loyalties and functional thinking influenced initial meetings; however, with real commitment and effort, breakthrough was achieved.

Cook (1994:30–4) has developed an interesting model of successful team performance, building on the work of the Management Charter Initiative, the National Health Service Training Authority's National Standards Grid and the Top Management Competency Model developed for South East Thames Regional Health Authority. The characteristics of successful team performance are shown below with comment regarding how each was manifested in the Yorkhill team:

- *Co-operation* – between team members whilst confronting problems constructively. The team described a turbulent beginning as they all approached the problem from different perspectives; however, they managed to channel these differences in a constructive way.

- *Activities and disciplines* – using systematic but adaptable work practices. The project worked with both formal and culturally recognized systems and processes, but at the same time allowed informal communication to take an important place.
- *People* – clarity regarding roles and competences and balance in team roles. A broad range of functional roles were represented and as the project developed the team came to recognize the strength which came from a mix of personality-related roles and behaviours.
- *Advancement* – developing individual and team performance. Clearly the team developed in terms of its effectiveness as the project evolved; however, individuals also describe a powerful personal learning experience.
- *Brief (Mission)* – sharing a clear brief and action orientation. This was clearly defined in the terms of reference that the team were charged with.
- *Leadership* – in one person or shared and responsive to the task. Whilst there was a co-ordinating leader each member might be seen as having led the initiative in their own areas of the Trust.
- *Environment responsiveness* – scanning the environment to identify trends, ideas and opportunities. This was a major activity which all members of the team engaged in and reported back to the team on, through the formal meetings.

To summarize some of the learning points which can be drawn from this case study and used in other organizations, ten key points, or rules for effective teamworking are proposed below.

1. Ensure support of the team from the highest level in the organization.
2. Make this support known throughout the organization – raise the team profile.
3. Provide clarity of vision and team objectives – make it challenging.
4. Create a sense of individual and collective responsibility.
5. Form alliances and open channels of communication with other teams.
6. Involve co-opted members to support the core team.
7. Encourage informal as well as formal relationships to evolve.
8. Ensure a mix of technical and behavioural profiles when selecting members.
9. Involve some team members with previous experience of teamworking.
10. Publicize results and celebrate successes.

REFERENCES

Belbin, R.M. (1993) *Team Roles at Work*, Oxford, Butterworth-Heinemann.

Cook, A. (1994) 'The Capable Team: a new approach to defining team competency', *Competency*, Vol. 1, No. 3, Spring 1994, pp. 30–34.

Hale, R. I. & Whitlam P. J. (1997) *Towards the Virtual Organisation*, Maidenhead, McGraw-Hill.

Katzenbach, J. R. & Smith, D. K. (1993) *The Wisdom of Teams*, Boston, Harvard Business School Press.

TEAM MEMBERS

Mrs Linda Fleming	Director of Contracts Team Leader
Mrs Myra Dunn	Assistant Director of Finance
Miss Susan Dick	General Manager, Operations
Miss Cath McColl	Service Manager, Surgical
Mrs Joan McGhee	Business Manager, Surgical
Mrs Lynn Robertson	Service Manager, Medical
Mr Robert Fraser	Business Manager, Medical
Mr Joe Skinner	Service Manager, Anaesthesia, ITU and Theatres
Mr John Marshall	Contracts & Planning Manager

Part 4

CORPORATE QUALITY PERSPECTIVES FROM NORTH AMERICA

Fourteen

SEARS CANADA AND ANDERSEN CONSULTING

Quality partners focused on value creation

EDWARD MATIER
AND
DAVID OMHOLT

Fourteen

SEARS CANADA AND ANDERSEN CONSULTING

Quality partners focused on value creation

In 1993, Sears Canada and Andersen Consulting entered into a partnership to turn around the troubled retailer's merchandizing organization, which had just posted net losses of $91 million (Can.) the previous year. Dramatic results were realized in less than eight months after project kick-off. By focusing on quality and value, this chapter outlines how the team actually exceeded its aggressive targets so quickly – helping Sears post a $136 million (Can.) turnaround by fiscal year 1994. The project was awarded Andersen Consulting's 1995 Worldwide Quality-Value-Success Leadership Award.

INTRODUCTION

Sears Canada has long been considered that nation's largest and most successful department store. Its 110 full-line stores and catalog operations grossed almost Can$4.6 billion[1] this year and, most important, it is creating shareholder wealth like never before with its stock up more than 400 per cent[2] from 1992. However, five years ago, the picture was far more dismal. Entrenched in a sluggish economy, consumer confidence levels hit historic lows,[3] and Sears Canada was losing money to the tune of Can$91 million. In addition, the retail scene was undergoing sweeping changes: thirty major Canadian retailers declared bankruptcy, and twenty-two major US retailers went 'north of the border' to steal pieces of the ever-shrinking disposable income pie. Most notably Wal-Mart, with its deep pockets, had bought out Canada's Woolco locations in a six-month period, pouring a quarter of a billion dollars – and lots of Wal-Mart experience – into them. The Canadian marketplace truly became a challenging puzzle to solve.

Sears knew that if it was ever going to regain its shareholder returns and market share of old, it had to adapt to the new business landscape. Such adaptation required taking a 'clean sheet of paper' and rethinking *every* policy and procedure it had created during its forty-year history. Rather than solely look externally to match industry best practices, Sears, in partnership with Andersen Consulting, chose to leapfrog the competition by defining new retail industry best practices. A very successful turnaround story ensued.

> This endeavor is the most significant reshaping of methods and procedures in the company's history and we are choosing to act quickly in a revolutionary, rather than evolutionary fashion . . . these types of demands require that we are willing to question all of our assumptions, beliefs and behaviors about what is possible, what can be done and what needs to be done. (Don Shaffer, CEO and President of Sears Canada, 1993)

PLANNING THE TRANSFORMATION

The first step in planning the transformation was to engage key members of the organization in the Master Planning effort. These members were recruited from all levels and functional backgrounds. This made for an effective balance of top-down 'innocence' and bottom-up 'know-how'. It also ensured key personnel brought in early to the new operating models, as they would eventually be asked to sponsor them before the organization at large. It was the first step in putting quality back into the procurement process.

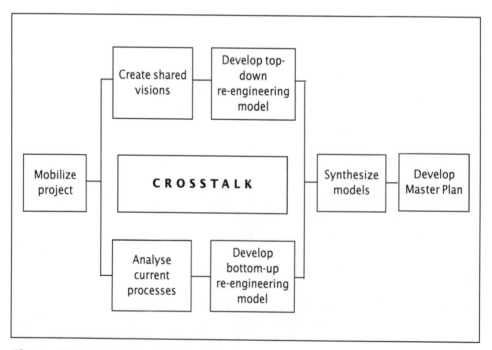

Figure 14.1: Master Plan development

From the onset, the Sears Canada/Andersen Consulting project team (hereafter referred to as the project team) adopted the motto *Carpe Diem* or 'The Time is Now/Seize the Day' to maintain the sense of urgency about the transformation. This rallying cry served to inspire the project team as *everything* was put on the table for re-evaluation

Scope

- Organizational structure, size, reporting relationships, and roles.
- Procurement policies, practices, and processes.
- Supplier base.
- Network configuration and merchandize flow.
- Enabling systems, such as EDI (Electronic Data Interchange).
- Measures and incentives.

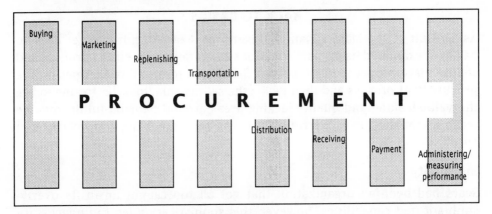

Figure 14.2: Scope of the transformation process

Goals

This broad scope was backed by bold goals. These goals had the customer as top priority. Every clean sheet of paper started with the customer in mind and worked backwards from there. Sears also knew it had to forge relationships with innovative suppliers who were equally dedicated to customer service. These suppliers had to enable Sears to make good its customer promise of being in stock with the right merchandize, when it was wanted. Key project goals included:

- Fulfil customer commitment by being in stock with merchandize that is wanted, when it is wanted.
- Fulfil customer commitment in send-later merchandize[4] by meeting all customer demand and delivering on time.
- Reduce holdover from previous seasons so more dedicated selling floor space could be allocated to fresher merchandize for the customer.

- Look beyond national borders to work with suppliers to reduce their costs of manufacture and ultimately pass those savings on to the customer.
- Work with suppliers to increase reliability of ship dates and accurate order quantities through a rigorous but fair compliance programme.
- Significantly reduce overall supply chain cycle time:
  - Order preparation.
  - Supplier lead times.
  - Inbound transportation.
  - Facility processing.
  - Outbound transportation to stores.
- Significantly increase inventory velocity and reduce regular markdowns.
- Improve productivity and morale of Sears' procurement organization.

BACK TO BASICS

As a result of the Master Planning exercises, Sears decided to get back to basics. It examined its primary functions as a retailer – procuring product and selling that product to customers. It first chose to focus its energies on the procurement process and then tackle the selling side. In order to ameliorate the value-leaking and quality-lacking areas around demand-fulfilment, the team established two overriding process redesign biases: *simplicity* and *speed*.

Simplicity

Sears had been an organization that got all too caught up in its overly-sophisticated capabilities; however, this sophistication led to unnecessary complexity. Too often this complexity impeded the company's ability to be nimble with the dynamic retail environment. The team decided to attack the existing organizational and process complexity, which was discovered to be the single largest driver of an uncompetitive overhead structure. Some examples:

Old processes	New processes
Thirty-seven product procurement methods	Four standard operational models: • Retail Continuous; • Retail Fashion; • Catalogue; • Big Ticket.
Many distribution methods	Only methods that maximize merchandize flow-through and minimize storage.
Thirty-one payment methods	Standard terms.

Speed

The project team quickly determined that an unnecessarily long cycle time (defined as recognition of product need to product availability for a customer) was the major culprit. It was driving excessive inventory levels and carrying costs, high markdowns, and most important, disappointing customers with stock outs and stale assortments due to being overspent with open-to-buy dollars.

In relentless pursuit of value, the project team developed a rapid implementation approach. This approach, it is important to note, did not depend on technology solutions with long lead times to remedy the problems, as no more than 10 per cent of the information systems staff was on the project. Rather, since it was the process that was broken, all technology would offer was a more efficient way to accomplish a faulty process. Thus, automating the procurement activities was *not* what was meant by a quality solution.

NO SKIMPING ON QUALITY

A quality solution *was* defined as one that would re-engineer *all* of the process rather than myopically addressing only some of the broken parts. Only a holistic solution would lead to a sustained competitive advantage. Such a solution had to:

- Adopt/create best practices in all areas of procurement: the strategy, the human capital, the process, and the technology.
- Engage management to personally sponsor the changes, ensure they are implemented, and achieve the results.
- Streamline and simplify the work.
- Reduce the total cost of the procurement process and the amount of inventory in the supply chain by shortening cycle times and ordering smaller quantities of goods more frequently (lowering carrying costs, shrinkage, etc.).
- Move to process-oriented workteam structures from functional silos.
- Develop a select group of strategic partnerships with innovative suppliers, increasing order volume and information-sharing in exchange for partnering with Sears Canada and operating within a thorough supplier compliance programme.
- Change measurement systems, focusing on end-to-end procurement process results (e.g. procurement scorecards), rather than on purely functional measurement.
- Infuse incremental quality into every step of the process.

The project team first set out to develop standard ordering practices to replace the thirty-seven methods that were driving up costs. As it developed these standardized practices, it also examined the organization and reviewed all the activities within the procurement process. What it discovered were problems germane to any functional organization.

- The company was organized around functions along the process. This meant that each function – administration, finance, merchandizing, catalogue, retail, marketing, logistics, quality assurance, supplier relations, MIS, etc. – had its own reporting relationships, organizations, measures, and agendas.
- Measurements, rewards and accountability were not focused around the end-to-end procurement process and results, but rather around functions and activities. As a result, inventory turnover, which is one of the most important measurements of the procurement process, was measured for just the inventory position/function. Other critical players in the process, such as buyers, were not measured directly on inventory, even though they had a direct effect on inventory turnover when they negotiated and purchased goods from suppliers.
- Activities and jobs were duplicated within the functions throughout the process. For example, retail, catalogue and merchandizing each had people dedicated to inventory management.
- Too many 'hand-offs' occurred within the process. For example, communication had to go up through the functions and across, rather than letting the people who worked within the process communicate across functional lines. Marketing decisions had to be run up through the marketing department, and buying decisions through the buying department. This structure made it difficult for buyers and marketing people to work directly with each other on a particular type of merchandize.

Once the project team had ascertained the scope of the problem, it planned a redesign of the organization based on people from several functions working together on a team to focus collectively on the end-to-end procurement process. Specifically, the project team did this by:

- Breaking down the functional organization into cross-functional teams organized around the end-to-end procurement process. One cross-functional team would be assigned to a particular type of merchandize. For example, one team would perform end-to-end procurement activities for children's apparel, one for hardware, etc. Team members represented each of the functions that was necessary to accomplish this: buying, marketing, inventory, finance, logistics, etc.
- Reducing the cost of the process and eliminating such redundant activities as multiple people-checking and rechecking inventory.
- Measuring the teams on the total procurement process performance (e.g.,

supplier compliance, stockouts, catalogue omits/back orders) and the total cost of procuring (i.e., inventory carrying costs and shipping costs – not just the invoice cost of the merchandize).

- Measuring individuals on collective, team performance (e.g., inventory turnover for a type of merchandize) – not just individual performance.
- Putting the teams in direct contact with their suppliers and customers, rather than running everything up through the functional hierarchies.

SENIOR MANAGEMENT'S HANDS-ON COMMITMENT TO QUALITY

Sears' senior management anything but divorced themselves from this undertaking. To make certain that all ranks of the organization understood the methods and goals of the impending effort, senior management did not commission anything to begin before it was clear that everybody 'got it' – including suppliers. As this truly was a sweeping change throughout the organization, affecting nearly every employee, senior management constantly communicated the vision. The Chief Executive Officer (CEO), Don Shaffer, and Senior Executive Vice President of Merchandizing, Bill Turner, took a very hands-on approach to sponsoring the change and communicating its impact. They went out on a 'road tour', investing significant face time with the workforce and supplier base via personal presentations – twenty in all – and through videos and regular newsletters.

In addition, weekly Friday morning meetings were held with the project team and top executives so that critical issues could be raised and resolved quickly. As a result of these extensive communication efforts, workers were afforded the chance of navigating the change-acceptance continuum (i.e., denial, anger, bargaining, acceptance, etc.). It became evident and reassuring to the entire organization that the executive team was committed to quality and that this personal handling was not just 'paying lip service'.

Once the general vision was understood and internalized by the entire work force, senior management mobilized live pilot workteams to run a proof-of-concept test against the new operating models.

PROVING THE CONCEPT WITH PILOT WORKTEAMS

The project team started by phasing in the design of the new business environment with the implementation of this environment, concurrently. The thought was rather than have every detail about every activity designed before the new procurement workteams are even put in place, the project team decided to take an iterative, 'strawman' approach: treat the new operating models as 'living, breathing' and foster a constant challenge/ continuous improvement environment. Piloting the new concepts with two live workteams would enable such a strategy. This way, the project team could conduct frequent quality assurance reviews. All in all, it was apparent that a quality redesign effort was to be a journey, not a destination.

The pilot workteams represented a cross-section of the merchandizing organization and included all four new, standardized procurement models. These workteams were truly empowered to be self-directing entities. Critical measures and goals necessary for achieving the desired business results were clearly articulated to them and included:

- Increased inventory turnover.
- Improved supplier compliance percentages.
- Reduced stockouts.
- Reduced regular (clearance) markdowns.

With four months of master planning under their belt and two pilot teams selected, the project team began training and orientating the pilot teams. These sessions were 'MC-ed' by Shaffer and Turner to show their support and to explain why things needed to change in order to make Sears successful again. The new measures and team accountability were explained, as were inventory turnover, stockout percentages, supplier compliance, markdown percentages and other measures. This information was critical since many people, because of their previous narrowly focused functional specialization, needed training on the basics of the procurement process.

CONCURRENT EVALUATION AND IMPLEMENTATION OF THE TRANSFORMATION

At the same time, the project team used the pilots as a testing laboratory to allow them to continue to design, in parallel, the other parts of the business environment for implementation :

- *Strategy:* Upper management needed to decide what to do with all the capital that would eventually be freed up as a result of the improved ordering practices, etc. Many of Sears' stores were in dire need of refurbishment, and this new cash flow could quickly be funnelled into store renovation projects. Also, there was a possibility that some warehouses could be closed because of the decreased inventory levels. Now, some real estate decisions might have to be made: Lease the space? Sell it?
- *Processes:* The project team further defined the procurement process designs and created 'practices' (procedures) to help the procurement workteams implement the processes; they created a supplier compliance programme which contained the terms and conditions that would need to be negotiated with partner suppliers.

- *Technology:* In addition to making some minor system enhancements to the inventory/ordering systems, other systems such as EDI needed to be tailored and implemented so that Sears and its suppliers could exchange information more quickly.
- *Human capital:* As the project team observed and learned from the team dynamics in the pilots, they began to design the organization above and around the procurement workteams. In addition, job descriptions/ grading, measures, rewards, performance evaluations, etc. were designed based on input from the pilot participants.

With pilot teams in place, EDI rolling, and the supplier compliance programme in operation, the project team began to work on improving the cycle time of the distribution network. To better meet customer demand, Sears had to rely less on forecasting. Thus, distribution time had to be shortened because it hindered Sears' ability to react to real-time fluctuations in customer demand.

Concept proven – full speed ahead!

Now six months into the project, the project team started rolling out additional procurement teams – four in June, five in July, three in August, two in September, and three in October – for a total of nineteen including the original pilot workteams.

The pilots allowed the project team to 'test the water' and refine the processes/practices, procurement workteam designs, job designs, training, measures, and rewards that came out of the master planning phase. The pilot team design was then extrapolated as the project team created the rest of the procurement workteams.

The management and support structure above and around the procurement workteams was also rolled out. In this design, the support groups were moved into one procurement-process-focused group that was focused upon the procurement process so the procurement workteams could have 'one-stop shopping' for their support needs. The support team was designed to look like the procurement workteams it supported – a quality assurance 'help desk'.

The project team then planned and conducted a two-day, off-site meeting with the workteam leads (National Business Managers) and the organization above and around the workteams (including Shaffer and Turner and their direct reports, Business General Managers) to allow them to work together. Going off-site was particularly important as individuals could break through the paradigms that were around them back at the home office. This way, innovative and unconstrained thinking could be fostered.

Before each procurement workteam was formed, an orientation session was held. The meeting was particularly valuable because participants in the pilot workteams gave testimonials to the soon-to-be-formed workteams on the success of the organizational and process changes. Those involved in the pilot workteams were dispersed into newly-formed workteams and remained there for three months before moving on to other groups. These 'roving' workteam members helped groups transcend their traditional functional orientations.

Some of the challenges the project team experienced with the new groups included the following:

- When the procurement teams were first forming, a learning curve had to be overcome (the project team facilitated this in their orientation, and called the stages: 'forming', 'storming', 'norming', and 'performing'). There was a tendency for the team members to feel as if their teams were understaffed. In most cases, the people were still performing activities from the old organization in addition to overcoming the learning curve of the new business environment. The 'roving' team members addressed these valid concerns via Business Improvement Sessions (BISs) with the workteam members to help identify bottlenecks, streamline/simplify the extra work, and teach the workteams to redesign their work on their own.
- Despite these efforts, old habits were hard to break. For instance, some people continued to answer the phone by saying, 'Marketing Department', even though it no longer existed as a stand-alone unit. Physical proximity was not enough to change old behaviours. The project team worked tirelessly to correct it, giving frequent coaching sessions to the procurement workteams.
- The goals on the scorecard were aggressive. A goals-setting management process was undertaken to ensure that the procurement team leads (and their management) bought in to the goals, and that they would support and drive them in their workteams. Without this strong management support, the workteams would never have reached their goals.

By January 1995 – less than one year after the pilot workteams were formed – the entire organization was reorganized and functioning. Tangible economic benefits had already been realized. Much of the capital that was tied up in excess inventory could now be redirected to refurbishing stores and to other strategic imperatives. The procurement teams were poised to perform into 1995 and beyond – and they did. The improvements continued, with better customer service, improved direct margin, reduced costs, improved supplier compliance, improved inventory management, increased speed, reduced cycle times, increased production, and optimized warehouse/distribution facilities. The quality performance speaks for itself.

RESULTS, AFTER ONLY EIGHT MONTHS!

- 50 per cent reduction in out of stocks (8 per cent reduced to 4 per cent).
- 65 per cent reduction in Big Ticket out of stocks/late deliveries.
- Reduction of $150 million in inventory (2.8 increased to 3.65 turns).
- 30 per cent productivity improvement in Merchandizing Department.
- 85 per cent of the business is on EDI/ASNs.
- 100 per cent supplier compliance tracking.
- Reduced cycle time:
  - Order preparation: 20 per cent reduction.
  - Supplier processing: 50 per cent reduction.
  - Distribution to stores/Catalogue centres: 65 per cent reduction.
- Exceeded Direct Margin plan.

WHAT CAN OTHER COMPANIES LEARN?

It is best to be a visionary company that changes before the change imperative is already at your doorstep. Sears Canada, on the other hand, was already in deep trouble – there was no option but to embrace change. However, the benefits it teased out in such a short time-frame were enabled by having the right sponsorship, the right amount of flexibility, and the right attention to quality, innovation, and teamworking. It illustrated the four requisite characteristics of a re-engineering effort (fundamental, radical, dramatic, and process) and fulfilled the charge initially set forth by Shaffer that this was to be a fundamental rethinking and radical redesign of business processes to achieve dramatic improvements.[5]

Sears also should be applauded for its put-the-customer-first mentality. The question inevitably was asked during each master planning session, 'How is this change going to affect our customers and their shopping experience?' It is evident by the way Sears' customers have responded.

Similarly, Sears did not forget its own people along the way. Senior management communicated the change plan, directly addressed employee concerns and empowered its people. By giving ownership of the business to the employees, senior management saw increased morale and synergy. Mary Tolan, Andersen Consulting's Global Managing Partner for the Retail Industry, agrees: 'The commitment shown by Sears' executive team to the project and to their people was remarkable. Their time and total immersion was critical to the ultimate success of the project.'

Although Sears placed great value on its employees' ideas and opinions, it saw the need for a fresh set of eyes. Left solely to 'insiders', Sears knew perspectives would be too narrow and breakthrough thinking would not be accomplished. Therefore, they turned to objective 'outsiders' who were not afraid to make waves and challenge long and widely-held assumptions. In the case of the Sears Canada/Andersen Consulting project team, the whole was definitely greater than the sum of the parts.

Another key element was the simultaneous focusing upon all aspects of the master plan – simultaneously a holistic re-engineering approach. The project team did not fall subject to the laws of maldistribution and focus on getting only a small percentage of the process totally right, as opposed to making the entire process incrementally more robust.

Last, the project team was tenacious in achieving results. Team members reached outside their comfort zones and questioned everything. They were courageous enough to throw out what was shown not to work during pilot testing and were celebrated for innovative thinking, no matter how counter-intuitive some ideas seemed at face value.

Stewart MacLeod, a VP and General Merchandize Manager for Home, Appliances and Electronics, summed it best: 'It's put the fun back into work . . . in my twenty-five years here, I've gone through many changes over the years – four or five major ones – but all they were were just big changes . . . this is a new culture; it's incredible.'

NOTES AND REFERENCES

1 Sears Canada Financial Statements, year-end 1997.
2 As of close of business day, 26 January 1998.
3 Conference Board of Canada, Index of Consumer Attitudes, 1997.
4 Non-take-with merchandize (e.g., Big Ticket White Good items).
5 *Re-engineering the Corporation: A Manifesto for Business Revolution,* Hammer and Champy, 1993, p. 46.

INDEX